# Additional Praise for B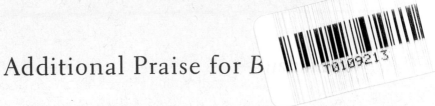

modernization of the Bronx Zoo, and herpetology in general, is revealed, as recorded through the observations and writings of Ditmars during his many years of employment with the institute where he strove relentlessly to arouse public awareness to the plight of the cold-blooded species with which he was so obsessed."

—Austin Stevens, herpetologist, author,
and adventure wildlife filmmaker

"It is striking that a considerable number of persons can trace their developing interest in herpetology back to their adolescent days reading the many books by curator Raymond L. Ditmars from New York Zoological Society. Those of us who have worked with bushmasters in the field and captivity feel fortunate to have had this wonderful opportunity. These magnificent creatures are unforgettable, the largest, most beautiful, and most compelling venomous snake in the New World. Author Dan Eatherley has captured their essence and the nexus with Ditmars—unearthing a plethora of new information about one of our famous and most productive herpetologists."

—James B. Murphy, Smithsonian National Museum of Natural History

"The world's greatest snakehunter, his quest for a legendary serpent, and a modern Boy's Own Adventure. Three stories elegantly intertwined in *Bushmaster*. Beautifully written and meticulously researched, I'm sure like me you won't be able to put it down."

—Nigel Marven, television presenter

"I picked it up and read it from start to finish without putting it down."

—Marc Morrone, animal breeder, author, and television presenter

"When I was a mere stripling my mother bought me *Snakes of the World* by Raymond L. Ditmars. My innate fascination for snakes soared to the skies with this book. But I never did realize what an incredible character

Ditmars was. In *Bushmaster* Dan Eatherley brings to life this enigmatic hero to uncounted, obsessed herpers."

—Romulus Whitaker, herpetologist, wildlife conservationist, and filmmaker

"This is an engrossing look at Raymond L. Ditmars, herpetologist extraordinaire and an inspiration to many. He has been brought back to life through Dan Eatherley's impeccable writing and practiced eye. A great read."

—William W. Lamar, herpetologist, GreenTracks, Inc.

# BUSHMASTER

# BUSHMASTER

## Raymond Ditmars and the Hunt for the World's Largest Viper

———◆———

## DAN EATHERLEY

Foreword by Desmond Morris

Arcade Publishing • New York

First Arcade Publishing paperback edition 2017

Arcade Publishing books may be purchased in bulk at special discounts for sales promotion, corporate gifts, fund-raising, or educational purposes. Special editions can also be created to specifications. For details, contact the Special Sales Department, Arcade Publishing, 307 West 36th Street, 11th Floor, New York, NY 10018 or arcade@skyhorsepublishing.com.

Arcade Publishing® is a registered trademark of Skyhorse Publishing, Inc.®, a Delaware corporation.

Visit our website at www.arcadepub.com.
Visit the author's website at www.daneatherley.com.

10 9 8 7 6 5 4 3 2 1

Library of Congress Cataloging-in-Publication Data is available on request.

Cover design by Erin Seaward-Hiatt
Cover photo of a bushmaster by Dean Ripa

ISBN: 978-1-62872-766-1
Ebook ISBN: 978-1-62872-555-1

Printed in the United States of America

To Clair, Merryn, and Hannah

# Contents

———◆———

Atlantic forest bushmaster (*Lachesis muta rhombeata*) — nineteenth-century engraving
(Courtesy of the American Museum of Natural History)

Some local names for the bushmaster (with suggested translations)

*Mapepire Z'anana*, Trinidad ("The Pineapple Snake")
*Matabuey*, Costa Rica ("The Ox-Killer")
*Konoko-Se*, Guyana ("The Forest Dweller")
*Cascabel Muda*, Costa Rica ("The Silent Rattlesnake")
*Plato Negro*, Costa Rica ("The Black Plate")
*Pico-de-Jaca*, Brazil ("The Stinging Jackfruit")
*Cresta del Gallo*, Venezuela ("The Rooster Comb")
*Verrugosa*, widespread in South America ("The Warty One")
*Diamante*, widespread in South America ("The Diamond")
*Surucucú-de-Fogo*, Brazil ("The One Who Strikes Repeatedly at the Fire")

*"To me, the haunts of snakes and other creeping things, have always been more attractive than the whirl of seaside and mountain resorts during the summer months."*

—Raymond L. Ditmars, June 28, 1900

*Summer 1896. The Bronx, New York City.*

JUST LIKE A COFFIN. Five feet long, three feet wide, and three feet high, the wooden box dominates the landing.

"The expressmen must have had some job getting it up here," muses the nineteen-year-old. According to the delivery note, the sender is a "MR. R. R. MOLE, PORT-OF-SPAIN." After three months the consignment finally showed up at port yesterday aboard the SS *Irrawaddy* of the Trinidad line, and just a few hours ago the crate was delivered by horse and cart to the large brownstone house on Bathgate Avenue. Dinner seemed to take forever but now it's over. Insisting that his parents remain two stories below, the young man can at last get to work with hammer and pry bar. He ignores the intermittent buzzes coming from the room adjacent to the landing. Forcing off the lid, he prepares for the draught of fetid air, a sure sign of a dead specimen, but is relieved to detect only a faint nutty odor. Under several inches of brittle straw lie various large burlap sacks, each knotted and labeled. Turning over a tag, he shudders as two words are revealed in a neat script.

LACHESIS MUTA

The sack expands and contracts in response to the breathing of its contents whose rough scales press a distinctive pattern against the fabric.

*Like the surface of a pine cone,* he thinks.

"Everything all right up there, Ray?" his mother's voice disturbs the youth's reverie.

"Fine. Don't anybody come up!" He needs to get a move on.

Heart pounding, the teenager grasps the bag above the knot and lifts it from the crate. It's disappointingly light given that Mole's note describes an animal of "about eight feet long." Books and articles had led him to expect a specimen of that length to be far heavier. Holding the sack away from his body, he enters a small adjoining room via a door fitted with strong springs. Glass-fronted cages are arranged in two tiers along one wall. Above them stretches the desiccated skin of a large snake, a python maybe.

The buzzing, emanating from one of the upper cages, intensifies. The teenager places the sack in a large empty cage on the lower tier and loosens the knot. He reaches for a broom handle; attached to one end is a piece of stiff wire twisted like a shepherd's crook. Using this, he inverts and raises the bag, hoping to coax out its tenant from a safe distance, but the animal is not cooperating and instead braces itself against the cloth, defying gravity. The beast does at least offer up a glimpse of alternating salmon-pink and jet-black markings. Impatient to see more, the young man whips away the sack with his hand, spilling the creature out into the cage.

He would never forget the turmoil of impressions etched on his brain in that instant: the snake's length far exceeding that suggested by its weight; the keeled scales lending the skin a rasp-like quality; the waxy sheen of the animal; the blunt head; and, set above pinkish jowls, the reddish-brown eyes with their elliptical black pupils. In the moments these features take to register, the front half of the reptile's body rises to form a huge "S" while the glistening pink tongue forks at the air.

Then the snake advances.

In horror the teenager backs away, knocking over a chair.

The reptile follows.

Never has he encountered a viper actually prepared to pursue him. In his experience, even the most venomous of snakes are cowards and, unless cornered, flee at the first sign of trouble. With the staff he tries ever more forcefully to check the giant reptile's progress, attempting to lift and push it back, but the limbless body of his adversary slides over the hook like jelly. The snake is between him and the door, cutting off any hope of escape. The buzzing is now an uninterrupted, deafening drone.

Downstairs his mother drops her knitting. "That was *definitely* a crash I just heard, John."

"Relax, my dear. Ray seems to know what he's doing," responds her husband with little conviction. They both glance nervously at the ceiling.

And still the serpent advances.

The inch long fangs and excessive amounts of venom for which this species is notorious dominate the young man's thoughts. Can this snake know its own power? Can that dancing tongue taste his fear?

The teenager has almost nowhere left to go when, in his peripheral vision, he notices a broom. He flicks it behind him with the crook of his staff. Retreating another step, in one motion he grabs the implement and shoves the bristles sharply into the face of his pursuer. The snake pauses, pulls its body into a tight coil and beats out a rhythm against the floor with the strange horny tip of its tail. The youth catches his breath. Saved!

Broom in hand and more confident, he advances on the reptile. Several additional firm jabs encourage the serpent to turn and creep toward the cage. The teenager gently raises the snake's chin with his staff, enabling the viper to glide into its new quarters. He slams shut the glass door to the cage and slumps to the floor, gasping and prickled by sweat.

Now for the boas.

# Foreword

—•◦•—

WHAT EXACTLY IS IT about snakes that fascinates us? Surely no other form of wildlife provokes such fear, such disgust, such curiosity, and, for many, such love and reverence. It's something that has long puzzled me. Indeed, more than five decades ago, my wife Ramona and I devoted an entire book to this enigma. In *Men and Snakes*, we traced humanity's unique relationship with ophidians throughout history. This intimate link is evidenced in the crude thirty-thousand-year-old serpentine finger smearings in the Rouffignac Cave of central France and the rather more elegant rock paintings made by the San people of Southern Africa. We see it in the powerful religious significance that snakes have held for many cultures throughout the ages, from Aztec Mexico where the ringed boa was associated with the fecundity of the earth as well as wisdom, to the ancient Greek cult of Asclepius, which saw snakes as healers. The twin snakes entwined about the staff of Hermes, the caduceus, remains a symbol of medicine to this day. In Judeo-Christianity, the snake is held responsible for Adam's expulsion from the Garden of Eden and all the woes of the world that have followed. The snake has been used as a weapon of war, as sport, as food, as entertainment, and even as a pet.

Sometimes merely the idea of snakes affects us in a mysterious way. Every age, however, throws up a few men and women who are truly fixated on these odd creatures. Think of Steve Irwin's sensationalist television shows, or C. J. P. Ionides, who made a name for himself in the 1950s collecting deadly black mambas in East Africa. I would argue that Raymond Lee Ditmars, the subject of *Bushmaster*, was a game-changer in this rarefied field. As the twentieth century dawned, here was someone who not only collected, studied, and wrote about snakes, but for the first time made it his special mission to enlighten and educate the general public. For Ditmars, defending these misunderstood and actually rather vulnerable creatures from hatred and ignorance was a calling, a vocation. In the introduction to our own book, we expressed the hope that a greater familiarity with the snake would foster a more sympathetic attitude toward a much used and abused animal. This was certainly the way Ditmars saw it, and, for a few short years in the 1930s whilst his expeditions in search of a bushmaster in South America were making front-page headlines, the United States, a nation in the throes of the Depression, found itself infected by "snake fever" too.

Yet, less than a century after his passing, the name Raymond Ditmars registers with few people besides the baby boomers who had devoured his still-in-print writings in the late 1950s and 1960s. It's my hope that *Bushmaster*, a fascinating book about a fascinating man, will introduce this important figure to a new generation of nature lovers. Snake people are special, and the greatest of them, like Ditmars, are inspiring in their devotion to one of the most extraordinary forms of life on this planet. He described his respect for snakes as having "a religion all his own"—and nobody was more devout.

Desmond Morris
Oxford, United Kingdom
October 2016

The bushmaster, as it appears in Raymond Ditmars's 1931 book, *Snakes of the World*.

# PROLOGUE

## *His Unwavering Grip*

*"The Bushmaster is a bold and particularly dangerous snake, inclined to deliberately edge toward the intruder, bringing the lateral, S-shaped striking loop to nearer and better advantage. Its great length of fangs and large amount of poison render a well-delivered stroke of the utmost gravity."*

—Raymond L. Ditmars, *Snakes of the World* (1931)

———◆———

BY THE 1990S, BRISTOL, an ancient city in southwest England, could boast a lively cultural history. The poets Samuel Taylor Coleridge and William Wordsworth likely enjoyed a brandy or two in one of the countless public houses here in the 1790s. Perhaps they argued over slavery? Much of the former port's wealth was then generated by shipping Africans across the Atlantic. In recent years a series of popular music acts had emerged from Bristol and its environs, Portishead and Massive Attack the most prominent of these. Cary Grant was born here, so were the Plasticine heroes Wallace and Gromit. Darth Vader was played by a Bristolian although James Earl Jones gave him voice, the gentle agricultural tones of the West Country actor considered more hobbit than dark lord. The spray-painted stencils of guerrilla artist Banksy continue to mark out the city.

Yet for me, Bristol's attraction was its status as the global center for wildlife filmmaking. The British Broadcasting Corporation's Natural History Unit had been churning out programs here for decades, including all of David Attenborough's highly regarded documentaries. Dozens of smaller independent production companies specializing in wildlife had emerged in recent years, making shows for the BBC or overseas broadcasters such as the Discovery Channel or National Geographic. So in 1996, with a newly minted zoology degree under my arm, I headed for the "Green Hollywood" with half-formed thoughts of filming exotic creatures on tropical islands.

After several years not filming exotic creatures on tropical islands—in fact, not filming very much at all—things had finally been picking up. A brief spell at the BBC had led to employment as an assistant producer at an independent. I now had successful film trips to Indonesia and the Americas on my résumé. But the repercussions from the terrorist attacks on New York and Washington just four months earlier were being felt in unexpected places, and natural history filmmaking was not immune. Business in the independent sector was already in the doldrums. Budgets had been slashed and even the BBC was tightening its belt, choosing to produce more new programs in-house and loath to fund ideas from independents.

Before 9/11 our particular outfit might have weathered the storm thanks to a strong relationship with a major broadcaster across the Atlantic. We had just produced two films about serpents for National Geographic Television featuring veteran herpetologist Rom Whitaker. *Snake Hunter North America* and *Snake Hunter Costa Rica* saw the Indian-based but American-born host return to snake-hunting haunts from his childhood and catch up with old acquaintances. Along the way, viewers learned about serpents and other wildlife. The shows, blending natural history with adventure, were pitched somewhere between the sensationalism of Steve Irwin and David Attenborough's restrained style. *Snake Hunter* had attracted good audiences and we were now researching ideas for further installments. The scenarios were coming thick and fast: Rom drops in on an Italian snake festival, Rom catches mambas and spitting cobras in Africa, Rom swims with sea snakes off the coast of Malaysia. We were also developing a new program idea about a viper that had briefly appeared in *Snake Hunter Costa Rica*. It was known as the bushmaster.

This particular snake had fascinated Rom since childhood when he read about it in a book entitled *Thrills of a Naturalist's Quest*. Published in 1932, this is one of several autobiographical accounts written by a certain Raymond Ditmars, curator of reptiles and mammals at the New York Zoological Park, familiarly known as the Bronx Zoo. In the book Ditmars describes how, as a kid in late nineteenth-century New York, he started bringing snakes home as pets. Venomous species living near the city were added to the reptilian menagerie, including rattlesnakes and copperheads, the latter named for their reddish-brown pattern. After much resistance his parents yielded to their son's hobby, by the mid-1890s surrendering the entire top floor of their house to the expanding collection.

Matters came to a head when young Raymond received a crate of snakes from Trinidad. (Customs rules were laxer in those days.) In a chapter called "Episode of the Bushmaster," Ditmars describes excitedly prizing open the wooden box dispatched from the West Indian island by the enigmatic Mr. R. R. Mole, a newspaper publisher and fellow serpent aficionado. Among the tropical boas, rat snakes, coralsnakes, and fer-de-lances in the exotic consignment was the star of the show: an eight-foot-long bushmaster in good condition, which, the delivery note stated, Ditmars should "be extremely careful with liberating." On its release, and ticked off for being cooped up for several weeks, the viper supposedly chased the young snake devotee around the room, the rest of the family downstairs oblivious. With the help of a broom Ditmars persuaded the bushmaster to slither into a cage and lived to tell the tale. "I figured it had received one of the surprises of its life," he writes, "and it had certainly given me the worst jolt of mine."

While researching the Costa Rica program I had gathered a few basic facts on bushmasters. The serpent inhabits rainforest from Brazil to southern Nicaragua. Like rattlesnakes, another group of venomous snakes confined to the Americas, the bushmaster is a pitviper, so called for the shallow depressions on both sides of the head between its eye and nostril. These pits are lined with temperature-sensitive cells connected to the visual centers of the brain, enabling the snake to pinpoint prey with stereoscopic heat vision in total darkness. Bushmasters are not the world's largest venomous snake—that accolade probably goes to the king cobra of Asia—but a bushmaster killed in Trinidad reportedly exceeded twelve feet in length, making it the longest of all vipers.

Bushmaster venom isn't the most toxic either, although the volume potentially delivered in a single bite makes the snake extremely dangerous, not least because the fangs, sometimes attaining two inches in length, inject the poison deep into the flesh of victims. And if those death-dealing teeth snap off, backup fangs wait in the rear, ready to swing forward and report for duty. In his 1648 natural history of Brazil, the physician Guilherme Piso reported that bushmaster bites quickly caused pain, dizziness, colic, delirium, and fever. Soon after, the blood rapidly corroded and boiled up through the nostrils, ears, and even the hands and feet. Death came within twenty-four hours. Not for nothing that in Costa Rica the snake was affectionately known as *mata buey*, the "ox-killer."

The bushmaster's scientific name, *Lachesis muta*, is just as dramatic. Lachesis was one of the three Fates of classical mythology who determined the length of a person's life, while "muta" means "silent," hinting that the bushmaster is a rattlesnake that has lost its noisy appendage. That the snake vibrates the peculiar burr-like tail tip when annoyed just adds to this impression, although in truth other snakes perform similar defensive behavior and scientists now believe that bushmasters are only distantly related to rattlers. Despite this, the bushmaster is still known as *la cascabela muda* in many regions. The viper's murderous reputation had attracted attention in martial spheres too, where "bushmaster" could refer to an Australian military vehicle, a regiment of the Arizona National Guard, and a firearms manufacturer.

Like many other vipers, the bushmaster is an ambush predator, taking patience to a new level: groundbreaking field research led by the Cornell University scientist Harry Greene showed that one specimen in the

Costa Rican forest spent two weeks in the same spot until it caught a rodent. The bushmaster is the sole viper in the Americas known to lay eggs; others, such as rattlesnakes, bring forth live young. It is thought the mother stays with her clutch to guard them—an unusual behavior for snakes.

The Colombian biologist Isidoro Cabrera with the skin of a bushmaster (*Lachesis muta*), c. 1950. In life, this snake, a female, exceeded nine feet in length. (Photo by Federico Medem. Courtesy of William W. Lamar)

FOUR years on and I was amassing supplementary detail to put in the pitch document for the television program on the bushmaster. I investigated other aspects of the biology and mythology surrounding this mysterious and deadly serpent, gathering tidbits from the Internet and poring over neglected textbooks in local libraries. I grew more interested in Ditmars, too. Rom Whitaker had explained that the curator's stories had sparked his enthusiasm for all things reptilian. Others said the same thing. In 1956 the herpetologist Clifford H. Pope acknowledged a lifelong indebtedness to Ditmars for stimulating his interest in reptiles and was among many regarding the zoo man's works as classics. Newt Gingrich was another unexpected devotee. The former US speaker recalls writing to his hero for advice as a twelve-year-old: "I got a very nice letter back saying he had died the same year I was born." Rom tells a similar story. For *Time* magazine, Raymond Ditmars was simply "the best-known snake man in the U.S."

Reading further, I learned that celebrity had come early in Ditmars's career. As a teenager he began extracting venom from rattlesnakes and other deadly species, manipulating them with all the skill and precision of a surgeon twice his age. The poison was passed to scientists seeking cures for snakebite. This rare pastime caught the attention of city newspapers, with whom he established a lasting and fruitful association. A few years later the New York Zoological Society appointed Ditmars assistant curator in charge of reptiles at the impressive new zoological gardens in the Bronx. Over his lifetime Ditmars produced seventeen books and a wealth of articles on natural history, his influence and interests extending far beyond the world of snakes, lizards, crocodiles, and turtles. He also delivered countless public lectures and was among the first producers of natural history films. In 1934 Ditmars appeared in *Who's Who*, sharing the pages with Josef Stalin and Mickey Mouse. He was friends with Theodore Roosevelt and the millionaire industrialist Andrew Carnegie. When he died in 1942 at the age of sixty-five, Raymond Ditmars was a national institution. He had even been immortalized a year earlier in a successful movie. *The Lady Eve*, a romantic comedy directed by Preston Sturges, opens in the Amazon rainforest (actually a botanical garden close to Los Angeles). A stout, bearded professor passes Henry Fonda a rare snake called Emma in a box to be delivered to "Dr. Marsdit." "Keep her warm as you get farther north," says the scientist, "and sometimes let her out of her box to play a little."

Astonished that I had known nothing about such an illustrious figure, I sought Ditmars's other books, all out of print for decades. I discovered that the hair-raising incident with the bushmaster kindled an obsession to catch a specimen for himself from the wild. Ditmars studied, wrote about, and filmed all manner of animals, but the viper continued to gnaw at him. In several of his books he reproduced the same ghastly photograph of a bushmaster. Despite the evil cat-eye stare, the snake in the picture was dead, its maw fixed open in a half grin, half sneer, the tusk-like fangs straining indecently at their fleshy sheaths, desiccated tongue forks tickling the chin.

In later life, Ditmars's vacations were spent hacking through Latin American forests in search of a wild specimen. These quests caught the public imagination, making national newspaper headlines during the 1930s. The bushmaster was Moby Dick to Ditmars's Captain Ahab, but unlike in Herman Melville's famous tale, the idea here was to capture and keep alive the lethal and elusive quarry. When the occasional bushmaster collected by others did turn up in the Bronx Zoo reptile house, the specimen invariably died within weeks. Perhaps this enigmatic denizen of the forest was simply not meant to be caught?

I trawled archive film footage websites for motion pictures of the celebrated snake man. Searches for "Ditmars" generated disappointingly few hits and none featured any kind of snake, let alone bushmasters. All I could find was a single black-and-white newsreel from 1933 entitled "First Look At Vampire Bat." The footage is brief. A trim, balding gentleman in an immaculate white suit stands in windswept gardens, somewhere on the grounds of the Bronx Zoo. He holds a live bat that, the accompanying notes state, comes from the Chilibrillo Caverns of Panama. Ditmars could be saying something, but the clip is mute. The bat struggles uselessly, the curator gently pinioning each wing in his steady hands. I later discovered that this was the first time a living vampire bat had been exhibited in the United States. By the 1930s Ditmars was at the height of his fame and the vampire bat garnered him yet more publicity. However, in the background was the bushmaster, tempting Ditmars to return to the tropics for just one last look.

I suggested that our bushmaster film might include a flavor of this quest, revealing Ditmars as the archetypal snake-hunter blazing a trail for the likes of Steve Irwin, with whom modern audiences would have been familiar. But 9/11 changed all that. The only program ideas National Geographic now wanted had to feature the mountains of Afghanistan, Osama bin Laden's hideout, or anthrax, his supposed latest weapon against the West. Snake films were out. My company had to let me go. Life went on. I rejoined the BBC and worked on other shows.

But what I wouldn't realize for several years was that, just like the Panamanian bat, the long-dead curator from the Bronx Zoo now had me in his unwavering grip. Close by, the bushmaster too lay in wait.

# 1

# Working up Snakes

*"Poisonous snakes have always fascinated me. Just how and when this fascination started I can't remember."*

— Raymond L. Ditmars, *Strange Animals I Have Known* (1931)

———•◆•———

*July 26, 1891. Central Park, New York City.*

"LOOK WHERE YOU'RE GOING, son!" hollers a police officer. But the fair-haired youth is oblivious as he careers through the traffic that even late on a Sunday clogs the intersection of Seventh Avenue and 110th Street. He slips between two drays loaded with crates and reaches Warriors' Gate, a large gap in the low stone wall bounding the northern edge of Central Park. At last, a pause for breath. He has after all just run most of the way from his house some six blocks distant.

He is soon off again, sprinting across lawns and hurdling flower beds, only one thing on his mind: to get to that wild northwestern corner of the park before sundown. He was a mere boy in knickerbockers when he first discovered garter snakes basking on the rocky ledges and outcrops beyond the old Blockhouse. Years later the serpents still fascinate him, especially on warm summer evenings like this one when he can spend hours marveling at the lithe movements, the flicking tongues, the scales glistening in the fading light.

But today will be different. Something catches his eye that stops him dead. A poster is fixed to a tree trunk: SNAKE SHOW AT THE MENAGERIE.

7:30PM TONIGHT. PROFESSOR GEORGE R. O'REILLY EXHIBITS HIS REMARKABLE COLLECTION FROM AROUND THE WORLD.

"Just my luck," he laughs. "A snake show starting right now, and here I am at the far end of the park!"

Half an hour later and the panting, sweaty teenager staggers toward the sheds and open-air enclosures housing elephants and bears, monkeys and wolves. The stench of animal waste floats in the evening breeze. Two camels watch mournfully as he passes into the former arsenal, a castellated building now serving as the menagerie's administrative offices and whose entrance hall is the temporary venue for tonight's exhibition. He's surprised to find a sizeable crowd of visitors filing respectfully past several dozen glass-fronted display cases arranged on trestle tables. Perhaps not everyone in this city hates snakes after all.

The youth begins inspecting the cases, each labeled with its reptilian contents. CRIBO. FER-DE-LANCE. PUFF ADDER. PARROT SNAKE. Many species are new to him although he does recognize the olive-brown colors of a water moccasin. Nicknamed the "cottonmouth" for its habit of gaping a whitish maw at enemies, this snake is a venomous native of the United States, chiefly the waterways of the South where it is more dreaded than its cousin the rattlesnake. The moccasin is said to strike on the slightest provocation—and without the rattler's boisterous warning. One case is marked TIGER SNAKE—EXPERT RAT CATCHER (FROM TRINIDAD). Coiled motionless within is a yellow-and-black serpent whose length he puts at about four feet. A live mouse has been placed in the same case: supper. The rodent is agitated, approaching and repeatedly sniffing at the reptile. At one point it even clambers over the snake's head. The teenager watches, hoping for a kill. Nothing happens so he moves on.

At the far end of the hall, a newspaper reporter with pen and notepad questions two smartly dressed, vociferous gentlemen.

"Oh no, it's a simple enough task," booms one of the latter, the County Clare accent unmistakable. He is tanned, has an athletic build, and sports a closely cut brown beard and mustaches waxed to an upward point in the French style. "You use your forked stick to pin down the snake, then grasp him behind the head and fling the rest of his body over your shoulder. The animal can coil around as much as he chooses after that."

"Although, mind you keep a firm grip on his neck," adds his colleague, "or there'll be trouble! Isn't that so, O'Reilly? Ha ha!"

As the trio descends into laughter, the teenager advances on O'Reilly. "Excuse me, Professor, but which is your favorite snake species of them all?"

"Well, young man, what's your name?" replies O'Reilly, his blue eyes still smiling.

"Ray, I mean, Raymond."

"Well, Raymond, my favorite species, eh? That's a tricky one. You saw the cribo over there, did you?"

The youth nods.

"That fellow loves to eat other snakes, including the poisonous ones, and he'll take on vipers almost double his size. To me that's mighty impressive . . ."

O'Reilly pauses.

". . . but for pure majesty it really has to be the snake we've just been talking about: the bushmaster! Or, as my friend Mr. Libert here from Trinidad knows it, the *mapepire z'anana!*"

The two words are pronounced slowly, deliberately.

"While other deadly vipers such as fer-de-lances inhabit the lowlands close to human population," continues the Irishman, "the bushmaster lurks in hilly regions, deep in the vast forests of South America. He's damned difficult to find. But when you do, watch out! He sometimes grows more than thirteen feet in length. His fangs are of a *wondrous* size and his venom is *copious!*"

"And he's strong too," interjects Libert. "Body's thick as a man's arm and he can launch himself over three-quarters of his own length!"

"Goodness me!" The teenager is enthralled.

"Yes, you undoubtedly need your wits about you when taking a bush-master," says O'Reilly, "although I didn't have too much bother subduing one in Trinidad a couple of years ago. Eight-footer turned up in Chagua-nas after I offered a reward."

"Is it in your exhibition tonight?" asks the young snake enthusiast.

"Alas no, Raymond. The specimen lasted but a few days. In my expe-rience, the bushmaster never takes well to captivity."

Many other questions follow. Toward the end of the evening Ray returns to the tiger snake case finding much the same situation: no telltale bulge in the snake, its cage mate alive and well. Indeed, the rodent now appears relaxed, sitting back on haunches cleaning whisk-ers just a few inches from doom. Still the snake fails to stir, not even a tongue-flick. Either that snake's not hungry or he's made of India rubber!

---

THINGS were going well. For years I had been filming interesting wildlife in exotic places, including on some tropical islands. Raymond Ditmars and bushmasters were all but forgotten. Or were they? Passing through London one day I found myself with time to kill. Instinct led me to the Natural History Museum and, in particular, its library, where an after-noon could be whiled away perusing classic works crowded with vivid illustrations of zoological specimens. I gravitated toward the snake books. A 1742 edition of Charles Owen's *An Essay towards a Natural History of Serpents: In Two Parts* looked amusing. Topics covered included "Fiery Serpents that infested the Camp of Israel" and "Divine Worship given to Serpents by the Nations." Also catching my eye was *Ophiolatreia*, an anonymous "exposition of one of the phases of phallic, or sex worship" which was "privately printed" in 1889.

Then I pulled out an 1825 edition of Charles Waterton's *Wanderings in South America, the North-west of the United States and the Antilles*. Waterton was a Yorkshireman, minor aristocrat, and tropical traveler. *Wanderings* details a decade's worth of explorations beginning in British Guiana, where his family had estates. Various encounters with wild beasts including jaguars, insects, and birds are described. At one point Waterton wrestled a boa constrictor, trussing its jaws with his braces. But what really struck me was his description of another snake: "Unrivalled in his display of every lovely colour of the rainbow, and unmatched in the effects of his deadly poison, the *counacouchi* glides undaunted on, sole monarch of these forests," writes Waterton. "Both man and beast fly before him and allow him to pursue an undisputed path. He sometimes grows to the length of fourteen feet." *Counacouchi* was the local word for bushmaster.

Whether the explorer had actually seen one was debatable, but the snake obviously had a reputation. My interest in the bushmaster reawakened, I sought further descriptions and in another nineteenth-century volume I learned that the snake had a curved claw on its tail, supposedly planted in the ground as a fulcrum for pouncing on victims. One equally fanciful report had the snake "erect on the tip of his tail in the midst of a Brazilian road and barring the way as effectually as an eighteen-pounder." In that country the bushmaster went by the name *surucucú* referring to the mysterious whistle it was said to emit in the dead of night. *Peee-ooooooo-ooooooo-wheet!*

I could have lingered for hours but had a train to catch. I considered photocopying some of the more interesting pages, but the copy price was high.

"You can take photos of the pages," suggested a middle-aged male librarian seated at his large, elegant desk.

Luckily I had brought my digital camera and prepared to snap away.

"But you'll have to fill this in." I was handed a yellow form.

Having completed the paperwork I again readied the Lumix and pressed the shutter button.

This prompted the unmistakable sound of throat-clearing.

"Please don't use a flash!"

This was reasonable given the age of the books, but daylight was fading. Admitting defeat, I went home.

But something had clicked. During those few hours I had lost myself in a bygone era of discovery and travel. My fascination both with bushmasters and the American zoo curator they had so obsessed flared with new intensity. I spent the next week tracking down and ordering as many of Ditmars's books as I could, titles like *Strange Animals I Have Known*, *Confessions of a Scientist*, and *The Book of Insect Oddities*. The book prices were occasionally eye-watering, suggesting his works were still in demand. Of most interest was *Snake-Hunters' Holiday*, describing a collecting trip to Trinidad and British Guiana in the summer of 1934. The goal had been to trap a live bushmaster.

This now sounded like my kind of holiday. But why? I had no desire to catch a viper myself. Lacking the expertise of a Rom Whitaker or a Steve Irwin, nothing would have been more reckless.

Yet the quest still appealed. Putting down *Snake-Hunters' Holiday*, I resolved to go to New York and learn more about Raymond Ditmars. I would trace his career, follow in his footsteps, visit his haunts. My snake-stalking skills honed, I would then head down to South America and try my own luck at finding a bushmaster. How difficult and dangerous could it be? After all, bushmasters were responsible for just 0.01 percent of reported snake bites in Latin America. I tried to ignore the nagging possibility that because accidents occurred far from civilization, bushmaster bites were underrepresented in the figures, and that if I was bitten, the outlook wasn't great. The locals seemingly knew this. During the filming in Peru of Werner Herzog's 1972 movie, *Aguirre, the Wrath of God*, a lumber man was struck twice in the leg by a bushmaster. Legend has it that, without missing a beat, he lopped off the limb.

The Central Park Menagerie, New York City, 1893. A malodorous cluster
of ramshackle sheds, cages, and open-air enclosures.

"Ten years ago there's no way I would have walked up here alone."

Regina strode ahead along the narrow path skirting a bulky protru-
sion of gray schist. Crowning the outcrop was Blockhouse Number One,
the sole survivor of forts built in 1814 to ward off a British attack that never
came.

"Really?" I said, peering up at the rudimentary structure. Nestled
among the oaks and maples framing the northern perimeter of Central
Park, this seemed a peaceful enough spot despite the hum of traffic from
West 110th Street down the hill to our right. Earthy, sylvan odors filled
the cool, early autumnal air.

"Yeah. Even in the mid-2000s, this part was still notorious for mug-
gers, drug-dealers, prostitutes."

The Central Park Conservancy had spent three decades and almost
a billion dollars restoring Manhattan's premier green space. In the 1970s
the park was in decline, and few ventured above 96th Street, but as the
conservancy steadily worked its way north, the lowlifes were driven off.
This corner of the park, known as the North Woods, was a "hold-over

area," among the last to be restored. The conservancy now maintained wildness of a different sort here, removing invasive plant species such as Japanese knotweed, Chinese wisteria, and Norwegian maple while re-planting native oaks, maples, elms, tulip trees, and sweet gums. Dead wood wasn't tidied away but left to rot, providing habitats for invertebrates.

"Things still happen, though," she said as we paused for breath, "This *is* New York."

Just twenty-four hours before, I had flown into the city, the plane tracing the coast of Long Island before slowly descending toward Kennedy airport. A few hundred feet beneath me, surfers bobbed on the green waves of Atlantic Beach. Then, earlier today I had rendezvoused with Regina Alvarez at Central Park. A conservancy employee for nineteen years, Regina now taught at a small city college but maintained her links with the park. We had gone first to an area Ditmars had pronounced a snake haven: some rocky bluffs between West 104th and 105th Streets. But the only sign of life was dog-walkers chattering in a nearby clearing, their animals cavorting across the grass.

Regina had already softened me up for disappointment during email exchanges. The serpents in the park now seemed to be exotics, unwanted pets such as king snakes or boas. Raccoons, red-tailed hawks, and other predators had probably wiped out the natives. Yet merely visiting one of Ditmars's earliest haunts provided a minor thrill in itself.

Half an hour later we emerged from the North Woods onto West Drive to be confronted by an unbroken stream of joggers, a form of New York traffic peculiar to Central Park. Waiting for an opportunity to cross, I stared up at the skyscrapers looming over the trees on the horizon.

Regina caught my gaze. "You used not to be able to see buildings from here, but in 2009 we had a storm one night. Lost five hundred trees in fifteen minutes."

The soil in much of the park was shallow, barely covering the bedrock, and offered tree roots scant purchase when high winds swept in from the Atlantic.

"Some people like seeing the skyline from the park, others hate it," continued Regina. "They want to forget they're in the city."

While snakes seemed nonexistent, other species were doing better. Beavers and chipmunks were making a comeback, and not long ago a coyote nicknamed Hal padded in.

"The theory is he came in along the Metro North Railroad," said Regina.

"Shall we head to the Central Park Zoo?" I asked as we weaved through a party of gasping seniors.

DURING the nineteenth century, just as today, the northern end of the park was a semiwilderness rarely disturbed by the landscape gardeners who focused on the neat flower beds and elegant avenues elsewhere. In the spring and summer months of the early 1880s, a blond-haired little boy would creep up to the ledges here after school, eager to see the dozens of garter snakes and brown snakes stretched out on the warm rocks. Non-venomous but exciting, several exceeded a yard in length. In the early days he would just watch. Then he started stuffing them in his pockets. On the weekends the young naturalist could spend an entire day gathering snakes in the park, occasionally recruiting others to the cause. With the twenty-five cents his father gave him for lunch he would buy a pickle for a penny and doughnuts for a nickel. He gave the rest to other boys in return for green chicken snakes and garter snakes. Central Park's reptilian treasures fueled a passion for the lowly that had manifested itself in the boy long before his family had moved to the city.

Raymond Lee Ditmars was born in Newark, New Jersey, on June 22, 1876, to John Van Harlingen Ditmars, a furniture dealer, and his wife, Mary. He had one sibling, an older sister named Ella. Ditmars senior was of Dutch ancestry and a veteran of General Lee's Confederate army, hence his son's middle name. Raymond was an instinctive herpetologist in its truest sense. The term derives from the Greek *herpeton* meaning "creeping animal," and as a toddler he would root about in the back yard for anything that crawled low to the ground. That meant ants and grasshoppers and caterpillars and frogs and turtles. Yet watching was not enough, the animals had to be held, had to be collected. One story has Ditmars training ten toads to dance in the parlor, the amphibians supposing the carpet to be grass. His mother warned her little blond boy that he would soon be "all full of warts."

The 1880s saw the Ditmarses relocating to a four-story apartment house in Harlem. That's when Raymond started his adventures in Central Park, a few blocks to the west. Summer vacations were spent at Gravesend Bay in Brooklyn. For Raymond, the entertainments of nearby Coney Island were not the only attraction. In time the bay would suffer industrial pollution and was even used to dump military waste, but when Ditmars was a boy its salt marshes and sand dunes were pristine. Alive with turtles, crabs, and snakes, it was a habitat ripe for exploration. Once, aged twelve, Raymond found a pair of garter snakes among the cattails and begged his parents to let him bring them home. The answer was "No," although he subsequently saved another garter snake from a stoning by his friends, secreting it in a soap box in the garden and feeding it bread and milk. He was later permitted to keep a dozen or so harmless types in his bedroom during winter months, provided they didn't appear in the parlor or at the dinner table.

The boy's interests ranged beyond the small and slimy. Thrilled by his father's war stories, Raymond hankered after danger, adventure, and travel. He fantasized about becoming a fireman. The perils inherent in such a career were tantalizing. Equally seductive was the opportunity to ride colorful vehicles drawn by magnificent horses or the Amoskeag and La France steam-powered fire engines. Many contemporaries shared such passions, but the yearnings stayed with Ditmars. His love of deadly reptiles would become the most obvious manifestation of a penchant for risky situations, but other hazardous natural phenomena were also attractive. Volcanic eruptions, lightning storms, and hurricanes fascinated him.

Ditmars devoured accounts of mysterious lands and exotic creatures. The French American anthropologist Paul Belloni du Chaillu, famed as the first white man to prove the existence of gorillas, was an influence. Like other explorers, du Chaillu sold animal specimens to zoos and museums to bankroll his expeditions. Additional funds came from lecture tours and bestselling books. A passage in the 1861 classic *Explorations and Adventures in Equatorial Africa* chimes with Ditmars's own benevolent view of serpents. Conceding that snakes were "dangerous animals," du Chaillu considered their presence "a great blessing to the country" in their destruction of "great numbers of rats and mice, and other of the smaller quadrupeds which injure the native provisions." Moreover, they were "peacefully inclined, and never attack man unless trodden on." Such enlightened attitudes are, however, absent in a later book that reports du Chaillu's encounter with a large serpent close to a waterfall. The "ugly" black-and-yellow creature had a triangular head "showing that he was venomous." As the snake slipped into the water, the author reached for his gun: "I had not to wait long before he appeared, when I fired the load of small shot, broke his back, and the reptile sank to the bottom." A second serpent "just the color of the dead leaves" was spotted lying across the path. Du Chaillu bludgeoned the animal with a stick, decapitated it, and took the body in pieces back to the camp as food for his hunters.

Negative responses such as these are, of course, the norm for most of us. This is what made Raymond Ditmars so unusual. Why did he love snakes when disgust, hatred, and, above all, fear of the cold-blooded seems hardwired in humans? Carl Linnaeus, an eighteenth-century taxonomist, described reptiles and amphibians as "foul and loathsome animals" with "their cold body, pale colour, cartilaginous skeleton, filthy skin, fierce aspect, calculating eye, offensive smell, harsh voice, squalid habitation and terrible venom." It was for these reasons, he asserted, that the Creator had not exerted his powers to make many of them. But as much as we are afraid of reptiles so have we long been drawn to them, especially to serpents with their unfathomable limbless motion and their alien,

unblinking stares thought to fascinate and terrorize prey in equal measure. So important have snakes been for us that they may even have shaped
our belief systems, with some resurrection myths reportedly inspired by
the way snakes are able to slough off their skin in one go like an unwanted
stocking, emerging clean and bright. For Ditmars, and for generations of
herpetologists since, perhaps what was key was the *mystery* surrounding
serpent nature.

Writing in his early twenties, by which time he'd extended his snake-
hunts far beyond New York City limits, Ditmars offered a clue to the
fascination. During a ramble in the Pennsylvania woods he noticed in the
grass "a slender snake, whose delicately striped body resembled a dainty
bit of ribbon," steadily consuming a tiny toad. Pausing to watch the proceedings, he witnessed the arrival of another, much larger, serpent. The
latter promptly grasped the smaller snake by the head and "swallowed
feaster and toad until only an inch or so of wriggling tail protruded from
its mouth." Detecting "the human intruder" the engorged reptile "turned
quickly and disappeared whence it came." For Ditmars, this "curious little
tragedy, so quickly enacted and among such queer creatures" reinforced
his interest in the serpent race, prompting him "to collect and study the
habits of these creatures."

While du Chaillu's attitudes to serpents may have been ambivalent,
the young Ditmars would have been left in no doubt as to the opinion
of another adventurer of the time. For George R. O'Reilly, an itinerant
newspaper editor and school professor of Irish origin, snakes were an abid-
ing passion. As Ditmars would later write, O'Reilly had "been in nearly
every temperate and tropical country in the world in his search and study
of serpent life." The live specimens were then dispatched to zoos in North
America and Europe. His experiences ranged "from the ludicrous to the
other extreme. In Africa he was worshipped by the natives, and in the
West Indies was regarded as a raving maniac."

The tools of O'Reilly's trade were simple: opera glasses to spot his
quarry, a long forked stick to catch it, and a calico bag or two in which

to bring it home. He also carried an eight-foot butcher knife and chain-smoked Havana cigarettes, their blue fumes supposedly keeping mosquitoes at bay. Much of the snake-hunting took place in Trinidad, where O'Reilly had once made his home, and in nearby Venezuela and British Guiana. He later moved to Newark, New Jersey, with some five hundred snakes as housemates, a good proportion of which he had bred himself. De Kay's snakes, ribbon snakes, garter snakes, watersnakes, and other harmless varieties rubbed up against venomous copperheads, water moccasins, and rattlesnakes. According to Ditmars, the collection was "positively alarming" to the uninitiated and wherever O'Reilly "took up his abode" the entire district became "immediately uncomfortable." When interviewed by the *New York Sun*, O'Reilly forbade the reporter from printing his address for fear that his neighbors might "present a petition to the landlord requesting that the serpent expert be ignominiously bounced."

As with Ditmars, the motives for keeping snakes were not obvious. O'Reilly told the paper that he did not sell or exhibit them, but amassed them "simply to be the better able to study their habits closely." Aesthetic qualities were an important element as the opening passage in one 1892 article written by O'Reilly makes clear: "As we find every color of the rainbow used by nature in the adornment of birds and insects, so among the serpents do we meet with the same lavishing of tints, not less striking in brilliancy of contrast, not less subtle in harmonious blending of shades, not less delicate in tracery of pattern." The Irishman never missed an opportunity to emphasize other noble attributes. "I consider that snakes play a most useful role in creation, even the most venomous kinds," he once said. "In every country snakes prey upon the smaller destructive animals, and are thus the farmers' friends."

O'Reilly even performed surgery to save badly injured animals. He was once brought a copperhead by a local farmer whose son had damaged it with a pitchfork during a difficult capture: "The snake was nearly dead when I got it, but as I'm something of a snake doctor, I set at work to save its life." The copperhead lived and that night gave birth to nine young.

(Ditmars would later prove similarly adept at such veterinary work.) Despite O'Reilly's assertions that snakes were a private affair, at least one public exhibition is recorded from 1891, when the professor—still living in Trinidad—had brought seventy-five specimens representing thirty distinct species to the Central Park menagerie.

The teenage Raymond Ditmars probably visited the show, since the menagerie was Central Park's other main attraction for him. During the 1860s, park employees started receiving animals as gifts, mainly unwanted house pets, but also such exotic species as an alligator, a peacock, a boa constrictor. Presently, a malodorous cluster of ramshackle sheds, cages, and open-air enclosures grew up in the south-east corner of the park to accommodate them. Some exhibits were donated by military officers from far-flung locations (General Sherman left an African cape buffalo here), others came from the traveling circuses of P. T. Barnum and others taking a break during the winter. The menagerie represented the city's only substantial animal collection and at its height more than seven thousand daily visitors would gaze upon the bears and monkeys, elephants and camels, eagles and macaws. People then moved on to view stuffed versions in the nearby Arsenal which, for eight years, served as the temporary home of the American Museum of Natural History until the museum's first permanent building opened in 1877. Was it the roar of lions, commonly heard across this southern corner of Central Park that drew the crowds despite the stench? Who knows, but the free entry price must have been part of the appeal, above all for the indigent masses of the city's slums and ghettos.

Mammals and birds predominated, but snakes and other reptiles were sometimes displayed and it was these that most interested the young Raymond Ditmars. He befriended the keepers, exchanged animal husbandry tips and once helped a ten-foot-long boa constrictor slough off its skin by draping it with a wet blanket. Snakes in captivity often failed to shed, leading to serious infections. Dry conditions were the chief cause, and moistening the reptile usually did the trick.

During visits to the menagerie Ditmars met another influential figure, a genial medical doctor named C. Slover Allen. Although expert in ear, nose, and throat maladies, natural history was Allen's true calling. "Every object in nature had for him a fascination which impelled him to study the animate or inanimate with equal ardor," wrote his obituarist in 1893. Early publications focused on hawks, ducks, and other birds, but the physician switched his attentions to an enduring problem: finding a snakebite cure.

While he never did arrive at a solution, Allen gathered valuable data on the water moccasins and rattlesnakes, which he trapped during vacations to Florida. The venomous snakes were maintained in a Fourth Avenue laboratory where the doctor extracted their venom. This hazardous procedure—euphemistically known as "milking"—involved grasping the serpent by the neck and applying its jaws to parchment, cheese cloth, or a similar material stretched over the mouth of a glass beaker. As the snake bit into the membrane, it sent two jets of lethal fluid into the collection vessel. Allen demonstrated his reptiles at meetings of the Linnaean Society of New York City, the leading naturalists' club of the day, of which he was an enthusiastic member. When the experiments were completed, the serpents were handed over to the menagerie. Just like his hero Allen, Ditmars would spend holidays collecting snakes, and he too would become a public educator on all matters reptilian.

A FEW minutes later, Regina and I stepped back into Central Park at the East 64th Street entrance. A sign on the stone pillar to our left read To THE ZOO AND CAFETERIA. Rather than slog the forty or so blocks south, we had caught an MTA bus down elm-lined Fifth Avenue. In front of us stood the redbrick polygonal towers of the old Arsenal building, with which Ditmars would have been familiar. He would not have recognized much else around here.

In 1983 the Central Park Zoo, as the menagerie had been renamed, was demolished. After five years and $35 million of investment, the Central Park Wildlife Center was born under the stewardship of the New York

Zoological Society. Gone were the cramped, depressing, jail-like cages that had prompted one parks commissioner to call the zoo "a Riker's island for animals." In their place was a series of innovative, naturalistic, and spacious exhibits arranged into tropical, temperate, and polar climate zones. More animals were on display now, but those requiring space, such as lions, elephants, and hippos were moved elsewhere, causing some people to grumble.

Interviewed by the *New York Times*, the society's then general director Bill Conway made no apology for the improved animal welfare standards: "This is a mini-zoo to show things likely to arouse people's interest and sense of caring." That meant whizzing squadrons of penguins viewable from new underwater angles and tropical birds freely fluttering between trees. As well as entertaining and educating visitors, the society wanted to generate sympathy—and funds—for conservation projects around the world. A modest entry fee was charged for the first time, which did not dent its success.

Three decades later and the place still seemed popular with New Yorkers and tourists alike. Time was limited so Regina and I didn't go into the zoo. Instead we wandered to a small lake called The Pond at the southernmost extremity of the park, where turtles thrived in the shadow of the nearby old Plaza Hotel. I imagined an obdurate guest insisting upon a bowl of turtle soup and a bellboy being ordered across the busy street with a net.

Regina looked at her watch. "Perfect timing."

She pointed back at a row of brick archways close to the Arsenal. Atop them the George Delacorte musical clock jolted into life: a goat, a penguin, an elephant, a kangaroo, a bear, and a hippopotamus, each posed fancifully in bronze, were set spinning. The tune of a well-known nursery rhyme ding-donged out across this frenetic corner of the park.

DITMARS realized that even more exciting serpent-hunting adventures could be had beyond Central Park. As a teenager he extended collecting trips far and wide. Sorties were made across the Hudson to the bluffs of Fort Lee, New Jersey, where ring-necked snakes and hognoses could be snared, and past the Statue of Liberty to Staten Island, always a reliable place for keeled green snakes. Another green-colored type of snake, just as gorgeous, favored the meadows of Plymouth County, Connecticut, while large black rat snakes foraged on rocky ledges the length of the Hudson River Valley. He would sometimes find them draped across tree boughs. Were they asleep? It was hard to tell with an animal lacking eyelids.

After the thrills of tracking down and snatching these sleek, fast-moving creatures, Ditmars loved sharing his experiences with others. In January 1893, aged sixteen, he formed the Harlem Zoological Society with other youths who shared his passion for nature. In the warmer months, the boys, each sporting a little triangular silver pin with H.Z.S. in blue, scoured the Bronx Park and surrounding countryside for turtles, salamanders, lizards, butterflies, beetles, moths, and, of course, snakes. His friend Charles Ward Crampton later remembered Ditmars as "a great companion. Hardy, untiring, considerate, never let a branch fly back in your face, always took turns going first, never showed off, always generous in dividing up the spoils." The creatures were brought back for examination and discussion. One report has Ditmars using tweezers to help a garter snake shed its skin while his colleagues looked on in amazement. The *New York World* reported that the boys met fortnightly on Thursday evenings at the houses of different members where "exceedingly clever and well illustrated" original papers would be read out. Ditmars was portrayed as "working up snakes." Indeed he possessed "one of the finest live collections of these repulsive reptiles in New York city," which he "affectionately" handled. Included was a six-foot-long "thunder snake" from California and two Florida diamondback rattlesnakes "whose bite is the most deadly of their kind." The youth had not caught them himself; he had acquired them from his friend Dr. Slover Allen, who had died a few months earlier. Nevertheless, by this point Raymond Ditmars had graduated from the nursery slopes of snake keeping and was now testing himself with some truly formidable animals.

According to the *New York World*, the Harlem Zoological Society boasted associate and honorary members, including a certain "Prof. Beutenmüller" who "takes a great interest in the boys and their work and encourages them in every possible way." In fact, Ditmars's association with the professor went beyond the mere sharing of amateur pursuits, for William Beutenmüller, curator of entomology at the American Museum of Natural History, was by now also his boss.

# 2

# Pleased with a Rattler, Tickled
# with its Fang

*"There is probably no class of creatures less known, more hated, and unjustly persecuted than reptiles; but observation brings about a transformation of ideas in the minds of their most persistent enemies."*

—James N. Baskett & Raymond L. Ditmars, *The Story of the Amphibians and Reptiles* (1902)

———⊶◆⊷———

*October 23, 1894, American Museum of Natural History, New York City*

THE SOUND OF HURRIED footsteps on polished red tiles reverberates down the length of the corridor. Removing hat and scarf, he passes gloomy exhibition galleries to his left and right. The occasional display specimen is visible by the gaslight seeping through from the brightly illuminated hallway: a regiment of impaled beetles, the spirals of an ammonite, a stuffed tiger-cat with unblinking marble eyes. The aroma of pickling alcohol hangs on the air.

Ahead, the grand door to the museum library is open. Ray is relieved to see that for once he's early; most of the fifty or so seats arranged in rows for tonight's meeting are empty. Several members stand in a huddle at the opposite end of the chamber, some are smoking pipes. Bearded and scholarly looking, their focus is another man, equally bewhiskered. He's sitting at a huge reading table that is covered in green cloth. Ray identifies him as Dr. Joel Allen, head of the museum's Ornithology Department and president of the New York Linnaean Society, the scientific organization at whose gathering Ray is hoping to speak.

Engrossed in talk of the evening's agenda, none of the men notices the timid eighteen-year-old hovering at the doorway.

"So we'll start with Mr. Dutcher's encouraging news on the protection of the terns on Great Gull Island," says Allen, leafing through papers. "Mr. Granger will next read out Dr. Shufeldt's article 'Peculiar phases of color assumed by certain birds.' Sadly the surgeon himself is unable to attend this evening." This last comment is met by grumbles from his colleagues.

"Then Mr. Foster has asked to list the published records on birds of prey found in the vicinity of the city. We'll close as usual with general discussion—but we won't have long as the library must be clear by ten."

Ray shudders at the final words, for it is during the period of "general discussion" that he intends to read out a scientific paper: a summary of field observations from the rattlesnake colony he has been visiting for the last two springs in the scrub oak woods of Connecticut. He draws from his jacket pocket a piece of paper. It is his carefully written article entitled "Notes on some Species of the Genus *Crotalus*, with a brief Review of the Genus." He mouths through it silently for the hundredth time. His hands are shaking. With bird matters dominating the schedule, who is going to be interested in his snakes? More learned members arrive. People start to sit. Chatter builds. Still Ray lingers at the library door.

Presently, a skinny youth of about his own age breezes past, a cylindrical package under his arm. It is William Beebe (pronounced "*bee-bee*"), who is already making a name for himself in the ornithological community. Ray surmises that the parcel contains a stuffed bird of some variety. Sitting down in the back row next to an elderly gentleman, Beebe unwraps the packet to produce a barn owl, pale and lifeless. Although the specimen appears ordinary enough to Ray, Beebe's neighbor is transfixed: "Goodness, I've never seen one of that size before! Well done, my boy. Where did you bag it?"

"Oh, quite close to my house in East Orange," says Beebe. "And I mounted it myself—"

A sharp call to order comes from the president's table and a respectful silence descends on the library. Momentarily emboldened by Beebe's example, Ray slips into the chamber, he too taking a seat at the rear.

As feared, the ensuing proceedings are devoted largely to bird talk. Almost two hours later and after a dozen motions have been voted upon, Allen at last signals the general discussion. "I am afraid we've rather run out of time," he says, "but if any members or visitors have anything pressing, and more importantly *brief*, to say, now's the time."

Ray holds aloft a trembling, damp hand.

"Yes, you boy, there in the back row!" exclaims Allen.

With thumping heart, Ray clears his throat and begins to rise but to his astonishment realizes he's been beaten to it.

"Thank you, Professor Allen," a smiling Beebe is already on his feet. "Perhaps the esteemed members would like to examine my specimen of *Strix pratincola* collected in the New Jersey woods this summer? I have prepared it myself."

Ray sits back down and watches in anguish as Beebe's owl is now passed reverently among the appreciative members. Precious minutes tick away. Finally, Ray can take no more. Springing to his feet once again he tries to catch Allen's eye.

"Meeting adjourned!" comes the response.

*New York*
*January 30th 1893*
*Prof. W Beutenmüller*

*Dear Sir,*
*The new term in Raymond's school begins this week & as soon as the term begins we are expected to settle for the coming half-year's tuition. We are therefore anxious to know about the possibility of his receiving a place under your care & instruction in your department in the Museum.*

*So far as anything in the way of salary is concerned we care nothing about it. The knowledge to be gained is of exceedingly more importance & is all we desire.*

*His heart & mind are so completely set upon the objects of the Museum that we are satisfied his school would not do him much good should he continue in it.*

*Will you kindly let me know what the prospects are?*

*Very Respectfully*
*John V H Ditmars*
*162 W 116th Street*

I COULD not believe my fortune in coming across this short note written in an elegant, flowing hand. The day after my tour of Central Park I had headed to the American Museum of Natural History, entering the grand building via the security entrance on 77th Street. Stepping from an elevator at the fourth floor, I soon found myself in the research library. Try as I might I couldn't picture a nervous young Raymond Ditmars here clutching his paper in sweaty hands hoping to catch the eye of the Linnaean Society's president across a crowded chamber. But this large, airy room with its computer terminals, functional wooden furniture, and modern lighting was indeed the site of the museum's original library. The sole connections to the past were framed monochrome photographs on the walls capturing moments from the museum's history. One showed a museum porter maneuvering a large set of antlers. In another, a bearded scientist chips away at the fossilized carapace of a giant prehistoric reptile.

A helpful librarian in his late twenties named Gregory appeared and escorted me into the special collections room adjacent to the research library. I spent a pleasant hour or two rummaging through box file after box file of letters, posters, tickets, telegrams, and receipts. Although the documents were absorbing, I turned up little of relevance. An onset of light-headedness indicated to me that it must be lunchtime. This became something of a pattern; so engrossing was my research that the hours would just race by.

The quest for Ditmars now became a quest for food. Returning to the elevator, I found it occupied by a well-dressed old lady.

I asked for directions to the visitor's cafeteria.

"Oh, are you British?"

The woman, a long-standing volunteer at the museum and an apparent Anglophile, offered to take me to the staff cafeteria instead.

"It's much nicer there."

We left the elevator at a secret basement level for which a special key seem to be required. We continued to chat as she steered me through the bowels of the museum, a musty world of cinderblock tunnels and exposed cables.

"I know how you must feel being new in a place like this. You have a good word for it in England: 'gormless.'"

An hour later, in possession of a full stomach—and hopefully more gorm—I was back at work in the special collections. Almost immediately I found nestled among papers from the entomology department the 1893 letter from John Ditmars to Beutenmüller. Could I detect in it a hint of resignation? Was this a parent despairing that his son would ever make good? It was hard to say, but the sense of relief was unmistakable in a note written the very next day:

*New York*
*January 31, 1893*
*Prof. W Beutenmüller*

*Dear Sir,*
*Yours just received. Please accept my thanks for your kindness & the interest you have taken in my son.*

*The terms upon which you offer to receive him into your department are perfectly satisfactory.*

*He will call upon you & be guided by your direction.*

*I trust that yourself, the Museum & Raymond may all be mutually benefitted by the new relationship.*

*You will find him obedient & respectful.*

*With sincere regards*
*Respectfully Yours*
*John V H Ditmars*
*162 W 116th Street*

These two documents, priceless in my opinion, marked a defining moment in the career of Raymond Ditmars.

The American Museum of Natural History, New York City, c. 1890.
(Courtesy of the American Museum of Natural History)

THE young naturalist had spent his later school years at the Barnard Military Academy for Boys on West 126th Street. Little biology was taught at this 130-pupil institution, although Ditmars thrived on the starched gray-and-white uniforms, the brass band, and the drilling under the watchful eye of William Livingstone Hazen, the school founder. Hazen would subsequently fight in the 1898 Spanish-American War. An ex-soldier, Ditmars's father was keen for his son to pursue an army career, ideally at the prestigious West Point Military Academy located some fifty miles north up the Hudson Valley. The sixteen-year-old Raymond prepared for the entrance exams in 1892, but extracurricular activities with snakes and other lowly forms of life were to lead him in an altogether different direction.

It was inevitable, given his adventures in Central Park, that Ditmars would be drawn to the vast galleries of the American Museum of Natural History located halfway up the west side of the park. The museum's first permanent building, a five-story Gothic structure on 77th Street, was opened in December 1877 by US president Rutherford B. Hayes. Over the succeeding decades the museum swallowed up four city blocks and launched a golden age of exploration to deserts, forests, polar regions, and oceanic archipelagos. Ditmars would lose himself in the collections of stuffed, fossilized, pickled, and pinned organisms from around the world. Highlights included the forestry exhibit and a colossal life-sized sulfur-bottom model whale suspended from the ceiling.

Through the Harlem Zoological Society Ditmars met Professor William Beutenmüller, the museum's curator of entomology and a leader in his field. As a child Beutenmüller had gathered butterflies, moths, beetles, and bees from around his home in New Jersey before moving on to collect in the Black Mountains of North Carolina. He would later serve as president of the New York Entomological Society, editing the first eleven volumes of its journal. Whenever the young Ditmars needed help in identifying an insect, he made for Beutenmüller's office.

Realizing that the curator "endured, rather than enjoyed, this invasion of youth," Ditmars rarely lingered more than five minutes. However, one afternoon the young naturalist brought along an exceptionally fine set of small moths netted on the spectacular and crumbling cliffs of the Hudson River Palisades. So impressed was the entomologist by the skill with which Ditmars had pinned out the tiny pink insects that he made him an astonishing offer: "I'm looking for a young man to mount a series of moths and butterflies in this department. There will be a chance of working up in the museum." Ditmars, then just sixteen, was shocked and exhilarated. What an opportunity! For sure the head of the Ditmars house would need convincing but, as his January 1893 letters to Beutenmüller make clear, John Ditmars was sufficiently pragmatic to yield to, if not encourage, his son's calling in life, even if the financial terms were of no consequence.

Having won a small battle with his parents over choice of career, Raymond faced the far greater challenge of convincing them to let him keep his beloved snakes at home. A few years earlier, after much persuasion, he had wrung a minor concession from them: for a while, he had been allowed a pair of innocuous garter snakes that coiled quietly in their box in one small room of the Ditmars apartment. His family was seemingly reconciled to sharing the home with these serpents, which, after all, were no thicker than a little finger. But patience had worn out following Raymond's acquisition of a watersnake, an irritable but otherwise harmless species frequenting waterways across the eastern United States. This had required him first to obtain permission from his father, something he ingeniously achieved by pointing out the close taxonomic relationship between watersnakes and garter snakes. Then one day while everyone was out, he used his lunch money to procure the animal from a local pet store run by Otto Eggeling, a rotund and affable German. On getting the watersnake home Ditmars himself was perturbed by its size and aggressiveness. He contrived to conceal it from his parents before their return, installing the reptile in a cage to which he had fitted a sun porch extending onto the fire escape. The idea was that his parents would not be able to see the snake from inside the apartment.

Alas, the plan had been far from foolproof. Within days a member of New York City's Finest was knocking at the front door bearing a "combination complaint from the police and health departments." The neighbors were appalled by the spectacle of a serpent enjoying the sun on the fire escape and demanded the nuisance be removed. Only then did John Ditmars himself investigate the source of the grievance. The sight of the four-foot-long watersnake incensed him. Now *all* the snakes had to go, even those enchanting, inoffensive garters. The snake-hunting career of Raymond Ditmars had encountered its first serious setback.

To make matters worse, duties at the museum proved tedious for the young thrill seeker. The "series of moths and butterflies" to which Beutenmüller had referred was the product of a lifetime of collecting by the late Harry Edwards, a popular thespian and writer. "Mr. Edwards was an entomologist before he became an actor," reported a *New York Times* article the previous spring, "And, while he became one of the most finished artists on the stage, he never forgot his first love." Edwards had gathered his insects from rainforest treks, museum visits, and exchanges with fellow enthusiasts. No one knew quite how many had been amassed by the time of his death, and estimates varied between 250,000 and 300,000. Yes, you read that right: *more than a quarter of a million*. And with every delicate specimen that had to be fumigated, pinned, labeled, and cataloged, so Ditmars's initial enthusiasm for museum work drained away. If formal academic science meant this kind of drudgery, he wanted no part of it. "The monotony of that job was almost maddening," he once wrote. "It took about two years to thoroughly complete it."

The sole respite were rare field trips with "the chief"—days out to the New Jersey Palisades or to the Long Island orchards. Ditmars's stretch at the museum coincided with the 1894 emergence of periodical cicadas. Beutenmüller was compiling a monograph on these bugs colloquially known as "seventeen-year locusts" for their habit of emerging from the ground en masse every couple of decades to reproduce. The sight of millions of chirping insects covering every available surface was astonishing and the expeditions also represented gold-plated opportunities to hunt snakes and salamanders.

Ditmars continued to devote his free time to the pursuit of serpents, and by now he wasn't restricting himself to harmless varieties. Buzzing with timber rattlesnakes, the forested hills of Connecticut were a favorite early haunt, and near the house of his uncle, an inventor at the Colt arms factory. An old woodsman had mentioned a rattler den close to the town of Waterbury, and while still a schoolboy Ditmars started making regular pilgrimages to the site. Ever the optimist, he asked his parents whether he could bring a few home in a barrel. Of course not. But that did not stop the lad returning to the vipers that he likened to "velvet cushions" coiled here and there on the steep rocky shelves. He wouldn't just survey them from a safe distance; the budding scientist wanted to study their fangs. That meant getting close enough to pin the snakes down with a forked stick.

"What a thought for a mother!" Ditmars later wrote. "A youth of sixteen, alone on a ledge handling deadly rattlesnakes, with help far distant, separated by miles of rocks and scrub oak!"

Mercifully, he wasn't bitten. He seemed to have an uncanny knack for handling venomous snakes. Was it an innate skill, or was he just very fortunate? If it was luck, then one day it got even better. Ditmars convinced William Beutenmüller to allow him to keep live snakes at the museum. Back then, the institution had no reptile department, so this would have been the first time live snakes were housed here. Having saved up his vacation until the autumn, Ditmars returned to the Connecticut snake dens. By now he knew every fissure and cranny. "I came back with a big fine rattler," Ditmars would later recall with pleasure.

For a while the trophy was kept on his desk in a purpose-built wooden box with a plate-glass sliding panel. The long hours of insect preparation were now enlivened by reptilian buzzing. Sometimes Ditmars would gently withdraw the snake from its cage, allowing it to coil up harmlessly on the desk. Other reptiles were added to the collection, but such joys proved short-lived. One day, during a visit to the entomology department, the museum's president Morris K. Jesup poked the rattlesnake with his walking stick, hoping to provoke a buzz. The viper duly obliged, then took off, careering through a pile of mounted insect specimens. A week's worth of work was destroyed and Beutenmüller was apoplectic. The snakes had to go.

"An orderly place, like the museum, where things were stuffed, impaled on pins and well-behaved, was no place for a live rattler," was how Ditmars encapsulated the chief's argument. The snakes nevertheless remained in the museum, albeit consigned to a taxidermist's storage room in the attic. For the foreseeable future he'd have to clamber over the dismantled bones of elephants to get at his precious snakes.

"The taming of the shrew!" roared Peter as the needle-sharp teeth sank steadily deeper into his hand. After a few minutes of pulling back damp pieces of carpet, we had already encountered a tiny garter snake and a good-sized watersnake. Now Peter had a small mammal hanging off his right thumb. The herpetologist always wore heavy duty gloves for this kind of work and allowed the shrew to linger for a moment before carefully prizing apart its miniscule jaws.

Having drawn a blank in Central Park, I was now more determined than ever to see snakes near the city. While the bushmaster and other exotic snakes would one day fascinate Raymond Ditmars, throughout his life he remained fond of local species, especially those living within fifty miles of New York that were the subject of his very first scientific paper, published in 1895.

Thanks to Regina, I had made contact with Peter Warny, an ebullient Long Islander in his late fifties for whom all forms of reptile and amphibian were nothing short of an obsession. I had had no idea what Peter did for a living but he had promised me he would find me some local snakes, so that was all that counted. A few days after my visit to the museum's library, Peter collected me from my lodgings just north of Manhattan, and we traveled to a good spot he knew up in Westchester County.

Peter loudly expounded upon his wide-ranging interests as we weaved through the suburbs in his Ford Freestyle SUV. It was crammed with dipping nets, old pillow cases, plastic buckets, and a miscellany of other tools of the ecologist's trade. The fertile smell of pond mud was pervasive in the vehicle, which may have explained the driver's preference to keep his window wound down. In normal circumstances, I might have done the same, but even the dashboard was piled high with bric-a-brac. This included small metal boxes and a valuable hardback book about Ditmars that Peter had brought along for me. These objects threatened to slide out of the driver's window at every right turn.

Peter primarily worked as a consultant on wetlands for various organizations including the Nature Conservancy, the New York Natural Heritage Program, and the National Audubon Society. Peter found invasive herps, those brought in intentionally or otherwise by humans, as fascinating as domestic species. The former included the Asian python decimating native wildlife down in the Florida Everglades and a nondescript variety of European wall lizard thriving in New York City. Peter argued that the modern ecologist should be as interested in the "eco-phenomenon" of disturbed habitats as in pristine ones; exotic species were just as important as endemics. He called his study "urban ecology."

As we joined the freeway Peter at last closed his window. He turned to me.

"Which is the most invasive species of them all?"

"Humans?" I offered

"Right! *Homo sapiens!*"

Half an hour later and we were in lush deciduous woodland. The city seemed far away, although at regular intervals we passed sizeable timber or stone homesteads, most with an SUV or pick-up out front. We pulled up at one belonging to Peter's friend Steve Ricker. Steve was director of the nearby Westmoreland Sanctuary, a nature museum and 640-acre wildlife preserve established in 1957 to promote environmental education. The urban ecologist bounded out of the car to greet his pal before rummaging in the back of his vehicle for rubber boots and non-matching gloves.

Steve had allowed Peter to strew dozens of old carpets, tarpaulins, and wooden boards around his spacious backyard. The idea was that snakes would use them as shelters. That was a few months back, and now was time to see what had been lured. The snake traps were concentrated around a crumbling dry stone wall and in a disused vegetable patch. We set about lifting the moldering mats close to the wall, several so rotten they disintegrated. Now, I say "we" here, but in truth I was more comfortable letting Steve and Peter do the work. This being my first outing to true snake country, I felt it prudent to acclimatize gently. After all, who knew what might jump out at us?

Many traps were too wet but one soon yielded a three-foot-long watersnake that attempted to flee into a crevice in the wall. This was the same variety of snake that had landed the young Raymond Ditmars in so much trouble with the neighborhood. Peter and Steve joined forces to extricate the dark-colored reptile, which was doing its best to unload the foul-smelling contents of its anal glands on them, a favorite defensive response for many serpents.

"OK!" exclaimed a grinning Peter. Breathless and smelly, he held up the snake in triumph and began a spiel.

"This is *Nerodia*. Used to be called *Natrix*, the Old World water-snake genus that you still have in England. This is *Nerodia sipedon*." Peter turned over his struggling captive to reveal handsome belly scales, a collage of oranges, reds, and blacks on a cream background.

"Whenever I catch a snake I examine it head to tail. This looks like a female. I look at its eyes, its cloaca, I test the weight, to see how it's doing. And this one seems OK."

With that, he handed me the snake. I cautiously held it by neck and tail, and at arms length in case the contents of the alimentary canal were not entirely exhausted. Seemingly resigned to its fate, the watersnake hung like a dead weight in my hands. Occasionally, during my years in wildlife television, I had handled snakes—nonvenomous ones that is— and was now reminded of their cool, glossy, muscular bodies. I returned the watersnake to Peter, who bagged it and tucked the captive into his shirt for photographing later.

In short succession we found another three snakes among the rocks, all garters of varying sizes but none as impressive as the *Nerodia*. Extra delights awaited us at the vegetable patch. This area had a sandier substrate and delivered up an additional two species. The first was in the genus *Storeria*. Inspiration was apparently in short supply the day herpetologists settled on the common name: this small brown snake was known as the "brown snake," although sometimes it was called De Kay's snake. This was in memory of the naturalist James De Kay who published an important work in the early nineteenth century on the zoology of New York. According to Peter, the brown snake ate snails and bore live young rather than laying eggs.

The final section of carpet harbored an even smaller variety: a secretive, burrowing serpent in the genus *Carphophis*. It wasn't much larger than the earthworms and other invertebrates upon which it preyed. This one was called, yes you've guessed it, a worm snake. Peter informed me that the species was often associated with ants' nests, where it gorged on the larvae, its tiny, tightly packed scales affording protection from insect mandibles. My reward for picking this one up was a squirt of noxious musk, quickly drying on my hand like a line of white correction fluid.

My quest was bearing fruit at last. In the space of an hour I had now seen four separate species of snake, all of which Ditmars himself would have collected in the early days.

"Are we within fifty miles of New York City?" I asked, an all-important consideration.

"Sure," said Steve. "Maybe forty miles or less in a straight line."

I punched the air in silent jubilation.

DURING the 1890s the name "R. L. Ditmars" started appearing in the membership lists of learned organizations associated with the American Museum of Natural History. Among these was the New York Entomological Society, established after "New Yorkers rebelled at the idea of going to Brooklyn for meetings." Professionals and amateurs would congregate twice monthly in the museum library to discuss insect matters. By the age of nineteen Ditmars was its corresponding secretary. Years later Annie T. Slosson, a founding member, recalled conversing with the young Ditmars during a meeting at the museum. "He owned that he was not a real entomologist but liked all sorts of creatures and was devoted to natural history. In the course of our talk he finally confessed that he liked snakes better than any other creatures and told me sadly that he had his trials in the pursuit of ophidian study for, oddly enough, his mother and other female relatives objected strongly to the presence of rattlesnakes in the house!" Slosson noted that, like all real naturalists, Ditmars began young and postulated that even as a baby he would have been "pleased with a rattler, tickled with its fang."

Ditmars's memories of the Entomological Society centered on many field trips around the region. The collection party included two "rather stout Germans" who, "red in the face and perspiring profusely," would frenetically whack bushes with sticks in search of tiny moths. A well-tailored businessman named Otto Dietz, a beetle specialist, would meanwhile tap vegetation, catching his quarry in an upturned umbrella. He deposited the coleopterans in vials that were then tucked neatly into a vest pocket. Ditmars admired this relaxed approach to science. Dietz would "collect all day, flick the dust from his shoes with a handkerchief, and look ready to step into a smart hotel lobby."

Ditmars would one day prove himself a celebrated and prolific lecturer on natural history, delighting audiences across the country. But in these early years public speaking was a terrifying, if necessary, ordeal. After the botched attempt to address the Linnaeans on rattlesnakes he succeeded in delivering a short talk at a meeting of the Entomological Society. Rising to his feet Ditmars announced his paper: "The Serpents of Central Park." The topic prompted mutters of bemusement in the insect-oriented audience, but he had already sought permission from Christian F. Groth, a Manhattan jeweler and the society's treasurer.

"As unexpected to that gathering as a snowflake falling in a tropical jungle, the title and my introductory paragraph caused a stir," Ditmars later remembered, "but as I continued, they were interested; I could feel it." He went on to describe the varieties of snakes that lurked in the Park and the best places to find them.

Ditmars employed an expositional technique which would become a hallmark of his lectures: he illustrated the successful talk with live specimens, on this occasion nonvenomous snakes secured from the park ledges. The exhibits were wheeled into the library in glass-fronted cases by a museum floor man. Such was the success of his talk that Ditmars was invited by the Linnaean Society to publish an extended version of his paper to comprise all snake species within fifty miles of New York City. At Beutenmüller's suggestion Ditmars added a section on distinguishing "inoffensive and dangerous reptiles." The topic of snakes found in the vicinity of the city would become an enduring one for Raymond Ditmars.

An agreeable aspect of his period at the museum was exposure to leading scientists of the day in disciplines ranging from zoology to meteorology. One important figure was the anatomist Henry Fairfield Osborn, who encouraged Ditmars's interest in snakes. The son of a railroad investor, Osborn was then serving as curator of vertebrate paleontology while teaching zoology at the city's Columbia University. Ditmars records his first meeting with the debonair professor, who was often attired in a paisley scarf and corduroy trousers, as establishing a firm friendship, "which was to endure and become a strong, guiding influence."

Ditmars also made the acquaintance of the ornithologist C. William Beebe. One year his junior, Beebe was tall and slim and shared Ditmars's irrepressible enthusiasm for nature—although in those days Beebe seemed happiest when he was shooting and stuffing it. The pair encountered each other frequently at the evening lectures and grubbing about in the wilder reaches of Central Park. Unlike Ditmars, Beebe went on to a more conventional academic training, taking (but not quite completing) a degree in pure science at Columbia under Osborn's tutelage, but their paths would soon cross again. In fact, their careers followed remarkably similar trajectories. Not only would Beebe take up a job at the Bronx Zoo, he also made a name for himself as a photographer, natural history writer, and explorer. A rivalry might have been expected to develop between the two men, yet little evidence for this exists.

But of all the scientists with which the young Raymond Ditmars came into contact during his time at the American Museum of Natural History, it was another entomologist who would leave the greatest impact.

# 3

# Silent Death of the Black Night

*"The gathering of the collection presented unique experiences. Possibly I was just lucky in some instances, but a stubborn determination to fill those cages had something to do with it."*

—Raymond L. Ditmars, *Thrills of a Naturalist's Quest* (1932)

—⋄—

*Summer 1895, Florida Everglades*

"THEN THERE WAS THE *Powhatan*. Another rigged side-wheeler, and *huge* at that. Easily two hundred fifty foot long, and perhaps two and a half thousand tons. Among the largest in the fleet during the war. I believe she ended her days patrolling off Cuba."

Professor Smith pauses at a fallen cypress trunk, gently lowering his pack on to the carpet of desiccated palmetto fronds.

"Seems as a good a spot as any for luncheon, Raymond, wouldn't you agree?"

"Yes, sir. I'll make the fire."

The teenage assistant sets about collecting some of the many thorny stems and twigs strewn over the dry, baked sand. Yesterday in the shallow reddish waters of the swamp the explorers were protected by a canopy of wispy foliage, but here on the higher ground they feel the full force of the midday sun.

"And again her engine was mounted crudely on wooden supports," continues Smith, who scratches his beard then rummages in the bag to retrieve a can of tomatoes. "Please remind me to examine the engine of our steamer on the way home. The modern vessels of the Clyde Line now use the vertical triple or quadruple-expansion design, allowing for smoother . . ."

A loud hiss like a sudden inhalation followed by a sharp buzzing interrupts the scientist's discourse and sends a jolt of adrenalin through Ray's system.

Both men scan the surrounding vegetation and, there, in a clearing beneath a gum tree not ten yards away lies a massive diamondback rattle-snake. The serpent's head, broader than a man's hand, is suspended a few inches above the leaf litter. The rest of the chunky greenish body, with its distinctive pattern of dark lozenges edged in pale yellow, steadily draws into a coil. The stubby, ringed tail and rattle are a blur of movement, creating a continuous, loudening drone.

"A beautiful creature!" gasps Smith.

This is precisely Ray's sentiment. He figures the reptile to be at least two feet longer than either of the Florida diamondbacks he acquired from Dr. Slover Allen. Oh, how he should love to bring this one home! It's an impossibility, of course. Smith has over the last day or so sanctioned the collecting of one or two harmless snakes—a few kings, corns, and chickens—but Ray has no bags large enough to contain the colossus before him, let alone any means of safely capturing it. Moreover, he can well imagine the dim view Beutenmüller would take of his returning from a bug-collecting trip with such a monster.

"I know what you're thinking, Ray," grins Smith. "Don't worry, there'll be plenty of other chances for you to catch such specimens. Come on, let's eat. We needn't allow this fellow to put us off."

His young assistant agrees and, while Smith completes his musings on Civil War steam-craft, Ray builds a fire with the gathered kindling. With a jackknife he cuts the lid off the professor's can, releasing a draught of fruity odor. He opens another of his own and carefully places the cans over the flames. His heart is still racing. The giant reptile nearby closely watches these activities, punctuating each movement with a crescendo of rattling, a further swelling of its body, another flicker of the glossy, bifurcated tongue.

A few minutes later, though, the men are calmly settled on the cypress trunk, each munching on long slices of bread slathered with steaming hot tomato. This simple meal is tasty and perfect sustenance for hours of field-work and, Smith asserts, guards against dehydration. Ray's companion, nominally an expert in insect pests, has enthusiasms and knowledge ranging far beyond the narrow confines of his field of research. Throughout the three-day voyage south hugging the eastern seaboard to Jacksonville, and the subsequent explorations along the palm-lined banks of the Indian River and finally into the Everglade swamps, Smith has proven an author-ity on plants, soils, meteorology, and myriad other natural phenomena. He also has revealed a deep appreciation of such man-made inventions as the railroad, electric signaling, and steam engines; matters an entomolo-gist has no business knowing. And, most admirable of all, the professor has now demonstrated an enlightened attitude toward a much-despised animal. Most people Ray knows would have tried to exterminate the dia-mondback, or at best run a mile!

". . . the soil stratum throughout this area is, as I have said, terri-bly shallow, lying over a bed of coral. So any vegetation struggles to take hold." Smith is now warming to another of his favored themes, namely the threat posed to the Everglades by the introduction of agriculture.

"If they dig canals and dry out these areas for farming, there'll be a serious risk from fire. In my opinion, Florida could one day be reduced to desert."

Again he is interrupted, a low-flying group of wading birds prompting the men to squint skyward.

"Look at that altocumulus forming, could be a squall's brewing over in the Gulf," says the professor. "Expect to get a little wet this afternoon."

Talk of the weather excites Ray; at last, a topic about which he knows something.

"Sir, in the winter over New York, when there are streaky clouds, that's also a sign of an approaching storm," he mumbles, gulping down the last of his food. "I am real interested in the weather too. I have attended lectures at the museum about it and check my barometer every day. It helped me predict the '93 hurricane!"

This pronouncement impresses Smith, who launches into a discussion of cloud formations. Ray listens, rapt. The third member of the lunch party eventually regains its composure; the rattling slows and abruptly stops. The snake unwinds itself and glides from view into a thicket.

"Beautiful," says Smith.

All is quiet again except for the hum of cicadas and distant crackling of a snail kite.

⬥

In 1965 New York was razed to the ground. In the same year, San Francisco, New Orleans, and Chicago were also flattened, the Great Plains and the Old Southwest bulldozed. Fortunately these were only history-themed attractions at an amusement park in northeastern Bronx. Known as Freedomland, the ill-fated enterprise was the brainchild of a Texan named Cornelius Vanderbilt Wood who had located it in Baychester, a patch of salt marshes that were formerly the venue for a cucumber-pickling operation. Wood was an alumnus of the Walt Disney Company, but he struggled to emulate the success of his former employers and the park foundered. Opened to the public in 1961, Freedomland was ripped down just four years later. This wasn't Baychester's first brush with failure. A municipal airport had also been mooted here but never materialized.

Many suspect that the substantial profits to be realized from selling the land motivated Freedomland's operators to file for bankruptcy and, indeed, soon after wrecking balls had done their worst, construction companies moved in. By the 1970s apartment blocks and clusters of three-story townhouses sprawled over the three hundred acres once occupied by Freedomland. Co-op City, as the development was known now, boasted fifteen thousand residential units along with schools, sports facilities, shops, restaurants, churches, offices, and a weather station. It was the largest housing development of its kind in the country.

Now, standing in the salt marshes of New York's Pelham Bay Park, I could easily believe such assertions. The sky was overcast, the tide was out. Far on the horizon Co-op City's string of dreary high-rises were discernible against the gray sky. Hints of sea and sludge were conveyed on an easterly breeze. All three of us had stopped whispering, although Erik occasionally reminded Peter and me to keep our voices low. A few minutes earlier we had skulked past some tarpaulins strung over trees, clusters of plastic furniture, and a rusting cooking stove, the makeshift campsite in the mud and grass. The camp was devoid of human life, the occupants presumably out trying to make a buck. I felt pity and fear. How could anyone survive here among the empty soft drinks containers, chunks of Styrofoam, tires, plastic trims from automobiles, baseballs, the contents of the city's storm drains? Anything that could float had paused here awaiting the next high tide to carry it a little further toward the ocean.

Remarkably, this was among the better places to find snakes within New York's city limits. Leaving the scenic charms of Westmoreland Sanctuary behind us, Peter Warny had introduced me to Erik Zeidler, another snake-hunting pal, close to a disused landfill site and NYPD shooting range. Aged twenty, Erik had grown up in the area and had the *Brwooaanx* accent to prove it. He had been visiting these marshes for years and had agreed to show us a few good spots for snakes although impressing upon us the need to keep the exact location secret for fear of inviting disturbance.

Erik shared Peter's mania for reptiles, a passion that very nearly killed him as evidenced by an ugly brown scar at the base of his left thumb. During field research out West he was bitten on the hand by a timber rattlesnake. Typically, envenomations from this species take a few hours to kick in but Erik had already been studying and handling these snakes for a while. Venom had often splashed his skin and he'd also inhaled microscopic droplets. As a result, he had developed an allergy to the poison that made the bite doubly perilous. Worse still, the rattler had struck an artery, so the toxins flowed straight to his heart, whose beating slowed and twice ceased altogether. Thanks to a miracle, and forty-eight vials of antivenin, Erik survived. He credited a fellow herpetologist (who wished to remain anonymous) for saving his life. Not only did his friend pull Erik out of the woods, he also put the local hospital in touch with poison experts who offered vital advice on treatment over the phone. Although he no longer worked with venomous species, Erik's love of herps was undiminished. After a year at the University of Kansas he came home to start a company educating New York schoolchildren about nature. "I like to get to kids early before their parents have turned them against reptiles," he said. "I find them naturally very open to snakes." He illustrated his shows with live specimens, just as Raymond Ditmars had a century before.

Erik now marched off ahead of us toward a patch of tall grass.

"I've put out a few boards around here but the homeless people take them."

Once again, cover boards seemed the method of choice for attracting snakes. Meanwhile, Peter revisited his favored theme, urban ecology. He had noticed that the snakes he was finding near cities were shorter-lived than their rural counterparts. One explanation was that, with so many killed on roads, those individuals able to breed earlier were likelier to pass on genes. Over time the age profile of the snake population was lowering.

"Take milk snakes," said Peter. "They used to live for up to fifteen years, now you'd be lucky to see one older than seven years. They need to grow up fast and reproduce before they die."

Lawn mowers presented another menace.

"In the old days, cows were used to keep the grass down. They didn't affect the snakes, but mowing machines have hit certain species hard, particularly the green snakes which often get chopped up in them."

Peter was interrupted by an exclamation of triumph. Erik, who had momentarily vanished, reappeared from the tussocks grasping a small, colorful snake in each hand. He presented them to me.

"Here you are: one garter and one milk."

We had seen several garter snakes at Westmoreland but the milk snake, with its attractive reddish-brown pattern on a light gray background, was a new one for me. I held it up for closer inspection.

It seemed that even in twenty-first-century New York City, snakes were still close by if you knew where to look. Erik put it best: "If they can survive out here—and even *I* can't survive here—then there's hope for biodiversity!"

ORIGINALLY a practicing barrister, John Bernhardt Smith had left the law in 1884 to join the United States Department of Agriculture. Soon after he was appointed assistant curator of insects at the National Museum of Natural History in Washington, DC. By the time Raymond Ditmars got to know him in the mid-1890s, Smith was the New Jersey state entomologist based at Rutgers College and making a name for himself in the battle against salt marsh mosquitoes.

One day Smith asked Beutenmüller's youthful assistant to join him on an insect-collecting trip in the Florida swamps. The plan was to start in the Indian River district on the Atlantic seaboard and move on to the Everglades. The duo was soon steaming down the coast toward Jacksonville aboard a Clyde Line ship. This, the first of Ditmars's many ocean voyages, was a thrill. While some notable insects would be encountered, the true revelation of the expedition was the professor himself. Ditmars remembered him as "an angular man between fifty and sixty, who was alternately restless and nervous or completely calm." In fact, Smith could only have been in his late thirties at the time of the Florida excursion, perhaps his striking beard added a decade or two in the mind of his young companion.

The professor's enthusiasms did not begin and end with insects. He proved an accomplished botanist, an expert on the characteristics of soil and, like Ditmars, was a student of meteorology. Smith was furthermore an authority on railroad technology, conversant in steam engine evolution, and a connoisseur of the fighting craft of the Civil War. Such versatility inspired Ditmars, who later said that Smith "had fanned a flame of inquisitiveness, and unconsciously steered me toward prying into the 'why' of things, which developed into widely diversified studies." Ditmars had discovered that concentration on just one field, something drummed into him by his father, was not necessary for success. Snakes however remained paramount. The young man returned to the American Museum of Natural History with rekindled enthusiasm. Less overwhelmed by the tedium of his daily duties, he now threw himself into extracurricular activities.

Things were improving for Ditmars on the home front too. His father's furniture business was now thriving and by the mid-1890s the family had taken up residence at 1666 Bathgate Avenue, a spacious brownstone mansion in the Bronx. The address hints at the diabolical, but, after years of cramped lodgings in Newark, Harlem, and elsewhere, this was heaven for the Ditmars family, a sanctuary from the noise and grime of the city.

A semi-rural district north of Manhattan, the Bronx had recently joined Staten Island, Queens, and Brooklyn as a full-fledged borough of New York City, but when Raymond Ditmars gazed from the window of his top floor bedroom he saw fields and farmsteads. Although suburbia was encroaching from the south, in the late nineteenth century much of the Bronx remained agricultural. A sizeable and growing Irish community had existed here since 1800, and later on southern Italians came in huge numbers. Germans represented the largest ethnic group however. An entrepreneurial bunch, they ran most of the dairy farms, as well as establishing feedstores and breweries. An abundance of fruit and vegetables was also grown here on truck farms, named for the horse-drawn carts that brought the produce into the metropolis. Ditmars would have seen many such wagons passing the house laden with apples, lettuces, potatoes, tomatoes, beets, and cabbages.

As much as Ditmars loved horses, he loved snakes more. The move had triggered a redoubling of efforts to erode the family's objections to these misunderstood animals. Resistance finally crumbled and permission was again granted for him to keep a "few reptilian specimens." In truth, attitudes had softened somewhat since the watersnake debacle and Raymond had already been allowed a West Indian land crab and a tame lizard. Now with the entire top floor at his disposal, he set about establishing a world-class serpent collection. If reptiles had to be kept in the house, the infernal things could at least now be consigned to the attic, far from the rest of the family.

Assisted by "Chips" Coggeswell, a carpenter at the museum, Ditmars built wooden crates with sliding glass front panels. The boxes' interiors were smeared with wax to prevent muck sticking, a trick learned at the monkey house of the Central Park menagerie. Soon, a two-tiered series of empty cases—twenty-six in all—stretched fully twenty-two feet across the length of his attic room.

They wouldn't stay unoccupied for long. The neglected timber rattlesnake from the museum storeroom was among the first taking up residence at the smart new accommodation in the Bronx. Joining it in short order was a brace of water moccasins and another rattler, a six-foot-long eastern diamondback. All these serpents were highly venomous and inherited from Slover Allen. The late physician had also connected Ditmars with a dealer in Florida, from whom were purchased additional moccasins along with king snakes, indigo snakes, coachwhips, and other harmless species typical of the southern states. Meanwhile Ditmars himself caught as many varieties as he could from the local area; a single trip during one vacation yielded a fabulous booty of copperheads, black snakes, milk snakes, watersnakes, spreading adders, and still more timber rattlesnakes.

"Coiled in their cages, sullen, watchful, always with a lunging loop folding back the neck, were creatures I knew could thrust and stab with fangs that in an instant could create tragedy," he once wrote. "A bite was unthinkable, a frightful thing." He was all too aware of the terrible risks he was taking, yet the snakes, especially the big vipers, held a fascinating allure for him.

Ditmars knew his pets were sensitive beasts with discerning tastes. Unless precise temperature and humidity requirements were met, the snakes might fail to shed their skin or refuse to eat. Parasitic infections could take hold. With no books on reptile care then available, he would have relied largely on trial and error, and in the early years he doubtless lost many prized specimens through simple but excusable mistakes in husbandry. Good hygiene was critical, and Ditmars adopted "a studied system for cleaning the cages and polishing the glass fronts." Those panels needing attention were slid out and turned so that the dirty inner face was outside. If the occupant of a cage was venomous, special measures were taken: "The poisonous serpents were backed into a corner by sliding the glass panel open slightly, slipping in a sheet of metal, then backing them into a triangle, by following the glass with the metal as the former was slid back."

The biggest headache was procuring enough food, and of the right type. Without exception snakes are predators, each variety with strict dietary preferences. While many were content with rodents, Ditmars found that some wouldn't touch mammals, instead insisting upon cold-blooded prey. A few, notably the king snakes, would only eat other snakes. Such challenges mounted with each new acquisition and Ditmars was soon spending as much time trapping rodents, lizards, and frogs as he was catching serpents. Mice were usually in greatest demand, but if you knew where to go, procuring these in good numbers didn't present much difficulty. Ditmars relied upon a string of little restaurants close to Chinatown that were "dubious in everything but rodent collecting," while

46

another establishment in the Bowery proved a "rodent paradise." Setting off home one evening aboard a crowded elevated train, he had placed under his seat a box containing a dozen live rats. Shortly into the journey though he noticed that the snake food was escaping. "The course I chose was rather prudent than heroic," he later confessed. "I changed my seat to the opposite side of the car, and proceeded with the perusal of my paper, awaiting the upshot of the adventure with trembling heart." The upshot was shrieking shopgirls, whirling skirts, and a furious conductor.

Despite these pressures the snake obsessive kept a lookout for new specimens. Ditmars was cultivating a taste for the exotic; fantastic serpents were to be found overseas, far from New York City, and he wanted them. One day a small boa constrictor was sent to the museum. A native of Central and South America, the live snake had turned up in a consignment of tropical fruit unloaded from a steamboat at the docks. Ditmars was soon frequenting the city's hectic waterfront hoping for more reptilian stowaways. To increase his chances he persuaded stevedores to save rather than kill on sight any snakes they encountered. The workers were furnished with linen bags for the purpose. As a result, reported Ditmars, "some very pretty tropical reptiles of harmless kinds" joined the burgeoning collection.

His position at the museum enabled him to establish contacts with fellow serpent devotees from around the world. Years afterward Ditmars described "letters from India, from the West Indies and Brazil," followed in due course by "gifts, in the shape of boxes with sinister contents, which meant additional coiled forms with bizarre patterns." His parents seem to have regretted their change of heart but now it was far too late. "I could not give up the snakes," he went on. "Destiny had the whip-hand!"

Among these new overseas correspondents was a certain inscrutable newspaper owner from the small tropical island of Trinidad. His name was R. R. Mole and he would be the one to put Raymond Ditmars's first encounter with a bushmaster within spitting distance.

A DENIZEN OF THE FOREST (*LACHESIS MUTA*. A VIPER WITH HER EGGS.)

An early twentieth-century postcard from Trinidad depicts a captive bushmaster
(*Lachesis muta*) guarding her eggs. (Courtesy of Lise Winer)

RICHARD Richardson Mole was born on September 27, 1860, in Bridg-
water, a market town and port in the English county of Somerset. Like
Ditmars, Mole was engrossed by natural history and he too was drawn to
reptiles. Perhaps his interest was kindled by the adders and grass snakes
then common in the Somerset countryside. When Mole was five years
old his father, who was a pharmacist, died from a diseased heart. An
ill-advised measure of prussic acid is said to have hastened his demise.
Soon afterward Mole's mother, Eliza, took him and his younger brother,
Arthur, to live with her sister who was a schoolmistress in Wales. Disaster
struck again in 1874 with the death of Eliza from "pulmonary consump-
tion." Despite the tragic start in life, Mole thrived in the care of his aunt
and subsequently trained as a newspaper journalist, working on a variety
of provincial English titles.

At the age of twenty-five Mole left Britain for work as a shorthand
reporter for the *Public Opinion* newspaper on Trinidad. The Arawak
peoples who first populated this verdant tropical island within sight of

the northwestern coast of Venezuela knew it as *Iere*, Land of the Hummingbird. The modern name was coined by Christopher Columbus in 1498 for a distinctive trio of coastal hills. Trinidad had changed hands several times as Spanish, French, and British colonists exploited its natural resources. Sugar was among the most significant exports with much of the lowlands given over to plantations, while the hills were the preserve of coffee, citrus, and cacao growers, the latter planting gaudy, flamboyant, and immortelle trees to shade their crops. As elsewhere in the Caribbean, Trinidad boasted a mix of races and cultures, a legacy of thousands of African slaves forced to work the fields and, later on, indentured workers from China, Portugal, Madeira, and especially India.

This convoluted history of human migration and colonization echoed far slower natural processes affecting the island's wildlife. Over millions of years of geological activity and changing sea levels, connections had repeatedly formed and disappeared between the South American continent and the fragment of terrain that would one day be called Trinidad. These temporary land bridges allowed a complement of mainland species to populate the island, while a unique flora and fauna evolved during periods of isolation. Given the island's proximity to Venezuela, a modest exchange of animal species doubtless continued when Trinidad was cut off from the mainland. Clumps of floating vegetation could have served as rafts while some species including snakes may have swam the gap, which is today less than ten miles in places. One such strait, known as *Boca Sierpe*, the Serpent's Mouth, is well named indeed.

Trinidad was thus a biologist's dream with a remarkable array of animal species, including reptiles, something Mole quickly appreciated on his arrival in 1886. He was soon studying and collecting many kinds of snakes, lizards, turtles, and crocodilians. The serpents in particular were extraordinary, from high-wire artists such as the slender black-and-yellow *tigre*, which slinked along tree branches in search of rats or birds, to the tiny brown snakes burrowing in leaf litter on the forest floor. The swamps and lagoons of Trinidad were the domain of a tree boa that spent much of the time draped on mangrove branches like an untidy pile of rubber rings. Locals called it *cascabel dormillon*, or the "sleeping rattlesnake." Mole encountered the anaconda, or *huille*, there too. According to a few reports, perhaps exaggerated, specimens of this mighty aquatic boa caught on the island surpassed twenty feet in length. "The sudden daring of these lazy, stupid animals is very great," noted Mole in 1892, repeating a description used by the writer Charles Kingsley twenty years before. "Their brain seems to act like that of the alligator or the pike, paroxysmally, and by rare fits and starts, after lying for hours motionless and as if asleep."

Several venomous species also lurked in Trinidad, among them the beautifully ringed coralsnakes that preyed on other snakes. Then there was the dreaded local version of the fer-de-lance. Called *mapepire balsain*, this large and often angry pitviper plagued cacao and sugar plantations, inflicting painful and destructive bites on the workers. Some swore that the snake spat poison in tiny jets a distance of six feet or more. The bitten put their faith in herbal cures, chewing on the astringent roots of the manaco palm or taking powdered guaco, a relative of the sunflower. The remedies were entirely useless. The *mapepire balsain* met its match however in another serpent: the black cribo. Known on the South American mainland as the *mussurana* or *zumbadora*, this feisty constrictor was famed for hunting other snakes, seemingly immune to their venom.

But of all the serpents of Trinidad, one stood out as having the most mysterious and fearsome reputation. To the creoles it was the *mapepire z'anana*, the "pineapple viper," a reference to the roughness of the snake's body that resulted from curious protuberances on each scale. Others called it "the Silent Death of the Black Night." But the name by which the snake was most commonly known was "bushmaster," derived from *bosmeester*, a word supposedly coined by Dutch settlers on the South American mainland in the early nineteenth century. As elsewhere across its range, a wealth of myths surrounded the bushmaster in Trinidad. For instance, by night the viper would be drawn to the lights of a campfire, and when it struck victims were left conscious and paralyzed, to be eaten alive by ants and worms. According to another local superstition, the *z'anana* also stung people to death with the *pickah*, the horny spike at the tip of its tail. The bushmaster possessed almost supernatural powers; even if lopped off, the snake's head inflicted a deadly bite. Meanwhile its mate would lurk close by, ready to wreak a horrible revenge.

Luckily this ghastly creature was uncommon, although Mole learned that the snake was one of several which sheltered in the burrows of armadillo, agouti, and, notably, paca. Called *lappe* by the locals, the paca was a large spotted rodent prized for its tender flesh — once described as "partaking of the qualities of veal and pork" — and when its dens were unearthed a *z'anana* sometimes leapt out. In 1889 a hunter and plantation owner named Albert B. Carr had learned this the hard way, reaching into the den of a *lappe* he had just speared. When he withdrew the arm a snake he later identified as a bushmaster was hanging off his thumb. Carr survived thanks, he maintained, to the application of ligatures and "Melidor's Antidote to Snake-Bite." Given the happy ending some have questioned whether a *z'anana* was the culprit, although others point out that hanging on after a bite is in fact typical of juvenile bushmasters. Moreover, as shall be discussed, Carr's bite may have involved minimal envenomation. Whatever the truth, Mole himself certainly did acquire z'anana specimens from paca burrows. He never had much fortune keeping them going in captivity however, although he once got a bushmaster to swallow a mouse, and in July 1903 a captive female astounded him by laying "ten or twelve eggs, larger than those of a duck." Every other pitviper in the Americas, including rattlesnakes and fer-de-lances, gave birth to live young. Carr had already speculated that bushmasters might be egg layers, and here was proof.

When not snake hunting, Mole immersed himself in island life, marrying within two years of his arrival. His erect bearing, immaculate white suits, and "gentlemanly manners and literary talents," made Mole a popular fixture in colonial circles. He founded a printing press with his brother who had joined him in Trinidad, and in 1898 started his own daily newspaper, the *Mirror*, vociferously championing the causes of the island's black and mixed-raced intellectuals. In 1916, though, the colonial government shut down the paper, perhaps in response to the editor's outspoken views.

Soon after settling in Trinidad's capital, Port of Spain, Mole had befriended another naturalist of German extraction named Friedrick William Urich. Twelve years Mole's junior, Urich—or "Jangoons" as he was popularly known—shared the older man's passion for cold-blooded wildlife (and starched linen suits). Together they prepared an inventory of the colony's commoner lizards, snakes, turtles, and crocodilians, and the resulting paper, entitled "Notes of some reptiles in Trinidad," appeared in an 1891 edition of *Proceedings of the Zoological Society of London*. The Englishman would spend a good part of his spare time revising this list, and eventually produced a well-regarded book on Trinidad's snakes.

The same year saw Mole, Urich, and six other aficionados of local wildlife establish the Trinidad Field Naturalists' Club. The group survives to this day, Tobago joining in the 1970s. Early meetings were held at various members' residences, with Mole often in the chair, but Port of Spain's grand Royal Victoria Institute Museum later hosted the Club. Such an august society needed its own journal, of course, and Mole was the perfect candidate to oversee publication. The naturalists discussed all manner of botanical, zoological, and general scientific topics and made regular collecting excursions into remote sections of the island.

Wildlife was not the sole appeal of such trips. Describing a duck-shoot on the Caroni Swamp, Mole mentioned seeing a "pretty Hindoo girl" standing on a log, "the bracelets on her shapely arms shining in the sun, and the wind streaming her long veil out behind her—a capital picture. Near her is her mother, a withered old woman, dressed exactly like her daughter, squatting on the earth, hardly lifting her eyes from some task she is engaged in." The cry of "Duck!" from "a chubby little coolie" disturbed the reverie.

Notwithstanding the demands of work and a young family, reptiles remained a preoccupation for Mole, who found time to amass a good number at his home close to Port of Spain's busy waterfront. Live snakes in jars even graced his bedroom windowsills and he regularly encouraged his children to play with them. He meanwhile fostered good connections to the outside world, donating reptiles, living and dead, to overseas museums and collectors. These included George Albert Boulenger, a well-respected zoologist at the British Museum in London then compiling a *Catalogue of the Lizards*.

Always hungry to expand his collection, Mole launched expeditions to the South American mainland, acquiring serpents in both Venezuela and British Guiana. By the mid-1890s he was also putting out feelers for specimens from temperate zones.

The timing was perfect.

# 4

# The Master of Snakes

*"I've always felt that I wanted to own a rattlesnake ledge so that I could feel I was kind of mothering the whole gang of rattlesnakes and helping them along a bit."*

—Raymond L. Ditmars, *Life*, June 12, 1931

❖

*Winter 1898. East Fourteenth Street, New York City.*

HIS FINGER RUNS DOWN the residents list: "John W. Isham, Theatrical Manager . . . J. N. Collins & Co., Furriers . . . Edwin S. Penfoed, Merchant." Then the name he's looking for: "Charles H. Higby, Artist—fourth floor."

Something brushes the reporter's head: a gray bed sheet is draped from the fire escape above. He removes his new homburg and dusts it down, then prods Higby's doorbell, eliciting a faint buzz deep within the tenement building. He waits, careful to avoid eye contact with a nearby group of street hawkers huddled around a smoldering brazier. Snowflakes whirl past lazily. The door is opened by a tall, spindly man in his late twenties with a pallid complexion and thick dark hair hanging low over the forehead.

"Mr. Higby?"

"Ah, you must be Mr. Ditmars, from the *Times*," comes a solemn reply. "Yes, it is I. Do please follow me."

The thin man, who is wearing a crimson smoking jacket, leads the reporter up several flights of rickety steps to a door on the top landing.

The drab vestibule stairwell, reeking of mold, does little to prepare Ray for the room into which he is now ushered. The first item catching his eye is a human skull sporting a wig of long blond hair. It teeters, grinning, on the edge of a ceramic basin cluttered with pots, paint brushes, and glass bottles. Covering the walls is a richly decorated jute cloth, to which a miscellany of gaudy draperies, sketches, shields, swords, fishing rods, and other ornaments has been attached. Rugs, cushions, clothing, and marble statuettes are strewn across the floor, as are several wooden chests, their hinges crusted with verdigris. A mandolin rests against one wall. On an elegant table is a second, larger skull, possibly a horse's, within which a candle casts a radius of flickering luminescence. From the ceiling is suspended an iron lantern with red-and-yellow glass panels. A skylight casts a watery glow, its panes covered in dust into which grotesque faces, snakes, and other patterns have been traced. In the hearth a pile of glowing coals pulses heat uselessly across the cold studio.

The artist strides to the table and with frail, tapering fingers draws a small metal box from behind the horse's skull.

"Care for a smoke?"

"That's all right, Mr. Higby, I finished my pipe on the way over."

Calmly removing his scarf and hat, the reporter now spots some glass-fronted cages in one corner of the room. The closest contains a yellow-and-black-patterned serpent.

"That's a handsome king snake you have, Mr. Higby."

"Yes, Rex is splendid isn't he?" smiles Higby, lighting a cheroot. The studio air is soon spiced with an oriental aroma.

"Please do take him out if you wish."

Ray lifts the cool, gleaming reptile expertly from the cage, inspecting the gorgeous pattern; the colored striations even pass across the snake's burnished eyes.

"Where did you obtain him?"

"A dealer in Florida. Came with a feisty pine snake. Still need to tame that one."

Ray returns Rex to his case and asks to sit. Higby indicates a worn divan, himself selecting a leather pouf on which he squats cross-legged.

"Before we start I will insist upon something."

"Oh yes?" replies the reporter, pulling out a notebook and pencil from his satchel.

"You must write that I only keep *harmless* snakes. A couple of years back the *World* printed that I kept a cobra di capello. My landlord doubled the rent!"

"Of course, Mr. Higby," replies Ray. "Now, as you know, I am putting together a piece for the *Times* on the growing popularity of serpents. I've been speaking to scientists who, like me, keep them as pets."

The artist nods.

"I want to put across the good points about these maligned creatures and dispel the fantastic myths." Ray pauses, then says, "So what *is* it about snakes that makes you want to keep them?"

The artist springs up, rifles through papers on a table and hands Ray a small pamphlet. A theater program.

"This one I designed last year. What do you see?"

Four barely clad female dancers, arms linked, are pictured on the cover.

The reporter colors. "Well, I see some, er, charming young ladies."

"Yes, yes, but *around* the picture, what do you see?"

A series of elaborate decorative flourishes frame the photograph.

"Of course," Ray laughs, "Snakes!"

"Yes," Higby cries in delight. "Snakes! Beautiful, gorgeous, lithe snakes! What better inspiration could there be? Nothing is more graceful. And the colors never fail to inspire me. Wait here!"

Higby disappears through some velvet curtains into an adjoining room. Ray supposes it to be the artist's bedroom. Several minutes pass.

The reporter hears a crash and quiet cursing. Next the sound of wood scraping, followed by a groan.

"What the devil is he up to?" Ray thinks.

Abruptly the artist reemerges staggering under the weight of fully eight feet of yellow snake, draped over his shoulders.

"Meet Yao, the city's only albino boa constrictor!" beams Higby. "Got him down at the docks. Damned Chinaman drove a hard bargain though. But he's worth every cent. Did you know that the South America natives worship these snakes? Now, Mr. Ditmars, please continue."

An hour later and Higby has bid farewell to Ray.

"Now then, what was I doing?" mutters the artist. "Oh yes."

Back in the studio, he upends a wooden chest allowing a serpent to slither out onto a soft Turkish rug. Higby slides both hands under the snake causing it to hiss and snap at his fingers.

"Naughty pine snake!" tuts the artist who now lifts the snake high above his head, bringing it down gently over his shoulders, as he'd done earlier with Yao. Higby walks to a mirror to note the effect but the sudden movement unsettles the serpent, which throws a coil around his neck.

"Oh come now, silly fellow!"

The artist strides about the room pulling at the snake's coils but cannot find the head or tail which might have given him purchase. As the reptile's powerful muscles tighten, astonishment turns to anxiety . . . then to cold fear. His heart is racing, his vision blurring. He must get this thing off immediately. Returning to the mirror, Higby at last sees the tail behind his ear; just a tip, but enough to unravel his assailant. A close escape.

"Naughty pine snake!"

◄────►

YONKERS. Hastings. Tarrytown. Cortlandt. Peekskill. Croton-Harmon. The place names changed regularly as I moved north out of the city, the view through the grubby train window to my left did not. The vast rusty-brown escarpments of the New Jersey Palisades gleamed in the morning sun. At their feet lay the cold blue of the Hudson River, a mile or more in width.

My ambition to visit the same timber rattlesnakes dens close to New York City that Raymond Ditmars himself frequented had proved challenging. Populations were already declining in the curator's lifetime from habitat destruction, and in the seven decades since his passing the species had been extinguished from much of its former range, the rate of disappearance accelerated by bounty hunters and poachers. The rattler now survived in a few isolated pockets of suitable terrain, the precise locations of which were jealously guarded by a handful of scientists and conservationists who had devoted careers to the snake. My early requests for assistance had been rebuffed by the more well-known gatekeepers. I couldn't blame them. After all, who was this Brit declaring an interest in a now-obscure American zoo man and his snake-hunting exploits? "To cooperate with your project," as one emailed reply went, "as admirable as it may be, would be to invite too much publicity and scrutiny concerning the localities where we have done much of our own work. This sort of collaboration would, we feel, be detrimental to the animals that we so fervently have strived to study and protect for decades."

This reluctance to help was in large part explained by the actions of a single individual. Rudy Komarek, who had not long ago died aged seventy-nine from a heart attack, was the classic backwoods man, complete with the obligatory nickname, in his case "the Cobra King." Like many before him, Komarek saw a commercial value in the rattlesnake dens of the northeastern states and spent decades poaching specimens for the pet trade, exporting most to Europe. When challenged in the 1970s by William Brown, a young scientist studying dens in upstate New York, Komarek only intensified his activities. In response Brown and his allies successfully lobbied for legal protection for the species. But this didn't stop the Cobra King, who continued flouting the law for over a decade. Multiple fines, a deportation from Kansas, and several stints in federal jail during the 1990s failed to temper his destructive behavior. According to one famous story, Komarek enjoyed antagonizing the scientists by clearing out their rattler study sites and sticking taunting messages on adjacent rock piles. He later moved to Florida, where he ran a website reportedly selling detailed maps of snake dens.

Conservationists estimate that Komarek removed some six thousand timber rattlesnakes from dens across New York, Connecticut, and Massachusetts; the poacher himself claimed almost double that number. Many hold Komarek personally responsible for the near extermination of the species across swathes of New York, Connecticut, Pennsylvania, and New Jersey. Others consider exotic disease and habitat loss the more significant factors. Compared with other snakes, timber rattlesnakes require large ranges to prosper and are often the first to go when development erodes suitable habitat.

Before leaving the United Kingdom, I had at last made contact with someone who had studied reproduction in timber rattlesnakes and was prepared to take me to some dens on the strict understanding that I kept the locations secret. I happily agreed and even promised to let him check what I wrote in case I revealed too much. Now, as the Poughkeepsie-bound train swept past yachts, tugboats, wading birds, rotten jetties, and the razor wire of Ossining prison (the original "sing-sing"), I sent a text to the scientist confirming I was en route. In time, the cliffs on the far bank softened to hillocks, carpeted in forest. A line of mist drifted over the water.

IN his 1932 book *Thrills of a Naturalist's Quest*, Ditmars recalls with pleasure the day, over three decades earlier, that a letter "generally addressed" arrived at the secretary's office at the museum: "The writer was R. R. Mole, owner of a newspaper in Port of Spain, Trinidad . . . Mr. Mole appeared to be an enthusiastic observer of serpent life, with a collection of living specimens. He was desirous of obtaining a series of the North American species for study—and wished to exchange living specimens of his area!"

Ditmars was thrilled. Here was an opportunity to obtain wonderful new snakes. The only downside was having to reciprocate with some hard-won trophies of his own. Many species in his cages were replicated however, so he could spare a generous variety of local specimens for Mole. The inventory he put together was impressive:

"Two timber rattlesnakes, two copperhead snakes, two water moccasins, two king snakes, two coachwhip snakes, one indigo snake, one chicken snake, four black racers, one mountain black snake, four spreading adders, two milk snakes, six striped snakes, six water snakes, six ringneck snakes, twelve brown snakes."

Ditmars placed the serpents in labeled linen bags before packing them into a single large crate for shipment to Trinidad. All he could now was wait.

One evening many weeks later he came home from the museum to a letter bearing Trinidad stamps. Mole had replied! His note confirmed that the North American snakes had reached him without a single casualty. Mole listed the serpents he was sending in return. They included fer-de-lances, coralsnakes, emerald tree snakes, and yellow rat snakes. Also on their way, two boa constrictors "six and ten feet long respectively." But the real star of the consignment was "one bushmaster." Mole had delayed the shipment until he was able to secure a "fair" specimen of Trinidad's enigmatic viper. The *z'anana* had been captured uninjured in a plantation not far from Port of Spain. Although the snake was "rather young"—a mere eight feet in length—Ditmars was cautioned to "be extremely careful in liberating" it.

Mole had dispatched this cornucopia of tropical snakes to New York aboard the steamship *Irrawaddy* of the Trinidad Shipping and Trading Company. Ditmars was beside himself with excitement as the vessel had already completed the eight-day voyage and was docked in Manhattan. The following morning saw him at the waterfront negotiating with customs officials to expedite delivery of a five-foot-long wooden box to the Bronx. And, twenty-four hours afterward, the crate was resting innocently on the landing outside his snake room. Why had Mole so blithely sent a herpetological parcel bomb to someone barely out of short pants? Ditmars himself may even have been puzzled. As he wrote many years later, Mole and others hearing of his collection of rattlers and water moccasins, "probably figured the owner to be staid and of mature years."

Ditmars had quite a time of it transferring the bushmaster from crate to cage. One of the boa constrictors gave almost as much trouble, albeit without the threat of poisoning, as this species was non-venomous. Most of the Trinidad serpents had traveled in burlap sacks but Mole had packed the two constrictors loose at the bottom of the crate. According to Ditmars, the six-footer sported "elongate saddles of chocolate brown" against a pale tan background, the markings "merging to crimson on the posterior third, where they alternated with areas of cream color." Its larger companion was just as gorgeous, with a "loud pattern and colors, even for a snake." The smaller of the pair offered no resistance as Ditmars conveyed it from the landing to a cage adjacent to that of the unruly bushmaster, even "gazing slowly and interestedly about the room."

By contrast, as soon as the hefty coils of the ten-foot-long constrictor were lifted from the crate, the snake anchored itself by the tail to the upper post of the banister and refused to budge. As Ditmars tried to drag the snake, whose body was as thick as a fire hose, its head waved wildly, "tongue lapping the air with forked tips widely extended." It was at that awkward moment that his entire family ascended to the landing to investigate the commotion. Alert to the danger faced by his son and the destruction liable to be wrought upon the delicate banisters, John Ditmars snatched up the snake staff and prodded the tail of the intransigent boa. The effect was instantaneous: the boa relinquished its anchor point "with a flourish" and inertia sent both it and its new master crashing through the doorway into the snake room. Ditmars's parents and sister looked on in horror as the constrictor now threatened to live up to its name, the massive coils all but enveloping the perceived adversary. But the ten-footer proved a gentle giant and, rather than striking out, deigned to be guided into new quarters. Ditmars had been lucky. "Boa constrictors vary in temperament," he later wrote. "Some are gentle, some irritably snappy, while others are devilish."

Despite the fanfare attending the bushmaster's arrival, in his writings Ditmars doesn't linger on its fate. We know that soon after its installation the viper had adopted "a precise, three-layered coil," a promising sign, as was the subsequent appearance of water droplets near the drinking bowl suggesting the snake was taking sips. Ditmars wrote that "its satanic dignity had not been seriously disturbed," but his assessment was premature, for the precious specimen refused food and soon perished. The snake-fancier was still inexperienced in reptile husbandry and, as shall be seen, bushmasters are remarkably fragile in captivity. Who could blame him for quietly ignoring this early failure?

Ditmars and the serpents he was amassing up in the Bronx caught the attention of the city's newspapers. According to the *New York World*, he was "intimately acquainted with the ways of reptiles, having no less than two dozen boarding in his room." This was surely an underestimate, as other reports have Ditmars managing a "private collection of three hundred living snakes." The *World* article continues: "it may be said that it took his family two years to become reconciled to his pets, and that the housemaid is never accused of wearing his neckties or helping herself to his perfume."

One story from 1897 had greater impact than most. Kate Swan, a feature writer at the *New York Journal*, had encountered Ditmars in the American Museum of Natural History. The pair allegedly fell into conversation whilst admiring the skeleton of a whale. Learning of the young man's unusual hobby, Swan arranged to interview him at length back at his Bathgate Avenue residence. Over several hours Ditmars expounded upon his captives in detail and discussed other serpentine topics including the exciting research then being conducted to develop a long-sought antidote to snakebite. Possibly inspired by his late friend Slover Allen, Ditmars had started milking his own collection. Despite the fact that the merest slipup could prove fatal, he gradually stockpiled dozens of vials with shining amber and greenish crystals of snake venom. Comparing the different colors, he later correctly deduced that toxicity might vary from snake species to species.

A few days after Swan's visit Ditmars was proudly surveying an illustrated two-page spread under the headline "The Master of Snakes." The piece was largely accurate, although the twenty-one-year-old who had left school with few qualifications was tickled to see himself referred to variously as "Professor" and "Curator." As Ditmars recalled, the story prompted a surge of correspondence "from all parts of the East asking questions about snakes. It looked as if a lot of people had had these queries on their mind and awaited hearing of a reliable source to have them answered." His new status as "expert" would be an enduring one. For the rest of his life a good proportion of each working day would be spent replying to such enquiries, a responsibility he took seriously. Raymond Ditmars was the best kind of teacher: someone for whom no question was too stupid or too-often asked.

Thanks to the *Journal* article he attracted the interest of a leading venom scientist, the Philadelphia-based physician Silas Weir Mitchell. Although failing to find an antidote, Mitchell was the first to demonstrate that serpent venom consisted not of a single toxic agent but a complex mixture of active ingredients. Mitchell would befriend Ditmars, his approbation spurring the younger man's later endeavors to develop and distribute effective antivenin.

Others made their way to 1666 Bathgate Avenue which, noted the *New York Sun*, became "a rendezvous of artists seeking living snakes to draw from, of snake enthusiasts, and of all those making a study of snakes." Ditmars would escort visitors up to the serpent room where he took pleasure in expounding on his animals. One section of the New York community had professional reasons of a different sort for making contact. These were snake charmers, mostly women, from traveling circuses who sought advice on feeding and caring for their animals. Ditmars's long-suffering parents now opened their door to a succession of flamboyant female performers politely asking whether "Professor Ditmars" was available. The ladies were sometimes a source of new specimens. Ditmars exchanged Mole's boa constrictor for an eight-foot-long Indian python belonging to a charmer called Olga. "It had lived in an atmosphere of tinsel and blare of circus bands," remembered Ditmars, "but to me it now assumed the dignity of the following entry in my notebook: 'Indian Python, light phase. *Python molurus*, variety *occelata*, probably from Madras. Female.'"

Notwithstanding his ingenuity in catching mice, sustaining dozens if not hundreds of snakes on a museum salary Ditmars described as "microscopic" was proving impossible. He was now experimenting with photography and had even built a small studio complete with sanded stage that further drained his resources. Ditmars was at a turning point in his life. Having abandoned all hope that their son would pursue a military career his parents were now pressing him to go into business. "This was understandable," remembered Ditmars many years later, "because my father was commercially successful and my uncles were nationally known experts associated with big enterprises. Any of them could have put me on the road to financial eminence. Naturally, when I refused to be drawn into the struggle for the Almighty Dollar, they all concluded that I was somehow lacking and would send up as some sort of disgrace."

Such views were excusable. At the time few could have foreseen that this ridiculous obsession with reptiles would soon lead to a dream career.

Raymond Ditmars, c. 1913—note the snake fang tiepin.

EDWIN McGowan was affable and handsome with graying sideburns. I put him in his early forties. Collecting me in his Honda SUV from the secluded railroad station, we headed for the wooded hills, via a much-needed coffee stop at a local gas station. He had a lot on his plate. As science director for the Palisades Interstate Park Commission, Ed was responsible for 110,000 acres of parkland, mostly undeveloped forest, as well as overseeing a small museum and zoo. Nevertheless, he shared my cagerness to get into the field, and while his interests weren't restricted to herps—he'd also studied bears and wolves in Alaska—the local rattlesnakes fascinated him.

Along the way Ed spoke about some discoveries he had made with the snakes. Over several seasons he had followed the movements of individuals that he had fitted with tiny radio transmitters. The research showed that females were more proactive in mate choice than was previously assumed.

"In the late summer, a female selects certain habitats, usually rocky outcrops, and undergoes a shed cycle. This lasts about three weeks and all the time she's exuding a scent attractive to males," said Ed. "But prior to shedding her skin she's unreceptive to suitors. Only after shedding will she mate with the attending male. The scar patterns I've seen on males suggest that during this latency period they wind up fighting for the right to mate with her."

The females were in effect playing prospective mates against one other to increase the chances of breeding with the strongest one. Even when it looked like a male had won the prize, Ed had witnessed a female putting a suitor through his paces.

"She would race away repeatedly for a short distance while he tried to maintain contact with her. It certainly seems to be a case of last guy standing."

We pulled off the highway onto a dirt track cut through a forest of oak and hickory. As beige dust kicked up behind us Ed spoke of his slight regret that his son, aged eleven, didn't share the same passion for nature. Soccer was his thing.

"I don't want to push him, maybe he'll get more interested when we start camping."

A few minutes afterward we were out of the car and booting up in preparation for a hike into the woods. Ed packed some gaiters for protection when entering true rattlesnake country later on. As I would soon discover, it was easy to step on one. Ticks were another peril, the tiny arachnids harboring several unpleasant diseases.

"So how do you go about finding rattlesnakes, Ed?" It was time I asked the million-dollar question.

Habitat was key. The snakes overwintered in hibernacula deep below the frost line in south-facing rocky outcrops. Early spring was the best time to look, when the snakes emerged from their dens, and then again in late summer as cooling temperatures prompted their return to the same sites—a behavior Ditmars likened to "the fall migration of birds." The rattlers typically hung around for a few days in multiple rock crevices near the den before going in. During the intervening months the serpents roamed widely on the hunt for prey, often white-footed mice, but also voles, squirrels, and rabbits.

We climbed past boulders of ancient granitic gneiss and traversed steep gray piles of accumulated rock debris, known as talus. Ed explained that rattlers, like most other snakes, go out of their way to avoid confrontation. "Camouflage is their first line of defense from enemies including us," said Ed. "If discovered, they'll retreat, maybe under a rock. Only when cornered will they puff up and start rattling."

Early on we found a piece of rattle and scraps of translucent shed snakeskin, signs we were in the right area. Like those of the bushmaster, rattlesnake scales bear a distinctive ridge. Time to don those gaiters. "Keep your ears open," advised Ed, "Sometimes they rustle the leaves."

It would be another two hours of clambering up and down the loose talus slopes before my companion, a few yards ahead, calmly said: "OK.

There's one." He stood back letting me find our quarry for myself. I tottered on the steep incline trusting the grip of my hiking boots and peered into various crevices for a good thirty seconds before finally glimpsing two yellowish coils and a small reptilian head wedged under a rock. The snake was glaring straight at me through a veil of cobweb, the tongue flickering ominously. I was less than six feet away.

As I pulled out my camera Ed removed the web with a stick giving me a clear shot. Soon after we found two more rattlers in nearby crevice, one snake dwarfed by the other. "That one's a neonate. Born a few weeks ago," said Ed.

Detecting our presence the youngster ducked into the shadows to re-emerge on the other side of the larger snake. We continued searching for a while more until it was time for me to head back to the city. We agreed to hook up again though a few days later.

"Next time let's try to find a big one!" grinned Ed.

AT the end of 1897 the "discontented, callow, vacillating youth," as Ditmars described his twenty-one-year-old self, took the fateful decision to abandon an incipient scientific career for better paid employment as a stenographer. Again, given the choice of new occupation, the parallels with R. R. Mole were uncanny. Ditmars received "sharp, but friendly, criticism of this step" from his superiors at the museum. In his spare time he had taught himself shorthand, learning to write it with both left and right hands, and joined an optical instruments company. Then he landed a position as reporter at the Court of General Sessions for the prestigious *New York Times*. This was thanks to an introduction to its managing editor Henry Lowenthal, who would become a "revered counsellor and friend." Ditmars now developed a nose for a good story and a journalistic writing style, skills that would serve him well. The career move surprised and pleased his parents who dared to hope that at last their house might be rid of snakes.

Ditmars's appointment coincided with the rejuvenation of the *Times*. In financial difficulties, the paper had recently been taken over by Adolph

S. Ochs, a newspaper magnate from Tennessee. Ochs invested $200,000 in the paper and steered it back to respectability and profitability. He later cut the price of a copy to one cent, which further boosted circulation. Biased stories and barely-disguised publicity items were dropped in favor of more objective coverage of current events and reports on the stock market. The sanctimonious advertising slogan "It does not soil the breakfast cloth" was employed as a dig against the muckraking "yellow journalism" of rival papers the *New York World* and the *New York Journal*, owned by Joseph Pulitzer and William Randolph Hearst, respectively. "All The News That's Fit To Print" was emblazoned on the front page, a motto that remains to this day. The Spanish-American war, which presaged the United States' emergence as a superpower, dominated the news during Ditmars's period at the *Times*. The paper was among those backing intervention to support Cubans revolting against their Spanish imperial masters. The young hack was meanwhile tasked with covering events closer to home. Indeed, the city's criminal courts were just a stone's throw from the *Times*'s offices on Park Row.

By now Ditmars was regularly lecturing on snakes in the evenings. To avoid the lengthy return trip to the Bronx he took to stuffing his satchel with live exhibits. The contents of the bag became a source of terror and intrigue for his fellow scribblers who speculated that at any moment a diamondback rattlesnake or water moccasin might burst free. The assistant night city editor ordered Ditmars to keep the satchel under lock and key and then to remove it altogether. As a compromise, it was eventually left in the office of Antonio Zucca, the New York City Coroner, whence Ditmars could access it day and night.

Ochs had introduced the coverage of court proceedings and another innovation, a Sunday pictorial magazine, that also directly benefited Ditmars, who was asked to write "around-town stuff." Stories decidedly serpentine in flavor began gracing the pages of the city's finest publication. The cub reporter now had a platform from which to evangelize about these much persecuted and misunderstood animals. In an illustrated article appearing in February 1899, Ditmars brought to wider attention his fellow snake hobbyists. As well as the artist Charles H. Higby, for whom snakes served as inspiration for his "peculiar work, elaborate in decorative effect," there was Frank Speck of Hackensack, New Jersey who possessed "a complete collection of the reptiles of the State" including "two lively black racers, which constantly dance up and down the glass front of their cage to the consternation of nervous callers."

Ditmars reserved his greatest admiration for Professor O'Reilly, "among the most enthusiastic collectors of ophidians," whose room "of ordinary dimensions" was crammed with "about forty cages, ranging in size from a packing case down to a soap box. In these cases snakes of all colors and sizes writhe and twist, and glare ominously at the visitor." Like Ditmars, O'Reilly invariably had a serpent or two about his person, carrying them in his pockets while riding street cars and railroad trains. Once, on a crowded Fifth Avenue sidewalk, he was prevented from saluting a lady because he had a serpent under his hat.

Ditmars enjoyed his period on the *Times* and although the days were long he kept his snake "collection spick and span in the few hours left over between newspaper work, traveling up and down town, and getting some sleep." He was already demonstrating his capacity for hard work. Ditmars might not get to bed until three a.m. and yet just six hours later would be aboard the downtown elevated train feeling "thoroughly refreshed." But if life seemed good after the monotony of museum work, it was about to get a whole lot better. Things were now afoot back up in the Bronx that would soon make Raymond Ditmars a household name.

# 5

# A Snapping Turtle in a Tin Bathtub

*"Science has done little to overcome the popular aversion to snakes. The modern scientist prefers to pickle his specimens and enter into heated squabbles with other scientists concerning the creatures' places in zoological nomenclature. And during this useless controversy all thoughts of the habits of these creatures, their life history, and economic importance, have been cast aside."*

—Raymond L. Ditmars, *The New York Times*, February 19, 1899

---

*November 14, 1898. Lexington Avenue, New York City.*

"OF COURSE, LADIES AND Gentlemen, ascertaining dimensions was no easy matter as you can well imagine, but last night we confirmed that the winning serpent measured . . ."

The speaker, mustachioed and in his early forties, sneaks a glance at his notes, then booms out across the cavernous hall: ". . . . at least *twenty-one feet* in length!"

The audience gasps.

". . . and tipped the scales at an astonishing *two hundred pounds!*"

Cheers fill the air.

The speaker waits for silence before continuing.

"So, the grand prize for the exhibitor with the largest serpent goes to . . ."

A pause for effect.

". . . Mr. Bartels of Greenwich Street for his Burmese python! Well done sir! A true giant!"

As the chamber explodes with applause an elderly, dishevelled man files through the crowd toward the podium, along the way receiving several congratulatory pats on the back. The speaker smiles and shakes Bartels's hand, presenting him with an engraved certificate and two blue ribbons to fasten to the neck and tail of the triumphant reptile.

"Thank you, Mr. Williams," grins Bartels, exposing tumbledown teeth.

Should the exhibition's budget have allowed, the trophies might have been fancier, perhaps a gold or silver medallions. The field of entries for this inaugural competition is strong nevertheless, and in any case the animal dealer looks satisfied enough as he tucks his awards into an inner jacket pocket and rejoins the audience.

Once the clapping has subsided again, Williams addresses the gathering. "Now, Ladies and Gentlemen, if you haven't done so already, I heartily recommend inspecting that stupendous python for yourself, and some of the equally impressive South American boa constrictors Mr. Bartels has brought along tonight. His stand is at the rear of the chamber. And don't forget, the first heat of the competitive snake charming contest begins in an hour's time. Indeed, if I'm not mistaken I can see the ladies readying themselves right now!"

The throng disperses. A young man advances on Williams, pipe fumes drifting in his wake.

"Good speech, Allen."

"Thanks, Ray," says Williams.

Both men turn to survey the spacious atrium of the Grand Central Palace. It brims with wire-top tanks, glass cages, and specimen jars. Turtles, lizards, frogs, and toads are displayed alongside snakes of many colors and sizes. Gigantic potted palms lend the proceedings a naturalistic feel while, here and there, signs forbid patrons from poking at the animals with umbrellas or canes. A hodgepodge of preserved snake skins and turtle shells decorate the walls.

"Is it true we're still a few cages short?" asks Ray.

"That's right," says Williams. "Hopefully they'll arrive tomorrow. Also, one dealer who'd promised us snakes preserved in alcohol palmed us off with pickled tapeworms instead. The cheek of it. As if we couldn't tell the difference!"

A former reporter on the *Times*, Williams now acts as press agent for various such fairs and conceived the idea for the reptile extravaganza during last year's Horse Show at Madison Square Garden. He shares Ray's opinion that the event should be as much educational and artistic as money-making. Both men are here to lessen the widespread antipathy toward cold-blooded animals, to demonstrate their virtuous qualities, perhaps even to boost their popularity as pets.

Ray and Williams tour the hall, arriving first at Ray's own reconstruction of a rattlesnake den. Sixteen vipers are coiled or draped amid rock piles skillfully arranged in a large cage to resemble the natural habitat. They form the centerpiece of a comprehensive display of snakes occurring in the vicinity of New York.

"I bagged all the rattlers close to the Palisades," explains Ray to his friend.

"And the copperheads came from Fort Lee," he adds indicating a cluster of beautiful red-and-brown forms in a neighboring enclosure. A dozen or so harmless snake species are also on display. Several signs emphasize these animals' value in ridding farmyards of rodent pests.

"I like your tropical specimens most," says Williams stooping to admire a deadly coralsnake, which, thanks to its red-and-yellow rings, resembled nothing so much as a lengthy stick of candy cane. In an adjacent mesh cage, two sizeable boa constrictors are peacefully entwined.

"Yes, me too. Some turned up on fruit boats, but most came from a fellow in Trinidad. Just wish I still had the bushmaster he sent me. Those fer-de-lances over there are from St. Lucia. Next best thing I guess."

The two men move on, tipping their hats to the artist Charles Higby—his albino constrictor Yao still going strong—and Frank Speck of Hackensack who is displaying representatives of all thirteen of New Jersey's snake varieties. Ray is familiar with many exhibitors, be they scientists or dealers in natural history supplies, amateur collectors or serpent charmers. Most originate from New York City or its environs, but a few have traveled from further afield, like Rochester's legendary Pete Gruber who is said to have survived a dozen rattler bites. "Rattlesnake Pete" is as celebrated for his ostentatious serpent leather jacket and fang scarf-pin as for his well-authenticated remedy for goiter, a cure achieved through the application of a live snake to the throat of the patient. Then there are the Brimley Brothers from Raleigh, North Carolina, and their snappy watersnakes and even snappier water moccasins. Several exhibitors are women, and indeed females constitute a good proportion of the visitors here this evening. The fact doesn't surprise Ray; the supposed affinity between serpents and the fairer sex is as old as the Bible, and indeed was recently immortalized by Oliver Wendell Holmes in his romantic novel *Elsie Venner*.

Of all the exhibits, one holds the greatest attraction for Ray. No specimens, living or dead, are displayed, just two notice boards to which sheets of paper are neatly pinned: architects' drawings for the new zoological garden.

"Seen this, Allen?"

He points at one diagram.

"It's going to be the serpent-house. How I should love to get involved in *that*!"

"Why not write an article about it? Get chummy with old Hornaday. See where that leads," says Williams.

"You know, Allen, that's not such a bad idea . . ."

―✦―

"THANK you," I called back having leapt a huge puddle, but the driver had closed the doors and was articulating the front end of his Bx9 bus back onto the broad, empty avenue. It was later in the morning than suggested by the charcoal gray sky. Although I was staying just three miles away, the journey had taken over an hour with all the stops and traffic. I was cold, wet, and behind schedule. I ducked out of the pelting rain under the brash awning of a deli and fiddled with my borrowed umbrella.

On the far side of the road a chain-link fence, perhaps twelve feet high and topped with several lines of barbed wire, stretched for about half a mile in each direction. The barricade seemed as much there to restrain the phalanx of mature pines, maples, and oaks from bursting forth onto Southern Boulevard as to keep intruders out. A wooden screen behind the perimeter mesh prevented even a glimpse of the treasures beyond.

According to my soggy map, a pedestrian entrance was sited further to the south. I crossed the boulevard, turned right, and after a minute's sloshing along the sidewalk arrived at an opening in the fence. Any doubt as to my location was removed by the words Bronx Zoo emblazoned on an archway above me against a turquoise backdrop of stenciled zoo animals and palm trees. In the sign's left corner was the square logo of the Wild-life Conservation Society. The New York Zoological Society had changed its name in the 1990s to reflect the global nature of operations, perhaps also to distance itself from negative connotations attached to zoos in the modern mind.

I followed a narrow avenue shaded by tall trees but floodwater soon halted my progress. My path was blocked. Beyond the pool were turnstiles and a zoo employee with an umbrella. She was chatting on a walkie-talkie. I failed to draw her attention. Not wishing to spend my first day at the Bronx Zoo in sodden shoes I retreated to the main road. Five minutes further along the boundary of the zoo brought me to its southern corner and an entrance for vehicles. Crossing the empty parking lot I reached another set of turnstiles manned by two more employees. I told them I had an appointment at the zoo library and was waved through without fuss. Perhaps my British accent reassured them.

I hurried along the walkways bordered with red oaks, passing signs for the CHILDREN'S ZOO, CONGO GORILLA FOREST, MADAGASCAR! The rain had softened to a light but insistent patter. Except for a dejected-looking young couple in matching yellow plastic ponchos and the occasional member of zoo staff zipping past on an electric buggy, I encountered no one else before arriving at a sleek, three-storied concrete and glass structure nestled in the zoo's northern corner. The Center for Global Conservation opened in 2009 and boasted such eco-friendly features as a microturbine energy plant and a green roof in which local grasses and shrubs had been planted to help regulate the building's temperature. Inside the building over a hundred staff were working to save wildlife and wild places around the world. It also housed the Society's library and archives. Had any documents relating to Raymond Ditmars and his hunt for a bushmaster survived? I pressed the door buzzer and waited.

USELESS! Wasteful! Not fair! The discussion over supper one evening in December 1887 had gotten serious and passions were inflamed. One can almost hear the guzzling of vintage sherry as the select gathering of lawyers, politicians, soldiers, and tycoons worked itself into a lather of indignation.

The topic that so incensed them was the threat posed to wildlife from indiscriminate or, as they put it, "unsportsmanlike" hunting. Industrial progress in the shape of railroad expansion and more efficient weaponry had left a trail of buffalo corpses across the Great Plains, while closer to home, in the Adirondack Mountains of upstate New York, deer herds were being ravaged by unrestricted hunting with dogs. Too often the line between noble sport, as practiced by these gentlemen diners, and the unfair, malevolent destruction of wild game was now being crossed.

Worse, animals were killed for mere profit. Something had to be done or soon there would be nothing left.

Among these rich and powerful men was Theodore Roosevelt, at the time lying low and smarting from a run of abysmal luck. The future president had lost a fortune when the previous winter had annihilated Elk Horn, his beloved cattle ranch in North Dakota. He has also come a poor third in a race to be New York City mayor. The single bright note was his recent marriage and honeymoon in Europe. Also in attendance was a naturalist in his late thirties named George Bird Grinnell. A decade earlier he had been an associate of Lieutenant Colonel Custer, but these days Grinnell edited *Forest and Stream*, the magazine of choice for North America's hunting and fishing fraternity. He'd also just founded the first Audubon society to protect the country's birds.

At some point that evening—perhaps at the passing of a cheese board or the finest Havana cigars—Roosevelt and Grinnell proposed a solution. They would establish a movement aimed at the "preservation of the large game of this country" through enforcement of existing rules and, where possible, the introduction of new legislation. At the same time, the Boone and Crockett Club, as it was christened in honor of the legendary frontiersmen Daniel Boone and Davy Crockett, would "promote manly sport with the rifle" and "bring about among the members the interchange of opinions and ideas on hunting, travel, exploration, on the various kinds of hunting rifles, on the haunts of game animals, etc." Despite the emphasis on killing—only those who had slain at least three species of large mammal could join—North America's first wildlife conservation organization was born.

The Boone and Crockett Club petitioned lawmakers and promoted its goals through books and articles, and saw early successes including the passing in 1894 of a federal bill to protect wildlife in Yellowstone National Park. In the same year Roosevelt was prompted by Madison Grant, an energetic young lawyer and fellow big hunter, to form a committee with a view of banning the murderous activities in the Adirondacks while creating a zoological society and park in New York City. The aim would be to collect and breed big game animals while providing a local center for scientific education.

The idea had in fact been pondered for years, not least as a new breed of zoological garden was now popping up across the country, with public education and general betterment the objective rather than grubby entertainment. In the years after the Civil War ended in 1865, twenty or more major "scientific" zoos had appeared, notable examples being in Philadelphia and Cincinnati. Then, in 1891, the National Zoological Park was founded in Washington, DC. Meanwhile, in London the Regent's Park Zoo had been going strong since 1828. The establishment of a first-rate zoo in New York was long overdue and, although popular, the cramped and stinking menagerie in Central Park was simply not up to the job. Roosevelt's committee, consisting of the lawyer and future US secretary of state Elihu Root, the architect C. Grant LaFarge, and Madison Grant himself, went before the state legislature in Albany to secure the Zoological Society's charter. William White Niles Jr., an assemblyman for northern New York City, offered crucial support. Niles was among many already calling for such a development. Further backing came from the press baron William Randolph Hearst.

Not everyone was happy with the proposal. New York's pet dealers worried that a new zoo would breed and sell domestic animals, putting them out of business. The owners of competing animal collections had similar concerns, some divining a conspiracy by the city's elite to abolish the Central Park menagerie, thus boosting the value of their Fifth Avenue properties. These latter fears were not realized in the short term at least; according to an 1899 report for the Department of Parks, the "Menagerie in the Central Park retains its great popularity despite the installation of the New York Zoological Garden." Others were meanwhile uncomfortable with the transfer of public land into private hands and, when the site was later proposed, pointed to poor transport connections.

Things moved fast nevertheless thanks to the power of Roosevelt's committee and its champions. On April 26, 1895, the state legislature incorporated the New York Zoological Society and provided "for the establishment of a zoological garden in the city of New York" with "the purpose of encouraging and advancing the study of zoology, original researches in the same and kindred subjects, and of furnishing instruction and recreation to the people." The society was empowered to "purchase and hold animals, plants, and specimens appropriate to the objects for which said corporation is created." The charter required that for at least four days of the week admission would be free of charge.

Roosevelt, the natural choice for the Society's president given his profile and early enthusiasm for the project, resigned less than a year after its creation blaming a heavy workload. The position went instead to the New York governor Levi P. Morton. But Madison Grant and his friend Professor Henry Fairfield Osborn were the real driving force. With funds promised by city authorities and a growing list of millionaire trustees, the pair now looked for someone to run the new zoo and somewhere to put it.

The first objective was met the following year with the appointment of William Temple Hornaday. Euphemistically described as "gruff and vigorous in his dealings with other people," the forty-one-year-old Midwesterner had made his name as the country's premier taxidermist at the Natural Science Establishment in Rochester, upstate New York. Founded in 1862 by Professor Henry Augustus Ward, the establishment specialized in advanced taxidermy, supplying realistically mounted animal specimens to museums then proliferating across the country. Hitherto, stuffed exhibits had been crude, bearing little resemblance to the animal in life. "A Fight to the Tree Tops" was Hornaday's *pièce de résistance* in which orangutans and gibbons were arranged in groups indicating social relationships and community activities. The creation, inspired by a collecting trip to Borneo, "aroused widespread comment and admiration" when unveiled at an 1880 meeting of the American Association for the Advancement of Science in Rochester. Numerous other exhibits followed.

Hornaday moved to Washington, DC, and honed his skills as chief taxidermist at the United States National Museum. When he visited Montana to "gather" American buffalo for stuffing, Hornaday's first-hand experience of the persecution of this symbolic species converted him from hunter to wildlife conservationist. A poignant moment was his discovery during the skinning of an 1,800-pound specimen that the unfortunate beast already carried four older bullets. In 1888 he was promoted to chief curator at the Smithsonian Institution's Department of Living Reptiles. While in Washington he lobbied for the establishment of the National Zoological Park, even choosing the 168-acre site at Rock Creek Park. In keeping with the zeitgeist, Hornaday envisaged the new zoo to be a wildlife refuge as much as a place for amusement and was a shoe-in as its inaugural director. Things turned sour though "due to matters of policy with which he was not in harmony." In 1890, months before the zoo's grand opening, a disappointed Hornaday left the capital to supervise a real estate company in—appropriately enough—Buffalo, New York.

That the recently minted New York Zoological Society could, six years later, lure Hornaday back to a public role in a scientific organization was a testament to the persuasiveness of its leadership. Not least as the preferred candidate had just turned down a similar job in Pittsburgh. Perhaps the starting salary of $5,000 per year—double that offered in Washington—also weighed in the balance. Whatever the truth, Hornaday was re-energized. Starting on a two-year contract, he would run the Bronx Zoo for the next thirty years.

Grant and Osborn encountered more difficulty in selecting a location for the zoo. The charter stated the park could be sited on any city territory north of One Hundred and Fifty-fifth Street. That left a lot of choice. In December 1888 the city had acquired, and protected from development, large tracts of cheap land to the northeast. The New Parks, as they were known, were the brainchild of John Mullaly, the editor of a Catholic Irish newspaper, who saw them as a means "to promote the sanitary welfare of the people, to secure to them opportunities for physical recreation and outdoor exercise, and to add to the prosperity and embellishment of our imperial metropolis." Not everyone was convinced. Some suspected Mullaly of a scam to boost the value of his or his associates' land in the vicinity of the proposed parks. Ironically, a young Theodore Roosevelt was among the cynics. Yet Mullaly, a shrewd political tactician, persuaded the state legislature to sanction the purchase. The initiative was, he insisted, "earnest, sincere, honest, and unselfish."

The New York Zoological Society's Committee now consulted *The New Parks beyond the Harlem*, Mullaly's book on the newly annexed territory. An early candidate was Pelham Bay Park on Eastchester Bay, whose sea breezes might help waft away the animals' stink, but the swampiness was unsuitable for hooved animals and mosquitoes were rife. Crotona and Van Cortlandt Parks were also dismissed.

By contrast, the Bronx Park ticked most boxes. Closer to the city, it was described as "sufficiently remote from all steam railways that its quiet is not broken by them." Long protected from development by the Lydigs, a a family of successful German farmers and bakers, the land was "a wonderful combination of hill and hollow, of high ridge and deep valley, of stream and pond, rolling meadow, rocky ledge and virgin forest of the finest description." Among unusual features of the park was the Rocking Stone, an enormous pink rock said to sway an inch when pushed. Deposited near the Bronx River in the last ice age, the ten foot tall chunk of granite on a high point among cedars became a popular landmark at the zoo, although safety-conscious officials later shored it up. The site was blessed with good water resources and excellent drainage. "Swamp influences" in the form of malaria were absent, although mosquitoes were troublesome and an open stream of sewage flowed for half a mile in the park's northwestern portion.

On July 1, 1898, the Society acquired 261 acres in the southern half of Bronx Park, the northern portion already earmarked for botanical gardens. A tour by Hornaday of fifteen zoological gardens across western Europe two years earlier bolstered the Society's confidence that the Bronx project would be "vastly superior." The new zoological park would stand "midway between the typical thirty-acre zoological garden of London, Paris, Antwerp, or Philadelphia, and the great private game preserve." During a lecture at the American Museum of Natural History in January 1899, Professor Osborn derided what was to be found across the Atlantic: "there is little or no natural scenery. Here and there attempts have been made to construct artificial hillocks and bits of rookery, but these attempts cannot be described as satisfactory. In our New York gardens there is every type of landscape that may be desired. The park needs little or no improvement except in the shape of walks, drives, and drainage."

Moreover, continued Osborn, animal welfare would be prioritized from outset. Captive specimens would be "as fully contented as if in their native wilds." The monkey house, for instance, would be fitted with a "perfect system of ventilation" and "roomy cages" offering "animals ample chance for exercise" and reducing risk of respiratory illnesses, principally tuberculosis. The speaker drove home the point with lantern slides contrasting the limited quarters endured by captives in European gardens with the grassy slopes and rocky inclines of the Bronx Park. The new development epitomized for Osborn the "American Zoological Park idea." The revelation, we are told, elicited a burst of applause from the audience.

THE rain clouds had dissipated and sunlight glinted off the surface of a lake adjacent to the Center for Global Conservation. A white swan stretched and flapped its wings, unsettling a nearby trio of wood ducks. It was five o'clock and I had exhausted the Ditmars archives. Just four boxfiles represented the entirety of the celebrated snakeman's official papers despite his more than forty years at the zoo. In fact, many records from the earliest years of the New York Zoological Society were now missing. Rumors suggest that much of the material, today so treasured by the zoo's archivists, was simply dumped sometime in the 1950s and what had been kept hadn't fared much better. The remnants of Ditmars's correspondence, for instance, were found moldering in the basement of the monkey house.

The surviving memoranda, letters, telegrams, and typed manuscripts spanned the years 1925 to 1928 and offered a fascinating snapshot of his life. Ditmars was entering his fifties and still in his prime. The enthusiasm for reptiles was undiminished as evidenced by the many letters answering queries on the subject. I lost count of the number of times he patiently denied the existence of the hoop snake. The hoary myth that mother snakes protected their babies by swallowing them was also tirelessly refuted; often the reader had, in reality, witnessed cannibalism, as many snakes are partial to consuming their own kind. When the curator himself once reviewed his mail, he discovered that, in just over a year, letters on that particular subject had come in from every state in the country.

The remaining correspondence I flicked through concerned the acquisition of new animal specimens. Would a bushmaster, perhaps, be mentioned here? No, was the answer. It was the end of the day and I had seen not a single reference to the reptile that in the early 1930s would come to obsess Raymond Ditmars.

SNAKES TO BE ON SHOW
TO FRIEND AND FOE.

COBRA
de
CAPELLA

And
CANNIBAL
SNAKES

FANGS OF A FIERCE ENEMY OF ANIMAL LIFE.

Article in the *New York World* marking the first American Intercontinental
Exhibition of Reptiles, November 14, 1898.

By 1899 William Hornaday was on the lookout for a reptile man for the
new zoo. Raymond Ditmars was the perfect candidate, but as with other
key turning points in his extraordinary career, the precise circumstances
by which he was appointed are hazy. The usual story, one Ditmars himself related, is that the *Times* dispatched him up to the Bronx to quiz

Hornaday about the new zoo. So bowled over was the cantankerous director by the young reporter's knowledge and love of reptiles that several weeks he later offered him a job.

William Bridges, a reporter on the *New York Sun* and eventually the New York Zoological Society's curator of publications, has a slightly different account. As he points out in *Gathering of Animals*, his candid history of the society published in 1974, Ditmars and the director were already acquainted, the latter having honored the Harlem Zoological Society with a talk on his favorite topic, "The Buffalo." And rather than interviewing Hornaday, Ditmars had instead spotted an article on the progress of the park in the society's December 1898 news bulletin. The twenty-two-year-old rewrote the piece for the January 2, 1899, edition of the *Times* and mailed it to Hornaday. "At present I am on the reportorial staff of the N. Y. Times," wrote Ditmars in his covering letter, "and have compiled the matter in the Bulletin in the shape of a newspaper article, which is enclosed herewith. If there is anything in the shape of press work I can do for the Society, it will be my pleasure to aid you in that direction." According to Bridges, Hornaday wrote back to Ditmars five days later complimenting him on his story that was "good and helpful, and very correctly written." He went on to offer him the position of "Keeper of Reptiles." The famous meeting may not have occurred at the zoo at all because Hornaday's letter suggested they talk over the matter at the society's office on Wall Street.

Ditmars had in fact recently proved his skills in organizing a major reptile exhibition as curator of the "American Inter-Continental Exhibition of Reptiles" at the Grand Central Palace on Manhattan's Lexington Avenue in November 1898. The event, the first of an annual series conceived by Allen Samuel Williams, a fellow reptile enthusiast and notable teetotaller, drew much press attention not least because Williams too had been a newspaperman. *Scientific American* emphasized its scale: "There have been small displays of snakes in museums and at the World's Fair but never a comprehensive exhibition. Certificates of merit will be issued for meritorious exhibits. Stuffed snakes and snakes preserved in alcohol will also be shown. It is expected that there will be one hundred and fifty to two hundred varieties of reptiles on exhibition." A reporter from the *New York Times* was meanwhile distracted by a "dispenser of alcoholic exhilarators" close to the venue whose signs promised "Snake Cocktails" and "Cobra di Capello Fizz" at fifteen cents a piece. The barman reportedly offered "to lay odds that they would produce more hallucinations at less expense and in a shorter given time than any modern drink ever invented."

Beneath all these thrills lay a serious conservation message. Ditmars was at pains to stress that snakes destroyed pests and thus, apart from rattlers and other "bad actors," should be regarded as friends. The exhibition demonstrated his ability to blend scientific information with entertainment to maximize publicity. Hornaday had taken a keen interest in the snake show and surely recognized this rare skill when hiring the young reporter. He later announced his new appointment—someone with no formal training in zoology—as "a thoroughly qualified expert in the care of reptiles in captivity, and also a man well versed in reptilian classification and life history."

Regardless of how Ditmars secured his new job, he had already visited the Bronx Park to view progress—or lack of. Years afterward he reported what he found: "The journey to the then remote Bronx ended at a cabin, where I was told about future elephant, lion, monkey, and reptile houses, deer and buffalo ranges. What I saw were rows of surveying stakes and men digging for a foundation." The collection then amounted to a bear cub, wolf pup, and "one snapping turtle in a tin bathtub."

Ground had been broken on August 11, 1898, for the winter birds house and through the fall and winter things picked up as wagon after wagon dumped loads of brick and stone, and gangs of laborers cleared away the wilderness of waving grass and bushes. Private benefactors including Cornelius Vanderbilt II, Jacob Schiff, and William C. Whitney poured in funds for the plans, buildings, and animals, while city taxpayers contributed equal sums for paths, grading, drainage, fences, and pavilions. Meanwhile, Bronxdale, a tiny settlement on the site with a cotton bleachery and one of the Lydigs' many flour mills, was demolished and today lies beneath the zoo's parking lot. Signs were erected banning locals from collecting firewood from the site. These were ignored at first so police officers of the 41st Precinct under Captain Hugh Fitzpatrick were tasked with keeping out vagrants.

By July 1899 some 250 men were at work, many of them Italian immigrants, a source of cheap skilled labor. Most commuted from the crowded lower East Side of Manhattan aboard the 3rd Avenue elevated railroad, the line then terminating inconveniently at Tremont Avenue, a mile or so west of the Bronx Park. Eight cents would buy a tram ride closer, but most workers completed the journey on foot. To avoid the hassle, many settled later in the Arthur Avenue area of Belmont near the zoo where a new "Little Italy" grew up complete with cafés, bakeries, and delis.

The new zoo would boast dozens of indoor and open air exhibits. To the satisfaction of Roosevelt and his fellow Boone and Crocketters, deer, moose, caribou, buffalo, and elk could now rove unmolested in generous natural ranges created by fencing off woods and meadows. An area was landscaped for burrowing rodents, an eighty-foot diameter circular prairie dog village, a three-acre lake for aquatic mammals, a beaver pond, and a pool for alligators. Dens for wolves, bears, and foxes were built.

Work also began on the animal houses, designed by Henry Heins and C. Grant LaFarge, the latter having stepped down from the society to avoid a conflict of interest. The buildings were conceived in the Beaux-Arts style, whose embellishments, monumental scale, and symmetry are also evident in the American Museum of Natural History, the Metropolitan Museum of Art, the New York Public Library on 42nd Street, and other landmarks of the period. Houses would be devoted to lions, monkeys, small mammals, elephants, antelopes, and overwintering birds.

Among the most ambitious structures was the aquatic bird house featuring an interior flying cage and aquarium for diving birds. Several hundred ducks would be housed in an adjoining aviary, crowned by an immense flying cage of steel girders and wire mesh. Large enough to contain mature trees, the cage would dwarf its counterparts across the Atlantic. A twenty-eight-year-old taxidermist and recent employee at London's Regent's Park Zoo named J. Alden Loring was hired to oversee the birds. Mammals were his responsibility too, but the workload proved unbearable. Weeks before the zoo's grand opening Henry Fairfield Osborn suggested Hornaday bring in none other than William Beebe as assistant curator in charge of birds. Like Ditmars, Beebe knew Osborn from the American Museum of Natural History and had cemented the relationship at Columbia University.

Of course, for Ditmars, the only building that mattered was the reptile house. Although the architecture and display cases would be inspired by its famous counterpart at the London Zoo, the New York Zoological Society wanted its reptile house to be a "model of its kind," incorporating "well-planned installations . . . a departure from stereotyped methods of exhibition." Hornaday himself prepared the ground plan, describing it as "an earnest effort to present carefully selected examples of the reptilian Orders, in a manner which may afford the visitor and the student a general view of the important groups of living reptiles." The latter included turtles, crocodiles, lizards, and snakes along with interesting examples of frogs, toads, newts, and salamanders.

Up to this time the lot of the cold-blooded was to be feared by the public, pickled in jars, and burdened with convoluted taxonomic names. For the first time living specimens "from all parts of the globe" would be viewed in surroundings "intended to represent their native wilds." At just twenty-three, Ditmars was overjoyed to be part of the venture.

# 6

# A Decided Awakening of Unbiased Interest

*"To the keepers in reptile-houses fall most extraordinary and dangerous duties. The handling of some of the smallest snakes, for instance, involves more danger than attendance on a large collection of lions, tigers and other fierce carnivora."*

—Raymond L. Ditmars, *The Youth's Companion*, August 1, 1901

———◆———

*November 8, 1899. The New York Zoological Park, New York City.*

AIR BUBBLES EXPIRE IN tiny explosions on the water's soupy surface heralding the appearance of a craggy reptilian head and snout. A translucent eyelid smears back, exposing an olive-green iris and a splinter of black pupil. A second alligator is already out and resting on a sandbank, and three more lurk somewhere in the organized confusion of resurrection ferns and Spanish moss, tillandsias and butterfly orchids, palmettos and bayonet cacti fringing the pool. Thirty feet above, silent rain freckles the glass of the conservatory roof.

Beyond the archway lies the magnificent central gallery of the reptile house, its red-and-yellow firebrick walls flanked with rows of display cases. A young man in a dark uniform, the words ZOOLOGICAL PARK embroidered on his cap, is watering one of the half dozen tree-sized ferns which are arranged in heavy pots about the hall. A second, older keeper in an identical outfit is polishing the cases for the third time that day. Moving from cage to cage, he passes king snakes and gopher snakes, black snakes and massive pythons.

Inanimate serpents are woven over shrubbery, draped over water bowls, coiled on bare concrete floors. Even the dozen or so newborn garter snakes are lethargic. Little happens here in daylight. But arriving at the venomous exhibits, the keeper finds a diamondback rattlesnake very much awake. The huge animal, noosed last month in the Florida swamps, has reared up to his own height. A reptilian puppet on invisible strings. The man shudders and not for the first time contemplates the strength of the glass that he now gives a cursory wipe. Barely an inch away, the rattler flickers a forked black tongue and presses its snout up against the invisible, frustrating barrier.

"All right fellers, you're in charge," calls out Ray, who has emerged from his office. Dressed in a military-style drill of gray with dark green piping, he strides across the central hall toward the lobby, passing a glass tank marked BATRACHIANS containing four enormous salamanders. "They'll be here in ten minutes, so I'd better be off."

"Yes boss," reply the weary keepers in unison. All three were up past midnight preparing the reptile house for the big day, but Ray seems as perky as ever.

The assistant curator pushes open the large wooden entrance doors, hurriedly closing them behind him to keep out the chill northwesterly. He passes between hefty square columns topped by their sculptural flourishes and out into the park.

He pauses, turns back, admires the reptile house. *His* reptile house. Under that slate roof with its elaborate cornice of carved animal heads is a world of responsibility: seventy-eight different species represented by sixteen alligators, thirty-seven amphibians, seventy-one lizards, ninety-four turtles, and almost three hundred snakes at the last count. And Ray is in charge of feeding, nurturing, and protecting every last one of them. He can hardly believe his fortune. Insensible to the dismal weather, he readjusts his tie, brushes down his jacket lapels and walks briskly into a leafless oak forest toward the north gate of the zoo.

"Here, let me assist you, Mr. Morton," says police captain Hugh Fitzpatrick offering his arm to an elderly gentleman with enormous gray whiskers. The Honorable Levi P. Morton, ex-state governor, former vice-president of the United States and now president of the New York Zoological Society is led from his carriage to a bunting-draped platform, temporarily erected on the terrace in front of the aquatic bird house. The latter's pediment is also bedecked handsomely in the American flag, a stone pelican standing sentinel at each corner. Thousands of guests have been conveyed on two special trains from Grand Central to Fordham station on the Harlem Division and then a short distance by carriage to the park's northwest entrance at Pelham Avenue and the Southern Boulevard. The wrought iron gates were opened at 3 o'clock precisely and Morton completed his journey to the bird house in his carriage. The rest dismounted and walked. A column of city bigwigs, millionaire industrialists, New York Zoological Society members—and very often all three— marching past extensive deer ranges and toward the huge flying cage adjacent to the bird house. A mass of less exalted citizens has attached itself to the throng: a thin man holding an umbrella and wobbling on a bicycle, bowler hat slipping over one eye; a lady hoisting her skirts to avoid a puddle while pushing a perambulator; a careening gang of children. This last offends Fitzpatrick who had expressly ordered his men from the Bronx Park's 41st precinct—out in force today—to keep such ruffians at bay. As the dignitaries take up camp chairs close to the lectern, they are issued with maps of the park, programs of the exercises.

Keen to expedite proceedings, Morton theatrically clears his throat. The standing contingent of the audience presses in, to hear the fine words, yes, but perhaps also in response to the miserable weather conditions. A shrill avian shriek issues from the bird house beyond. The whiff of ripe animal excrement occasionally blows through the crowd. Morton's contribution is brief. "Ladies and Gentlemen," he exclaims. "It gives me great pleasure to introduce to you the man who has done more than any other for the establishment of this zoological park, Professor Henry F. Osborn!"

Morton is guided to a seat—hastily wiped dry—and a younger man takes the stand.

"Fellow citizens, you are welcome to the opening of this park, which marks another step of progress toward the great New York of the future . . ."

Several other worthies give stirring addresses. "We hear so much said about New York that is bad," says city comptroller Bird S. Coler, "that it is time a better public sentiment were aroused, that we showed to the world what good things New York contains . . ."

An hour later and the speeches are at last over. Escorted by Fitzpatrick, Morton steps forward and lifts the rail in front of the stand. "Ladies and Gentlemen, I now take great pleasure in declaring the New York Zoological Park, and all its collections, open to the public!"

Standing next to the platform, flanked by fellow assistant curators Beebe and Loring, Ray cannot help but crack a broad grin.

---

"OH my God, it's a big snake, Daddy. Look how *huge* that thing is!"

"Hey Spiderman, come down from there."

"It's a dinosaur-snake!"

"Don't climb up there."

"Roar!"

The boy balanced on a ledge in front of an exhibit. His breath steamed the glass, his eyes popping. Before him was the dry forest floor of an African jungle: leaf litter, wood chips, tree branches, patches of hot white light, and right there in the middle of it all a single enormous snake, a pattern of black–and–white polygons running the length of its torpid body.

"What is it?" His father had caught up with his son and now cribbed information from a nearby sign.

"Oh, it's a gaboon viper. *Bitis gabonica*. The largest of the true vipers. Two-inch long fangs and a large quantity of venom make this among the most dangerous of snakes."

"Check out the nose on that thing!" said the boy, just an inch or so of glass separating him from the viper's snout which was topped by a grayish spike. "Look at his skin," continued Dad. "That color helps him blend into the ground when he is in the woods."

The snake was unphased and near motionless, except for the seemingly too-seldom inhalations which caused its whole body to rise and settle. Even if the gaboon viper could hear I doubted it would have responded to yet another enthusiastic child shouting and banging on the glass. Two million people visited the zoo each year, and most made a beeline to the reptile house.

At the time of my visit, the Bronx Zoo had no bushmaster on display, but the gaboon viper made for a reasonable substitute. Like the bushmaster, gaboons are sizeable, impressive vipers that lurk in tropical environments, although it was the African rather than South American tropics. They too have massive venom glands and huge fangs, longer even than those of the bushmaster. In both snakes, the fangs are hinged, swinging forward during a strike on prey and folding back neatly when not in use. This ingenious mechanism allows vipers to accommodate far longer fangs than are to be found in other venomous snakes. However, gaboons lack the heat-sensitive depressions in the face that give pitvipers such as the bushmaster and rattlesnakes their name. And, if the accounts are true, bushmasters grow much, much bigger.

My first view of the reptile house had been faintly disappointing. Some of the carved stone animal heads fringing the roof's cornice were obscured by a blue plywood hoarding on metal scaffolding poles. Algal growth stained the sea-green copper roofing; I later discovered that decaying concrete in the roof was being replaced. Remnants of desiccated ivy stubbornly clung here and there to the façade. The windows of the reptile house were boarded up, presumably to facilitate control of the light and temperature within, but this only reinforced the sense of dereliction. A black locust tree brightened the mood however. Fifty feet high, it reared over the front of the building scattering a confetti of tiny yellow leaves.

All was darkness as I stepped into the reptile house, now rebranded "World of Reptiles." Backlit signage and the reptile exhibits themselves offered meagre illumination and I almost stumbled over a life-sized bronze sculpture of a komodo dragon at the entrance. The floors and walls were covered in brown carpet. The faintly sweet odor of a thousand spilt sodas pervaded the warm air.

I already knew that little of the reptile house's original gothic structure would be visible. Peter Brazaitis, a former superintendent of reptiles at the Bronx Zoo—and someone I would soon meet—wrote that when he joined the zoo in the 1950s "the public display halls and exhibits had demanded a drastic modernization. A leaky roof, cold weather, and an insufficient coal-fired heating system had, over the years, cost the lives of many warm-loving reptiles." James Oliver, a successor of Ditmars's had ordered the complete redesign of the reptile house's interior. The main exhibits were gutted and a mezzanine level installed between the first floor and the roof to provide an additional storage and husbandry area. The imposing vaults Ditmars had known were now lost behind a low ceiling.

As my eyes adjusted to the conditions, I passed glass tanks with turtles, anacondas, and boa constrictors. One enclosure housed an Egyptian cobra, another had tree monitor lizards. A Fly River turtle with a comical pig-like snout caught my eye. Almost nothing moved, although a rattlesnake withdrew in apparent disgust when I photographed it; I had forgotten to switch off my flash. A collection of field biologists' tools formed another exhibit, recalling the displays of snakebite treatment paraphernalia that Raymond Ditmars assembled here a century before. The great man himself was not forgotten in the modern reptile house. An information board entitled A History Of Helping pictured the balding curator late in life. Sporting his trademark white three-piece suit, Ditmars was seated at a desk posing with a live python. Two assistants were on hand to steady the snake's body: a lady in floral print dress and beads and a moustachioed keeper. I returned to the front of the building. I was about to meet someone who knew what it was like to work at the Bronx Zoo reptile house.

The Reptile House at the Bronx Zoo, early twentieth century.
(© Wildlife Conservation Society)

ON July 17, 1899, the twenty-three-year-old Raymond Ditmars formally assumed the duties of "assistant curator in charge of reptiles" at the New York Zoological Park. The monthly salary was a modest $75, with a $10 allowance for room rent until accommodation at the reptile house was ready. He would not be elevated to full curator for another three years, but the job title was grander than "keeper of reptiles," the post offered by Hornaday six months previously. The position of chief reptile keeper—at $50 a month—went instead to Charles E. Snyder, whom Ditmars had met a year or so before while at the *New York Times*. The reporter had taken a day off to catch frogs in "the wilds of Jerome Avenue, in the Bronx" when he saw someone a bit older than himself "shinning up an electric-light pole to put new carbons in an arc lamp." The young lamp trimmer, also a naturalist, stopped what he was doing and gave Ditmars a hand. The pair continued frog-hunting aboard "an old buggy" Snyder was driving.

97

As Ditmars later wrote, his friend proved a "particularly intelligent and interesting fellow. I invited him to see my snakes and in turn he promised to bring me plenty of frogs."

By the time of Ditmars's appointment, the reptile house was more or less complete and he had little chance to influence the design. Construction had started back in August 1898. The New York Zoological Society prioritized the reptile house because, it later declared, visitors would be least familiar with its particular inhabitants. Approaching the one-story structure situated in the geographic center of the park close to a forest of ancient oaks, Ditmars would first have been struck by its size. Measuring one hundred forty-six feet in length and one hundred feet at the greatest width, the reptile house was the world's biggest. The Beaux-Arts building's cornice of terra cotta was punctuated with stone heads of crocodiles, turtles, frogs, and other reptiles, the creations of Alexander Phimister Proctor, a Canadian sculptor and lifelong member of the Boone and Crockett Club. As Ditmars passed through the south entrance flanked by white Ionic columns, he would surely have been awed by the central hall into which he walked. The grand east–west gallery, some one hundred fifteen feet long, was unbroken by a single supporting column. Instead, gently curving steel trusses, incorporating floral designs, spanned the forty-foot wide space. The girders braced a slate roof in which generous skylights were installed. The walls were of buff mottled brick, granite, and Indiana limestone.

Snakes and amphibians, or "batrachians" as they were often called, were to be allocated several dozen glass-fronted cages lining the great hall, while vast salt and freshwater tanks for turtles ran along center. An adjoining room would be devoted to terrestrial turtles, although at the time of the zoo's opening it served as a temporary lunchroom. The western end of the reptile house was given over to the spacious crocodile pool, the water heated to 90° Fahrenheit by concealed pipes. Beyond grew a green, jungly mass of palmettoes, cacti, yuccas, tillandsias, Spanish moss, resurrection ferns, orchids, and other exotic vegetation, the back wall cleverly painted to represent a Florida swamp—all under a glass roof. Stepping back outside, Ditmars would have spied, close to the southeastern corner of the reptile house, a natural depression thirty feet wide and sixty long in an outcrop of granite rock. With careful blasting, the society would extend the feature into a summer pool for crocodiles and alligators, with sea lions and penguins taking their place in colder months.

The cost of constructing the reptile house eventually exceeded $50,000—more than a million dollars in today's money—making it among the most expensive of the zoo's original buildings. Had Ditmars been brought in sooner he would have placed as much attention on the welfare of exhibits as architectural embellishments. The hopeless inefficiency of the reptile house's original coal-fired heating system in particular would kill off innumerable warmth-loving specimens. The use of natural wood for finishing the interior was another design blunder; so high was the humidity that the timbers needed re-varnishing every month.

To his parents' enormous relief Ditmars took his own snakes with him when he joined the zoo. At that point the attic collection amounted to forty-five animals, representing fifteen species, and it would form the nucleus of the reptile house exhibit. As well as serpents such as garters, copperheads, and rattlers and some turtles and amphibians, Ditmars's donation to the zoo included the skulls of a boa constrictor and rattlesnake. He also brought two alligators. One called Mose had been acquired back in 1892 as a sixteen-inch baby and had since lived in a tank of water on a window sill in the Ditmars household. Mose would become something of a fixture at the Bronx Zoo, surviving countless battles with other alligators—and subsequent stitch-ups—before being found belly-up in his pond one Sunday morning in 1934. By then he was eight feet in length and weighed two hundred pounds. Ditmars's contribution was surpassed only by fellow amateur herpetologist Morris Pearsall. In the same year, Pearsall furnished the reptile house with ninety-five serpents, supplemented with 291 smaller specimens destined as snake food. The population of the reptile house was further swelled by snakes native to the Bronx collected on the grounds by construction gangs. Notably absent on the zoo's opening day, however, was a bushmaster. Ditmars was yet to find a replacement for Mole's famous specimen.

The reptile house was in fact among the few large structures to be completed on time despite the frenzy of activity across the Bronx Park. The zoo's grand opening had been chalked for early summer 1899, but with the building schedule slipping and expenditure mounting, the society delayed it until the fall. The zoo's staff was meanwhile prohibited from talking to the press. The embargo was just as well given subsequent events. The trouble started on May 11 with the first arrival of animals ordered many weeks before. Their accommodations far from complete, the exhibits had to be housed in sheds and enclosures away from prying eyes. The secret yards quickly overflowed with "large water birds, alligators, snakes in glass-fronted boxes, lynxes, foxes, raccoons, bears, monkeys, squirrels, young antelopes" and more. A significant proportion of the animals perished in these inappropriate conditions.

Ditmars himself was soon caught up in an embarrassing incident. Over the summer he had added two enormous reticulated pythons to his reptile collection. One, known as Billy, disappeared from his wooden dry goods box, spreading panic among the construction workers. Hornaday and Ditmars found the fifteen-foot-long reptile sleeping in the zookeepers' temporary cookhouse. The zoo director promptly lassoed Billy, enabling the assistant curator to grip the serpent's throat. Two keepers then jumped the uncoiling snake, holding on with all their might as he writhed.

Although Billy was safely returned to his box, Hornaday was scared the episode would result in uncomfortable headlines. Yet such was the effectiveness of the news blackout that the story did not emerge for five months, by which time it was cold. The *New York Times* nevertheless later jested that, before its capture, the python "had left a trail in the earth that looked as though a small steamroller had been winding an erratic course about the animal yard." His feelings "deeply wounded by this unceremonious treatment," Billy fasted for several months in retaliation. The story had a sad postscript. In October 1899 a cold front swept the east coast and, with the reptile house heating not yet functional, one of the giant pythons—whether it was Billy is unclear—reportedly contracted hypothermia. Two weeks before opening day the snake died of "congestion of the lungs."

Despite the setbacks Hornaday gloated that he had played "a huge joke on the press," bringing in truckloads of specimens, with the newspapers and their readers none the wiser: "Very few people, if any . . . know that a great number of the animals are already in their quarters in the park, because I have kept the fact away from the papers, but now, as they are all enclosed by high board fences, so that nothing can be seen, I don't care, and you can tell all you please about the garden. The public had better keep away though, for they won't see anything until the opening day, when they will be welcome to come and see all that they can, and that will be a good deal if they see all there is."

CHRIS Hutson was a fresh-faced twenty-something, but by the time he had been appointed collections manager for herpetology at the Bronx Zoo in spring 2012, his resume already included positions at zoos in Chicago and Kansas. Like all reptile aficionados, it seemed, Chris had developed his interests early.

"I started breeding cornsnakes as a kid growing up in Wichita," he said leading me back through the reptile house to a carpeted door he unlocked and directed me through. "Later on I was encouraged to volunteer at the Sedgwick Zoo by the reptile curator, Jim Marlett. He was my 'herp mentor.'"

Even behind the scenes, much of the building's original structure was obscured by wood-effect paneling. Occasionally though, the carved stonework of an exposed doorway or pillar hinted at a grander past. The doors to the rear of each exhibit were marked with a notice: THINK BEFORE

You Open, and details of the current occupants. I was reminded of an article about Ditmars in a 1928 edition of *New Yorker* magazine. The curator used to ask those leaving his office late at night to proceed in darkness; switching on a light would disturb his animals. Visitors were advised to walk along the gloomy corridor until they heard the ticking of a clock signalling that they had reached the exit door. One guest who followed these instructions got the shock of his life when he stepped on a hose. He imagined it to be a huge snake.

Chris's office was adjacent to a kitchen and storage rooms. Shipping cases with air holes drilled into them crowded his desk. I spied a hardback copy of Ditmars's *Reptiles of the World* on a high shelf among newer animal guidebooks. Pinned to one wall were framed portraits of leading figures from the reptile house's illustrious past: curators James Oliver, Wayne King, and Herndon Dowling; and keepers John Toomey, Bill Holmstrom, and Stephen Spencook. Ditmars was there too, grasping a water moccasin while cajoling it to squirt venom into a beaker.

"Raymond Ditmars certainly was one of the most well-known fathers of herpetology," said Chris, offering his opinion of the reptile house's founding curator as we ascended to its second story. Up here, the cold, riveted steel of the roofing arches was now within reach. Natural light poured in from the original skylights. When Peter Brazaitis first climbed to the newly installed second floor back in the 1950s he discovered a treasure trove: "Two inconspicuous cardboard boxes lay against a wall, as though awaiting a final verdict in a trial that would decide what should stay and what should be erased from future memory. Beside the dust and crushed cement debris of construction, the boxes contained all that remained of the correspondence of Dr. Raymond Lee Ditmars." Brazaitis spent the ensuing lunch hours on the dusty floor reading the letters, "a smattering of the thousands" Ditmars had written during his time at the zoo.

Today the mezzanine level, double the size of the public space downstairs, served as a captive breeding area and was vital to the zoo's conservation program. Chris guided me past cage after cage, tank after tank, of rare species: Chinese alligators, frilled dragons, tentacled snakes, blue-tongued lizards, Komodo dragons. Water pumps and filters, air conditioning units, heaters, and ultraviolet lamps ensured that conditions would favor reptilian reproduction. Among recent successes was a litter of the highly endangered Hog Island boa. By the 1980s the pet trade had virtually erased this diminutive type of boa constrictor from its natural habitat, two small islands off the Honduras coast. Now, beefed-up protection against illegal collecting and the efforts of the Wildlife Conservation Society and others had helped wild stocks recover.

To minimize pressure on natural populations, most of the animals exhibited in the reptile house were acquired from captive breeders rather than in the wild. Nevertheless, Chris's team had a New York State collecting permit allowing them to catch a few local specimens each year just as Ditmars and his colleagues used to do a century before. Reptiles also came in from confiscations. Although keeping venomous reptiles as pets was today unlawful in New York, New Jersey, and Connecticut, such rules were by no means universal. In neighboring Pennsylvania, for instance, you just had to prove you were eighteen; and anyway, thousands of reptiles were now changing hands courtesy of the Internet with little regulation. Periodically, however, the Department for Environmental Conservation would uncover a cache of "hot" herps and turn them over to the zoo.

Chris led me into a well-secured room, stacked to the ceiling with white plastic crates containing venomous serpents. Most, it turned out, had been confiscated from a single address in Putnam County, New York. In June 2011, a fifty-six-year-old woman named Aleta Stacey was found dead in the bungalow she shared with almost seventy-five serpents, most of them venomous. Stacey, an experienced snake handler, was thought to have deliberately allowed a five-foot-long black mamba to bite her. Once her body had been removed officials from the Bronx Zoo reptile house had been summoned. The operation to gather up the snakes was so risky that two Medevac helicopters were kept on standby. "A lot of her snakes are still here," said Chris, "although I think Dallas Zoo took the mamba that killed her."

I was moved to wonder aloud why people wanted to keep such potentially lethal animals, and why zoos like the Bronx should care about them. One thing in their favor, argued Chris, was that the unique properties of their venom were inspiring new medicines, new types of anaesthetic. "But," he continued, "my true feeling is that if we don't have an appreciation for nature it devalues us. To me, things that exist naturally are more valuable than manmade things like cars or paintings, and some herp species are so endangered they're down to a hundred individuals. There are more Picassos than that."

WHEN the Bronx Zoo—or the "New York Zoological Park" as Hornaday insisted in vain it be called—was at last opened to the public in November 1899, the place was a construction site. The flying cage would not be completed for another eighteen months and the accommodations for monkeys, lions, antelopes, non-aquatic birds, and marine mammals were little further advanced. There was just one tarmac road reserved for business use and "Public Comfort Building No. 1," or the Rocking Stone Restaurant as it was better known, was still but an architect's plan. The reptile house at least was up and running and, by January 1900, the collection was flourishing. That month visitors could see 445 crocodiles, turtles, lizards, snakes, and amphibians, representing at least half of all specimens at the zoo. A year later and the figure had climbed to 663. The feeding requirement was more impressive still. According to the New York Zoological Society, the shopping bill for 1901 included "389 mice. 1,410 rats. 1,273 English sparrows. 366 rabbits. 531 pigeons. 232 chickens. 812 toads. 408 frogs. 26,900 live fish. 55 lbs. earthworms. 18,000 meal worms. 122 large pumpkins. 2,266 lbs. green vegetables (grass not counted)."

Ditmars's talent for breeding snakes (or at least keeping wild-caught gravid females alive in captivity long enough to lay eggs or give birth) was partly responsible for the population boom. Within a year of open-ing almost ninety specimens of reptile and amphibian had been born or hatched out at the zoo. The success rate would climb. In 1905, for instance, he raised 213 ribbon snakes, garter snakes, watersnakes, and rat-tlesnakes. "Never . . . have snakes in captivity been so prolific," reported the *New York Sun.* "Seldom, also, has the average of hatched eggs been so great. Only twenty-three of the eggs were barren." Indeed, the breeding program was sometimes a victim of its own success. One year Ditmars was forced to euthanize some young rattlers born in the reptile house "because of the impossibility of securing enough mice with which to feed them." Another time he quietly disposed of surplus watersnakes into the nearby Bronx River.

With so much to see, the reptile house was an immediate hit with the public. On weekends, police officers, keepers, park watchmen, and oth-ers were called on "to keep the crowds in motion and prevent congestion and discomfort." Soft music would be played to soothe the more timid of the visitors. Ditmars wasn't so naïve as to interpret the phenomenal pop-ularity of his exhibits as signaling a reversal of negative attitudes toward cold-blooded animals. As his successor James Oliver would write years afterward, "whether they like snakes or not, most people are attracted by them." But from the outset Ditmars saw the reptile house as an unrivaled opportunity to educate and enlighten a public who still believed the best snake was a dead snake. He thought long and hard about the arrange-ment and presentation of exhibits. The animals were grouped collec-tively to reflect taxonomic relationships, and accompanying each cage was printed matter illuminating the habits, physical characteristics, and geographic distribution of the reptiles in question. The accompanying text was also constantly refreshed. As Ditmars once explained, "the pub-lic has continually evinced a keen interest in the exhibit of the Reptile House, and the attendants are called upon to answer a great number of queries. It has steadily been the custom to answer on the labels, the ques-tions most frequently repeated, and the descriptive matter in the building is very complete." Later on, picture labels were introduced, helping visitors identify the animals. Large charts, illustrating the classification of venomous serpents, were also prepared, framed, and placed prominently.

Rather less effort went into the cages themselves, which, in the early years, resembled cramped prison cells with concrete floors, drab walls and a bowl of water. No indication was given of the habitat from which the animal was drawn, beyond a rock pile here, a dead tree branch there. All this changed in 1911 when the artist Ernest A. Costain was asked to create imaginative dioramas for the larger snake exhibits lining the north wall of the reptile house. Ditmars was perhaps influenced by Carl Hagenbeck, the German animal collector and trainer who often supplied North American zoos with Old World species. Hagenbeck had recently opened the world's first "barless zoo" at Stellingen in the Hamburg suburbs with hidden moats and other tricks creating unbroken vistas of animals. Removing the glass was hardly practical for deadly reptiles, but a series of living scenes with painted panoramic backgrounds took shape in the Bronx Zoo reptile house over the ensuing four years: a rattler den on a mountain ledge in Sullivan County, New York; a rocky shelf on the Hudson River Palisades inhabited by copperhead snakes; a bamboo glade crawling with Indian cobras and brilliantly-colored tree snakes. Ditmars pronounced the renovated cages "successful in every way" and was convinced the snakes appreciated their new surroundings too as they were "given opportunities to hide when they choose, although this latter habit makes it necessary to place a considerable number in a cage, in order that there always may be a certain number of specimens in view."

Such techniques are commonplace in modern zoos, which strive to enrich the lives of captives, but were rare in the menageries of the early twentieth century, particularly for cold-blooded species. Snakes and their kin were included for shock value alone. Detailed exposition of, and empathy for, these reviled animals was considered unnecessary.

Among Ditmars's other innovations in the reptile house was a glass exhibition case demonstrating the latest in snakebite treatment equipment, along with anatomical models and other objects relating to the venom apparatus of venomous serpents. The star exhibit, of course, was the impeccably preserved skull of a bushmaster.

Within a few years Ditmars's efforts to boost the popularity of reptiles started paying off. Writing in a 1906 *Bulletin* of the New York Zoological Society, the thirty-year-old noted a "decided awakening of unbiased interest" in cold-blooded creatures, "the greater number of questions" prompted by a "sympathetic interest." Not long before, the public had "looked upon the Reptile House as a great curiosity" passing "the varied series of scaly forms with considerable disgust." Now schoolchildren were even happy to hold harmless species such as the king snakes. As Hornaday once wrote of the reptile house, "it is safe to say that it has cured a greater amount of ignorance and folly than any other collection of the Park.'"

# 7

# *Reptilian Deviltry of the World*

*"The average wild animal has character, personality and conscience, pretty much like the average human being. He is temperamental, perverse, vicious, phlegmatic, diffident, and deceitful as the case may be. Entertainment lies in discerning these traits and adroitly checkmating them."*

—Raymond L. Ditmars, *Strange Animals I Have Known* (1931)

———◆———

*May 29, 1900. The New York Zoological Park, New York City.*

"Well, Charley, things have gotten a little out of hand down at Bartels."

Ray is seated at his rolltop desk. Before him are pamphlets, writing papers, shedded snake skins, and a pen holder and inkwell. Several glass jars harbor coiled serpents, misshapen baby lizards, and less familiar forms in yellowing alcohol. Suspended in one is the disembodied head of a viper, jaws fixed in a malevolent yawn, revealing a set of inch-long fangs.

"It appears our specimens are loose," continues the assistant curator. "Looks like we're going to have to go down there and collect them ourselves."

"Yes sir," responds Charles Snyder, hovering at the doorway.

Drawing on his pipe, Ray allows himself a moment to gather his thoughts. With display cases to order and the summer's collecting expedition in South Carolina to arrange, the last thing he needs is a trip to Greenwich Village. Still, he had waited months for this shipment to turn up in New York.

"Come on then, Charley. Let's get a move on," he says rising from his desk. "Hmm, let's see. We'll need nooses, two gunny sacks, and a good-sized valise. Oh, and before we go, please get someone to look in on Mose. Seems to have lost his appetite again."

As the head keeper hastens in the direction of the alligator pond, Ray unlocks the top drawer of the desk. He retrieves a hypodermic syringe and a metal box slightly larger than a cigarette case which bears the words CALMETTE'S SNAKE SERUM. He prays he won't need it.

Two hours later and Ray and Snyder have disembarked from the Third Avenue elevated train and are striding down Greenwich Street. It's late morning and the place is thronging with stevedores, delivery men, and fruit sellers pushing carts. The fragrance of rotten fish is inescapable.

"Hundred and Sixty, isn't it?" asks Ray again.

"Yes, sir. Almost there."

Ahead a small crowd has formed outside a shop. Two boys peer through the display window emblazoned with WILLIAM BARTELS EXOTIC ANIMALS. An old man with disheveled clothes rushes up to the assistant curator.

"Mr. Ditmars! Am I glad you're here!"

"Morning, Bartels."

The wizened animal dealer shoos people from the store entrance and with trembling hand turns a key in the lock.

"Everyone else, stay outside if you know what's good for you!" he declares.

Ray and Snyder enter, along with Bartel's attendant, a scraggy youth of perhaps sixteen. The dealer follows, closing the door behind them.

The hum of the streets gives way to shrieks, growls, hisses, and chattering from an assortment of cages and crates. Struggling not to gag on the aroma of animal droppings and sawdust, the visitors are led through the premises and via rickety stairs to a dim landing. Before them is a wire door secured with a hefty spring padlock.

"We had a shipment arrive from India via Hamburg yesterday," says the dealer breathlessly while his junior fumbles with the lock. "All birds, 'cept for one big teakwood case. Real heavy. My assistant brought it up here to open. Figured it had a python in it."

He pushes open the door, backs off. Ray and Snyder exchange glances and peer in.

The room beyond, twenty feet long and fifteen wide, is crammed with broken wooden boxes and other packaging, chest-high in places. A milky light from two mesh-covered windows bathes the scene. The reek of bird and rat excreta is unmistakable. Ray spots an Indian python lolling on a far shelf, a thick greenish-yellow body and flickering tongue.

"Sure, there was a python in it," says Bartels catching the zoo man's gaze, "but also a bunch of other snakes too, includin' the three kings we'd bin expectin' for months. All twelve-footers at least. Two of 'em are yours, ain't they? Well, my imbecile of an assistant dropped the box and ran out. So all the damned snakes got loose."

Ray edges into the room and, using a wooden shaft fitted at one end with a noose of chamois leather, he gingerly sets about lifting pieces of debris. The head keeper follows suit with a stick of his own, the sacks and valise in his other hand. An olive-green coil no thicker than a man's wrist protrudes from a pile about six feet away, and nestled close by is the yellow head of a cobra in profile.

"Here's one, Charley," the assistant curator murmurs. "Looks asleep. Go around behind me and open the door so we have a getaway. I'm going to stir him up!"

At that, comes the snap of the padlock. Snyder tries the handle.

"They've locked it, sir!"

"Infernal cowards!" says Ray. "We can't break down the door. It'll wake up them all up."

But is too late for that. The snake has sensed intruders and elevates the front third of its body, the neck flaring into a long narrow hood. Brilliant eyes fix the intruders with a piercing stare.

Ray readies his lariat.

"King cobra's a mighty good name for you my snakey friend," mutters Snyder as he picks up a nearby blanket with one hand, a heavy wooden slat in the other.

"Watch out, Charley, these fellers are fighters from way back!"

Sure enough, the reptile gives a shrill hiss like a muffled sneeze, and launches itself at the men, striking downwards and falling short by a foot. This is just as well since the cobra carries sufficient venom to drop an elephant. The pause enables Ray to slip his noose around the snake's head, pulling it taut, then to lower the thrashing reptile tail-first into his colleague's bag, releasing it in time to realize that two more cobras every bit as menacing as the first are closing in. With no opportunity to fasten the writhing sack, Snyder throws the blanket at an advancing snake as Ray turns his attention to cobra number three, which strikes at him and latches itself on the stick close to his fingers, fangs scratching at the wood, sickly yellow venom dribbling down. Ray maneuvers the cool, writhing body into an empty sack but the cobra starts chewing on the coarse material, preventing him from closing the bag. The zoo man's only option now is to shove both serpent and bag into the suitcase. Snyder at last ties his sack, swinging it into the same trunk whose lid his superior slams shut.

"Bartels!" roars Ray, fastening the straps of the suitcase. "Now, in the name of God, *open this door!*"

<hr />

"BACK in the thirties, Joe Ruf really ran the show. He was head mammal keeper and the toughest guy there. Started as a bear keeper. He used to go right into the dens with the kodiaks, blacks, and polars and beat the crap out of them if they showed any sign of aggression. They were all terrified of him."

Peter took another bite of his Siciliana slice. I did likewise.

"In the end, old Joe got glaucoma. He realized he had lost his peripheral vision one day when he found himself being gored by a reindeer."

It was two in the afternoon and we were seated at a pizza joint on Arthur Avenue a block away from the zoo. Peter Brazaitis, thirty years a reptile keeper in the Bronx, was going to take me back to his place in Connecticut, and tomorrow we would hook up with an old buddy of his, someone familiar with the country where Ditmars himself used to hunt for snakes. Before then I had been promised lunch at the best Italian restaurant in the Bronx, and it did feel authentic. Nothing fancy—true *Goodfellas* territory. A trio of young men, all tracksuits and slicked-down hair, huddled around a Coke machine, the occasional f-word audible. The long-established Italian community was now in retreat as Hispanics moved in but, as Peter later confirmed, these were "local boys." My pizza was tasty enough, although the cheese and tomato base lacked toppings. For my second slice I requested anchovies.

"All out," came the response from an aproned guy behind the counter.

I didn't push it.

Peter continued regaling me with stories. He'd started at the reptile house on $38 a week as a teenager in 1954, just twelve years after Ditmars had died. Not long into the job, he was taken aside by his boss James Oliver. It was time he learned how to handle venomous snakes. And what better species to practice with than a bushmaster? Peter managed to pin down the head of the six-foot-long squirming pitviper. But while picking it up, he momentarily lost his grip on the snake's twisting head, as venom sprayed from the bushmaster's mouth and streamed down his arm.

"Scared me silly."

Peter survived the ordeal and would work at the Bronx Zoo until 1988 when he was appointed curator at the newly rebuilt Central Park Zoo.

Peter had a deep knowledge and wry opinions of the inner workings and politics of the New York Zoological Society and its reincarnation as the Wildlife Conservation Society; he reveals much in his entertaining memoirs *You Belong in a Zoo!* Crocodilians were his passion and, with his employers' blessing, he had undertaken field trips across South America and to Pacific islands. The biological samples he amassed were eventually donated to the Yale University Museum in Connecticut when Peter retired in 1997. Now in his late seventies, Peter kept busy as a forensic herpetologist advising government officials in their fight against the illegal trade in endangered reptiles.

He was keen to stress that the keepers, not the curators, made the zoo run. "In the reptile house it was guys like Charles Snyder and John Toomey, Fred Taggart and Bill Holmstrom."

Despite this, Peter revered Raymond Ditmars and his book closes with a pilgrimage to his grave in Ferncliff Cemetery. Just north of Scarsdale, the snakeman shares his last resting place with such luminaries as John Lennon, Malcolm X, and Judy Garland.

"We stayed for a while," Peter writes, "conjuring up thoughts of his and our pasts, and the place where he and I had both spent the better parts of our careers. As we left we could only say, 'Thanks, Ray. Rest well.'"

Raymond Ditmars and Reptile House keepers force-feed an anaconda (*Eunectes murinus*), Bronx Zoo c. 1910. The practice was a last resort. (© Wildlife Conservation Society)

IT was a weekday evening in the early summer of 1901. A warning bell had sounded. The last visitor had ambled out, the gates closing smartly in their wake. In another ten minutes the sun would be setting. Save the occasional squawk or roar, all was quiet across the zoo, and nowhere more so than the reptile house.

Head keeper Charles Snyder walked into a small room away from the public areas. He carried a sack. Raymond Ditmars was there already, standing by a table in a butcher's apron. Stretched before him was a motionless black snake, perhaps six feet in length. A sweet alcoholic odor pervaded the room. Snyder upended his bag spilling the contents onto the table: a dozen small, green frogs, also dead. His superior was pleased with the haul, the fruit of just thirty minutes' pond-dipping in a nearby pool.

Ditmars prized open the snake's jaws and crammed a frog into its mouth. He used a small stick to force the amphibian further down the serpent's gullet. The procedure was repeated until the supply of frogs was exhausted and the reptile resembled nothing so much as a stuffed Christmas stocking. With the bloated animal in one hand and a snake stick in the other, Ditmars swept out of the room. Snyder followed. He too carried a snake stick along with a weighty bunch of keys.

The men entered a narrow passage, one of several running behind the reptile house exhibits offering rear access to each cage. Halting at a small iron door Ditmars nodded to Snyder who unfastened a padlock and rolled back the hatch a fraction. The gap was just wide enough to allow the curator to sling in the distended corpse of the black snake. Snyder slammed the door shut before the occupant could react. This was as well, given that the recipient of this unusual supper was a king cobra, among the reptile house's deadlier residents.

Elaborate procedures such as this were routine in the reptile house. Snakes were fussy eaters, nervous too. Most wouldn't feed until after hours when all was quiet, even then the sound of a watchman's feet in the hall or the banging of a remote door sent them retreating to their corners.

Ditmars and a keeper would therefore lock everyone else out of the building at night as they spent hours catering to their temperamental inmates; tiptoeing from cage to cage, their lanterns would pick out reptilian bodies writhing in gloom. Keeping the snakes warm was also important; they wouldn't feed at ambient temperatures below 70 degrees Fahrenheit.

The king cobras took fastidiousness to a new level. Not only was this species a cannibal, the snake meals had to be of just the right size. Ditmars learned to dupe one individual into accepting a black snake stuffed with frogs, as both stocking and filler were then available in good quantities on the zoo grounds, or further afield along the Bronx River.

The dietary behaviors and preferences of snakes intrigued Ditmars who published a well-regarded scientific paper on the subject. The measures taken to cater to the animals' peculiar tastes also made excellent newspaper copy. In 1900 Snyder revealed to the *New York Times* that he would hoodwink rat-eating snakes into taking beef strips sprinkled with hair shaved from a live rodent.

"The snake smells the rat's fur and dives in without loss of time," the keeper told the paper. "As for the rat, he doesn't mind being sheared at all, but seems to like it after a while. We often work the same racket on bird-eating snakes. In this case we have some of the smaller feathers from a chicken on hand, which we sprinkle over the meat."

The bigger pythons, boas, and anacondas often refused food on arrival at the reptile house. For instance, a twenty-seven-foot-long python procured in India at considerable expense went on hunger strike for three months snubbing repeated offerings of live rabbits, pigs, and chickens. Though giant constrictors could survive extended periods of starvation, their coats would dull, lessening their appeal as exhibition animals. Sooner or later niceties would be dispensed with in favor of brute force. A "system of compulsory feeding of large serpents" producing "very valuable results" was elaborated in an early report of the New York Zoological Society: "Mr. Ditmars prepares a string of dead rabbits, pigeons, or other food animals, and with the aid of several keepers, and the exercise of much skill and judgment, forces the whole collection down the serpent's throat. If the food is persistently disgorged, it is immediately re-introduced. Strange to say, food thus thrust by force into a serpent is properly digested, and assimilation appears to be as perfect as when it is brought about by more natural processes."

A dozen keepers clinging on for dear life as twenty-odd feet of enraged python threw violent contortions while rabbits or guinea pigs tied to a bamboo pole were run down its throat created a memorable spectacle for visitors to the reptile house. For a fee the zoo allowed visitors to lend a hand. Yet many months of force-feeding might be needed before a recalcitrant serpent ate voluntarily, and within a few years the practice was largely abandoned except for the most prized specimens including, as shall be seen, the bushmaster. As the *New York Tribune* observed in 1912, the "suffragette-feeding method was given up as unhygienic and an invasion of the reptilian right to be hungry. When Mr. Python indicates by opening his mouth, trying to swallow his partner's tail or otherwise that he is ready to dine, he will be presented with a thirty-pound pig."

Every snake was different. Another python, called Selima, purchased from a circus, thrived on human contact. On returning to the zoo from three months' sick leave Ditmars discovered Selima had died. During the absence his keepers had placed food in the snake's cage every five days but otherwise ignored it. When the python refused to eat, it had been force-fed and soon succumbed to "the dreaded 'canker.'" Ditmars suggested that "the snake, which had been accustomed to being noticed and handled, missed the many attentions previously received, and also missed the practice of feeding it by hand, and, under the changed conditions, worried and lost appetite; and its long fasting led to its death."

THE following morning saw us in Peter Brazaitis's red Toyota SUV hurtling west through the forested countryside lining the border of New York and Connecticut. The leaves were on the turn and the brilliant autumnal sunlight filtered through in yellows, greens, and browns. Once a strong-hold for the timber rattlesnake, this region was a magnet for Ditmars and his fellow snake-hunters. Though numbers had dwindled, the species lived on in many local place names. Rattlesnake Road. Rattlesnake Hill. Rattlesnake Mountain. Rattlesnake Gutter. Rattlesnake Ledge. We passed an old post office and railroad station. It was clad in white clapperboard, the Stars and Stripes fluttering out front. I fancied that, as a young man, Ditmars might have passed through here by train on early collecting trips. Later on, though, he would have driven himself, taking the old Route 22 from Bronx and returning with trunkloads of snakes, lizards, turtles, and frogs.

Our destination today was a neat house in a settlement called Dover Plains on the New York side of the state line. A compact, silver-haired man in checked shirt, blue jeans, and brown suede boots guided us in. Of a similar vintage to Peter, Norman Benson had been born on a farm a few hundred yards up the road and built this house himself back in the fifties. The Bensons had been working the land around here since the eighteenth century.

"Originally we had one hundred twenty acres with dairy cows, corn, oats, alfalfa," said Norman settling into a shiny red leather armchair. On a wooden coffee table close by was a television remote and small black bible.

"Rattlesnakes were common. You saw them in the yard, and on the stone walls until we made the fields larger. We gathered the hay by hand then so you had to be very careful: there could be a rattlesnake, black snake, or a racer under there. We had rattler and copperhead dens close to here."

The hills around Dover Plains were snakier still and would have been irresistible to Ditmars. The Scattercook Mountains and the Catrocks, named for the pumas that once lived there, were notably productive. And pinpointing the best spots was easy; the curator could have stopped in at any roadhouse and asked the locals.

Like Peter, Norman was too young to have met Ditmars. He did however remember a character called "Rattlesnake Nick"—real name Herbert F. Nicols—who, during the late 1940s, kept a booth at the summer carnival where he would fool around with venomous snakes, almost killing himself in the process.

"Nick was kinda fearless," Norman said. "On Memorial Day and Labor Day weekends he'd drive up to high rocky ledges in his Model A Ford and select about a dozen of the biggest snakes. He'd catch them by the tail. I remember as a kid he would dump the bags in front of our farm just to show off. Of course, they'd all be dead by the fall."

Whether Rattlesnake Nick had known Ditmars was unclear but Norman remembered him mocking the folks from the Bronx Zoo for wearing high boots when hunting the hills.

Over time, as both agriculture and persecution intensified, the serpents were no longer to be found making summer forays to the lower ground, and were seldom encountered even on rocky ledges high in the mountains. Norman maintained an amateur's interest in the timber rattlesnakes, their decline prompting him in the 1970s to write to the zoo asking if the large pilot black snakes still common on the farm might not be preying on the rattlesnakes' young. The letter found its way to Peter, who by a twist of fate also then lived in Dover Plains. The two men became friends, spending summers together snake-hunting in the Eastern Mountains. They identified five rattler dens on the ridges overlooking the town and conducted a population study marking dozens of individuals with tiny tags to keep a track on their movements, a little like the work Ed McGowan had done.

"One day I heard a rattling but couldn't see the snake anywhere," Peter recalled smiling at his friend. "Norman spotted it in the branches of a tree looking down at me at head height, the last place I'd expected to find one. Another time, there was this copperhead right next to Norman's knee which *he* hadn't spotted. Took it back to the zoo and it had thirteen babies. Afterward we turned them loose."

In a scene recalling Ditmars's own adventures with Professor Smith in the Florida Everglades back in the 1890s, the pair would often stop for lunch on the steep talus inclines, rattlesnakes coiled in the rock crevices all around them. Once a group of boy scouts in short pants appeared at the top of the slope and trooped down oblivious of the danger.

"We didn't let on," grinned Norman.

THE early years at the zoo furnished Ditmars with ample opportunity to hone his reptile husbandry and veterinary skills. The health of his charges, even the lowliest and most despised, was of paramount importance to him. Since childhood Ditmars had ensured creatures under his care received the best welfare. "My feeling for animals is actuated by a conscience which would be disturbed if I recalled any thought of their physical or mental welfare being wantonly neglected," he once wrote. All new arrivals at the reptile house received VIP treatment, especially the snakes that, according to one dubious report, were bathed in tepid water, fully rested, and massaged fortnightly with Vaseline "to bring about a re-establishment of the natural circulation, which has been in abeyance through lack of exercise." Remnants of old skin from previous sheds were removed, steam sometimes used to aid the process.

Such approaches were ahead of their time. In other zoos serpents were regarded as dangerous animals to be poked at with long bamboo canes and fed through trapdoors. Ditmars recorded the astonishment of a delegation from London Zoo visiting the reptile house in summer 1907 who "saw that we had doors in the rear of the cages on a level with the floors of the latter, and opened them freely to feed and handle the snakes."

Lacking any training in animal medicine Ditmars relied on initiative and common sense to diagnose and treat reptile ailments ranging from dental abscesses to broken bones. "Long, keen-bladed lancets, saws, tweezers, forceps, needles, hypodermic syringes, and fifty other polished instruments" each shining "like a mirror" were assembled in a glass-fronted case in Ditmars's office reported *Forest and Stream*. Even with the gravest conditions his instinct was to restore the patient rather than letting nature take its course.

Many of the injuries were sustained in fights between captives. Among the worst incidents concerned Mose the alligator who, in his first year at the zoo, received a mauling from a young crocodile sharing his tank. The gator's abdomen was torn open from snout to tail and the intestines protruded. The heart and lungs were visible through another laceration on the side. Determined to save this treasured friend, Ditmars lashed Mose to a plank, washed and replaced the guts and sewed him up. "The creature was so badly mangled," he later wrote, "I wasn't quite sure that everything had been put back just where it belonged. I placed the creature in a shallow tank of tepid water. Its wounds rapidly healed. Within ten days it was feeding." Mose would live another three decades.

Most operations were less drastic. At around the same time, the *New York Times* reported that another alligator had several corns removed from its feet. Following this course of chiropody the big reptile entered "a stupid condition," but within days was rallying. The paper recorded that "for the first time since his ordeal, he rose on all fours and, to the delight of the many sightseers opened his huge jaws as wide as they would swing and devoured his quota of fowl with evident relish."

Snakes were prone to mouth and head injuries from insect bites, the persistent rubbing of snout against glass, or, for venomous species, from the act of being pinned down and milked. Painful abscesses had to be drained, rotten fangs or jaw bones removed, dressings replaced. When treating venomous snakes Ditmars put himself at considerable risk, and the papers reveled in the danger. In 1901, an inflammation on a king cobra's head needed attention. "Nearly twenty minutes were occupied in the operation and every instant of the time Mr. Ditmars' arm and hand were within striking distance of the fangs of the most deadly snake known to naturalists," noted *Forest and Stream*. When the curator doctored a second cobra for necrosis of the jawbone, the *Washington Times* explained that because "the scales of the snake are slippery as glass he will have to dispense with gloves, thus running the risk of being bitten by a snake whose bite, unless treated immediately, is mortal."

Ditmars did what he could to minimize the risk. With another king cobra, he played on the serpent's cannibalistic tendencies, distracting it by tossing in a food snake. The meal half-ingested, the curator used it to maneuver the patient within range, allowing him to operate in safety while "the big snake's little yellow eyes fairly danced with fury." Ditmars was "not ashamed to acknowledge that when the iron door rolled to and shut off the danger his pulse had quickened to a substantial degree." And he was all for trying new approaches. During the 1920s, yet another king cobra with eye trouble was taken in a cage for an "ozone jag," to be precise, a bracing ride in sub-zero weather conditions strapped to the hood of the curator's car. "After a drive of about fifteen miles," Ditmars told the papers, "I figure this snake will be stewed to the eyebrows, so to speak, and while he is good and groggy, I'll take him out of the cage and operate on him."

Although the curator never once sustained a bite from the many deadly snakes he was handling, in the late summer of 1900 he did suffer a serious accident in the reptile house. While placing a dead specimen into a jar of formalin the container slipped through his wet fingers and shattered against a sink, a glass shard cutting his left hand and slicing veins and muscle. The wound went septic and amputation of the arm was recommended, but Ditmars's older sister Ella kept the doctors at bay and by the end of the year he had recovered, albeit with permanent stiffness in his left wrist.

As well as stitching up wounded animals, Ditmars worked hard to defend them against parasitic and microbial attack, devouring any available texts on the subject. The strict quarantine procedures observed in modern animal collections were unheard of. Dysentery, influenza, tuberculosis and other infections posed a constant threat in the early decades of the New York Zoological Park. In October 1901 an "obscure disease" killed off a chimpanzee and four orangutans. Ditmars traced the infection to Galápagos tortoises, which carried an amoeba fatal to the precious apes that had shared their accommodation during the summer.

A few years later the cobras started going down with flu. According to the *Washington Times* the reptile keepers hung the serpents out on tree branches and injected "a large amount of a solution of dioxygen" down their throats. Within a few hours "the snakes were pronounced out of danger." The "grippe" returned with a vengeance in 1919, and many zoo animals were affected by the same influenza outbreak that killed millions of humans worldwide. That same year an infestation of fever-bearing ticks wiped out five hundred snakes, although a twenty-three-foot-long regal python worth upwards of $1,000 was among those saved with a judicious dusting of "arsenical powder."

In time, most animals perished despite the best efforts of the reptile house staff and the exhibits constantly had to be replenished. Local snake-hunting expeditions ensured a supply of native reptiles and amphibians, but to source more exotic specimens Ditmars corresponded with a growing network of dealers at home and abroad. He bargained with backstreet animal peddlers, swapped rarities with other zoos, and dispatched letters "to government agents, explorers, missionaries, and captains of steamers touching at remote points" in the Old and New World tropics. Well aware of their drawing power, Ditmars prioritized the big and the venomous. That meant colossal pythons, lethal vipers, and cobras that could tower over a man.

The trapping of two fourteen-foot-long king cobra specimens loose on the chaotic premises of animal dealer William Bartels in May 1900 was but one of many dramatic episodes during this period. Other notable acquisitions in the early years included a "gorgeous" rhinoceros viper captured in the Congo by the missionary-anthropologist Samuel Phillips Verner and, in Ditmars's words, transported "in an ordinary basket for a distance of about five hundred miles, despite the hysterical complaints of his superstitious black carriers." Verner also presented the zoo with a gaboon viper from the Gold Coast (present day Ghana). When annoyed, the "villainous" snake inflated its thick body, exhaling "to the tune of a long hiss." A female fer-de-lance viper from the island of Martinique in the West Indies promptly bore to two dozen young, which, according to *Forest and Stream*, were "the first of their kind born in captivity." Adding that each was more or less as deadly as the mother, the magazine reported that the babies "are kept in a small glass case in a miniature fairy land of snowy gravel and ferns. The baby snakes are not over four inches long and so slender that a child's finger ring would easily encircle them."

Whenever possible Ditmars would head to the New York docks to greet overseas arrivals in person. He was there in June 1907 to meet a new twenty-eight-foot python, which, one newspaper asserted, "began to wind around him, apparently mistaking the scientist for a new variety of appetizer preparatory to a real meal." The curator is said to have pacified his aggressor by catching the snake behind the spread jaws, "a movement too quick for others and the python to see." Two years later Ditmars toured the great zoological gardens of Europe trading $2,000 and a cargo of rattlesnakes, copperheads, and water moccasins for forty-eight cases of new specimens. The trip's most awkward moment was his near arrest in London for transporting a jackal in a cab across genteel Hyde Park. Ditmars had to convince an English "bobby" that he "had no desire to stampede the horses or frighten British aristocracy." A Cape hyrax, a giant salamander weighing more than a small child and "a fine series of species representing the reptilian fauna of Australia" were among the 448 beasts accompanying the curator home aboard the SS *Minnehaha*. Most thrilling of all for the waiting press pack, starved in Ditmars's absence of good stories, was a Tasmanian devil which had spent much of the voyage biting off the wire screen from its cage.

The bushmaster was, of course, another early target. As Ditmars once noted, this "death dealer" was "always a sensation in a collection of reptiles" and orders were placed annually, specimens being gathered by R. R. Mole in Trinidad and Venezuela. Captives proved nervous, snappy and notoriously delicate, however, with four out of five perishing en route from their native forest. Those that made it to the Bronx Zoo lasted but weeks.

Decades afterward Ditmars recalled the horror with which William Hornaday viewed "the reptilian deviltry of the world" his young curator had marshaled in this formative period of the reptile house: cobras, kraits, and coralsnakes; death adders and buzzing groups of rattlers; and, on occasion, bushmasters as well. "Dr. Hornaday congratulated me but implored that in the name of heaven I watch those sinuous terrors like a lynx, so that none got away."

# 8

# A Sort of Freemasonry

*"I'm getting the car shined up for my annual spring snake hunting expedition. . . . We need a lot of snakes, and it's up to me to go out and catch them."*

—Raymond L. Ditmars, *New York Tribune*, April 10, 1921

———◆———

*Spring 1919. Hampton County, South Carolina.*

TAILS SWING LIKE LAZY metronomes. Withers convulse angrily. Yet nothing will disperse the cloud of biting flies plaguing the two pintos as they plod over the uneven sand hummocks. Their riders, both elderly men in broad-brimmed hats, seem as untroubled by insects as they are by the waves of choking afternoon heat rising from the saw grass. The temperature of the terpene-rich air must be into the nineties, but both Sam Greaves and Charles Horton are clad in trousers and heavy cotton jackets. Each grips his reins with thick gloves. The tops of their thick leather boots extend beyond the knee.

A short distance behind the guides is a buckboard wagon drawn by a third pinto. The vehicle bounces clumsily between live oaks and pines humming with cicadas. Ray sits in the driving seat, pipe in mouth. Charles Snyder is to the left carrying a wooden pole with copper wire noose, while in the second row is a third man, a medical doctor named Gilbert van der Smissen. Like Ray and Snyder, he is in his forties. Beside the physician is Clara Ditmars, by some margin the youngest of the hunting party. All are attired in the same thick canvas and high boots as their guides.

Having arrived from the Bronx just yesterday, Van der Smissen is the sole member of the party free of tick bites. Snyder is the worst afflicted with several ugly purple spots the size of dollar pieces on his arms. Chigger mites further torment the visitors, burrowing beneath the skin and causing its surface to rise in tiny red bumps like a scattering of paprika, although high boots and sulfur-dusted socks defend the lower extremities. Most of the parasites latched on last week during work atop an ancient rice dam down in the swamp proper. It was worth it though. Water moccasins, copperheads, kings, hognoses, and red-bellies are among a rich haul of serpents, along with a two-hundred-pound alligator hooked snorting from a small lagoon.

Today's collecting has been indifferent; the bulk of the wooden crates sliding about in the rear of the wagon remain empty. The highlight so far is a good-sized coachwhip snake that Snyder ran down near the reddish shores of the Savannah River. The curator himself picked up a pair of gopher tortoises basking on one of the corduroy roads of cypress logs laid by Sherman's engineers during the Civil War. That no alligators have been caught today is unsurprising because Ray asked Sam and Charles to stick to the higher ground in the hope of taking the first diamondback rattlesnake of the trip. At Clara's request the girls stayed behind at the clubhouse with grandfather Hurd. Even though Gladyce and Beatrice wear protective leggings in the field, their inclination to frolic in the high grass lining the trail or to forage for blueberries puts them at risk of venomous snakebite.

Presently Ray halts the wagon in the shade of a bald cypress.

"Looks like no rattlers again today," he sighs. There's something queer about this spot but he cannot place it. He takes a swig of water then yells ahead half-heartedly, "Hey boys. Guess we ought to call it a day!"

He leans back to hand the canteen to his wife. At that moment he understands: *that buzzing isn't cicadas.*

"Charley! Can you hear that?" the curator exclaims reaching for a pole. "There's a diamondback near here, real close."

Ray springs from the wagon and Snyder follows suit readying his noose and a muslin sack about three feet deep. The two guides wheel about on their horses.

"Is that it, Ray, just over there?" Clara points at a patch of saw grass not fifteen yards away.

She's right. Both Ray and Snyder now discern the spear-shaped head and the black lozenges of an eastern diamondback rattlesnake, its coils thicker than a man's arm. Estimating length is impossible: could be a four-footer, could be bigger. All they know is that it's a rattlesnake and they want it.

Snyder feeds his pole toward the viper whose rattling intensifies, as does the flicking of its forked tongue. With a swift, practiced move he drops the noose gently over the reptile's neck and pulls the wire taught. The diamondback writhes in surprised anger sending out an arc of venom over Snyder's jacket sleeve. No venom contacts his skin, which it might have penetrated through the numerous insect bites. The curator presses the snake against the ground with his pole, reaching down to clasp it firmly behind the head. The others look on in trepidation as Ray calmly lifts the reptile high in the air, clearing its sinewy body from the ground. The slightest slip now and fangs three-quarters of an inch in length could be sinking into his wrist, shooting into his veins enough venom to drop an ox. But, seconds later a muffled buzzing emanates from the bottom of Snyder's bag.

Dr. Van der Smissen applauds the display.

"Bravo!"

Two hours pass. The hunting party trudges through the grand gates marked with PINELAND CLUB and approaches the clubhouse down an avenue of oaks. Cedar shingles clad the two-story building, whose generous veranda is supported by palmetto columns. In a nearby clearing is a simple log cabin from which two teenage girls emerge and run toward the hunters. An old man trails at a slower pace.

"Oh, Pop, come and see what grandpa and I caught," pants the older of the girls. "We've got you a terrible big snake! A rattlesnake!"

Ray removes his pipe, a broad grin forming.

"You don't believe us," adds her sister, "but Gladyce heard him buzz and then we saw him almost under the bushes over there."

"I'm afraid it's true," nods Hurd catching up with his granddaughters.

"I teased the snake with a stick just like you do, Pop. I knew he'd coil up like a watch spring," says Gladyce striding toward a distant patch of huckleberry. "Then grandpa dropped a box over him."

The curator jumps from the wagon, signaling Snyder to follow. Ahead is an inverted wooden box of the type used for condensed milk tins, several stakes securing it to the soft ground. The girls stand close by.

"Probably just a rat snake," smiles Ray to his colleague as he nonchalantly kicks over the case. What he sees causes horror and admiration.

"Great Scot, Charley! Why, that's bigger than the one we bagged!"

For the rest of the trip, Gladyce and Beatrice will stay with the hunting party.

———————

"F*** me!"

I couldn't believe it. Just there, inches from where my right boot was destined to land lay one huge timber rattlesnake, much bigger than any Ed McGowan had so far shown me. My peripheral vision detected the serpent a millisecond before I was conscious of the threat, and triggered evasive action, specifically to launch myself at ninety degrees while releasing a stream of expletives. Inelegant but effective. How had I avoided the thing that, although sprawled out in my path, was quietly camouflaged in the dappled sunlight? I had read somewhere that our primate ancestors had bequeathed us a hardwired fear of snakes. Perhaps we had also inherited an escape response controlled by an ancient — dare I say reptilian — part of our brain?

"Pardon my French," I said.

If this was my reaction to a rattlesnake, what would happen if I found a bushmaster?

A week after our initial rattler hunt, Ed had invited me for another jaunt in the woods north of New York City. Among his many responsibilities was participating in a volunteer program responding to nuisance calls about snakes. When a venomous species was encountered by members of the public, Ed and his pals would pick it up and move it a short distance, more for the protection of the snake than the human. Several timbers had recently been reported close to a popular hiking trail, and Ed suspected that a den was nearby. The plan now was to confirm the sightings, find the den and reroute the path.

Driving back through the familiar woodlands, I noticed that the foliage was changing. Reds, violets, and yellows were now in the canopy. At one point a badger-sized creature scampered ahead of our vehicle, thought better of it and plunged back into the undergrowth. It was a woodchuck. The road wound higher. Sections of the Hudson River were visible hundreds of feet below.

"Washington had redoubts up here in the Revolutionary War," Ed told me. "He planned to fire at the British on the river. Seems a long way to shoot a cannonball."

We had parked close to a well-used hiking trail and made our way to a bluff fringed with bushes of black huckleberry. Tiny resin spots under the leaves, Ed pointed out, distinguished it from its close relative, the blueberry. Turkey vultures wheeled overhead. A blue jay surveyed us from an oak. After several minutes we'd seen no sign of a snake and it was only below the rocky outcrop that I had finally met my large timber.

"Well done, Dan," smiled Ed. "I walked right by and didn't see it!"

The snake was darker than the earlier specimens, the face almost black. From this range the keeled scales were easy to discern, prefiguring those I hoped to see on the bushmaster.

"It's in decent shape, not emaciated," observed my companion, nevertheless concerned to see blisters on the reptile's snout which could have signaled an emerging fungal disease.

The viper was motionless, content to lie there as we photographed it, then edged stealthily away into thicker scrub without so much as a quiver of the famous caudal appendage.

Ed noted the angle taken by the rattler; the species had a phenomenal sense of direction and at this time of the year was likely to be pointing toward its den.

"Come on," said Ed, "Follow me."

The marriage of Raymond and Clara Ditmars marked
in the *New York World*, February 6, 1903.

On Wednesday February 4, 1903, a twenty-six-year-old man and a girl more than a decade his junior were married. Clara Elizabeth Hurd was on the young side for Raymond Ditmars, which worried her father who counseled them to wait, but the two loved each other. Raymond's mother

Mary was terminally ill and wanted to see her son marry before it was too late. Clara's own mother had already died. The ceremony was conducted in the front parlor of the Hurd residence in the Bronx by a priest from the nearby St. Paul's Episcopal Church.

The guest list was restricted to immediate relatives and few details were released. But, hearing of the marriage, the newspapers filled in the blanks. New York's *The World* revealed that it was "a snake wedding" with "the delicately mottled integument of the only King Cobra in America . . . artistically displayed" among "the maze of roses and carnations on the table of the supper-room." Later on, continued the paper, Trilby, the couple's pet gopher snake "coiled himself around the white neck of the bride and, placing his face against hers, hissed the heartiest and sincerest of congratulations in her ear." Meanwhile, according to the *Saint Paul Globe*, a "trained band" of the "finest rattlers" from the groom's collection performed Beethoven's wedding march: "They range in tone from the little rattler with a high treble note to an eight-foot diamondback from Florida with a whir like an automobile striking a 70 percent grade. The effect of the eight rattling off, 'Here comes the bride' is said to be unique."

Stories of how the pair had met were similarly creative, most involving the heroic snake man rescuing his damsel from a rattlesnake during a visit to the zoo. In fact the Hurds and Ditmarses were neighbors on Bathgate Avenue and Clara had long idolized the handsome naturalist, tolerating if not sharing his interest in the cold-blooded. "Chicky," as Ditmars affectionately called her, would accompany her husband on snake-hunting trips for the rest of their married life, and the same would be true for their daughters Gladyce and Beatrice, born in 1904 and 1906 respectively.

That Ditmars would spend vacations collecting snakes even after landing a dream job at the zoo was a sign of a man obsessed. Of course, the rapid turnover of specimens at the reptile house and his subsequent involvement in venom research demanded a steady supply of deadly snakes, but animals could always be purchased from professional reptile collectors, and many were. However, nothing matched the excitement of catching serpents in the wild, and Ditmars stressed that the excursions were purely for pleasure. "I didn't like to be held down to any specified thing," he wrote in 1935. "I disliked making formal accountings and the like." Ditmars and his friends would pay their "respective ways with no thought of coming back with apologies for not getting the specimens we had been expected to collect."

In time the curator's snake hunts took him far from home, but in the early years meager resources limited his jaunts to the immediate vicinity of New York. Among favored spots were the higher elevations of New York's Westchester, Sullivan, and Dutchess Counties, the Ramapo Mountains that straddled the New York-New Jersey border, and the southern Berkshires of Connecticut. He later pushed into the wilder areas of Pennsylvania and Massachusetts.

The newspapers were fascinated by the curator's snake-hunting adventures, particularly now that a pretty young wife was involved.

"Catching a trout or a striped bass is looked upon as good sport by a good many women and I don't undervalue the excitement," Clara once told the *Washington Post*, "but snake hunting is far more interesting. There is not only the danger and excitement of the chase but the captives remain living things to be observed and studied, and, believe me, the creatures are well worth all the attention scientists give them."

Outlandish headlines and brazen embellishments were again the order of the day. In September 1904 snakehunters led by the twenty-eight-year-old Ditmars headed home after a successful summer's collecting in the Shawangunk Mountains of Sullivan County. The *Saint Paul Globe* reported shenanigans aboard the New York-bound train, revealing that the party's luggage of wooden cases contained "196 snakes of all kinds, including many large rattlers." Soon into the journey "Mrs. Ditmars felt something crawling over her foot, and, without attracting the attention of the other travelers, glanced down and saw a large rattler." She coolly apprised her husband of the fact who "grasped the snake tightly around the neck, and, as his wife opened the window, dropped it from the train." Unbeknownst to fellow passengers several other serpents escaped their boxes during the trip, the curator again handling each with quiet efficiency. When the train at last entered a tunnel, he supposedly seized the opportunity to hide the remaining snakes.

Ditmars initially visited collecting sites by railroad or horse-drawn cart, but by 1911 had switched to a touring car allowing considerably more territory to be covered. "In a period of seventeen days the car's speedometer showed we travelled over 300 miles of mountain roads," he wrote of a collecting trip near Black Lake in Sullivan County. "Several new ledges were hunted for rattlesnakes, and between tracts of snake country much collecting was done for the insect department." In 1914 he went further still, reporting to the New York Zoological Society that "over six hundred miles of road were covered, enabling the collectors to quickly reach and investigate many ledges, swamps, and other types of collecting grounds." The automobile also enabled him to respond rapidly to the first warm days of spring that tempted snakes from their winter dens. Still sluggish from hibernation, the reptiles were easy pickings if you could get to the right spots promptly. Ditmars's interest in meteorology came in handy here too, and he monitored atmospheric pressure for signs the weather was about to turn. In October 1911 he returned from the field with another memento, a small century-old cannon that he towed back to the Bronx under canvas. He had intended to decorate a lawn at the zoo with the artifact, but a "country constable" took a dim view, arresting the curator for "concealing a weapon." Ditmars secured his release after lengthy arguments before the local authorities.

From the outset, the excursions were social affairs. Ditmars loved sharing the thrill of the hunt with likeminded enthusiasts. Trusted keepers such as Charles Snyder or George Palmer, as well as old friends Adam Dove and Morris Pearsall, would join his wife and daughters on the trips. Writing in the 1920s the curator celebrated a "sort of freemasonry" to which snake-hunters belonged: it "is darn seldom one of these fellows gets bitten. They know how to handle snakes and they are intelligent men too." There was Jerry Miller of Sullivan County, "an odd sort of man who knows every crack and fissure in the rocky parts of the county that shelter snakes" and who once raged for days after hearing of the destruction by two farmers of "twenty-five rattlers they found entwined in a great writhing ball." Ike Whitbeck in the Berkshires was also a "devotee of the rattlers," and Henry Mallory of Great Barrington, Massachusetts, was "fascinated by the mottled skins." Years later another comrade, Arthur Gillam of Flushing, Long Island, would accompany the Ditmarses on their tropical expeditions. An advertising man by profession, Gillam was reputed to have "caught more poisonous snakes than anybody in the world," donating many to the Bronx Zoo.

Ditmars was at pains to differentiate his associates from the country folk they often encountered on their travels, "back-woodsmen" who claimed mysterious powers over serpents. Typically named "Rattlesnake Pete" or "Copperhead Bill," such characters spouted ludicrous myths and peddled worthless homemade snakebite cures—usually alcohol based. The curator wanted to encourage a far more rigorous, science-based approach to reptiles and by the 1920s was presiding over the Reptile Study Society of America. Part of a wider movement to protect serpents from mindless slaughter, society members visited snake dens in the spring and fall to observe, and sometimes try to catch, the reptiles. They shared information on serpents in their areas and lobbied for protection of "economically useful" species. The society would meet annually over a good dinner, performing stunts with snakes for the benefit of assembled journalists.

Ditmars never missed an opportunity to evangelize and propagandize. In July 1922, aware that Sir Arthur Conan Doyle and family were preparing to depart New York following a three-month tour of the United States, the curator dispatched a messenger to the docks which were swarming with journalists. Ditmars's man presented the famous novelist's

A watersnake (*Nerodia sipedon*) in Westchester County, New York, does its best to crap on the ebullient Peter Warny. In less than an hour we'd seen four local snake species which Raymond Ditmars himself would have collected for the Bronx Zoo.
Photo by Dan Eatherley.

Dr. Edwin McGowan, an expert on timber rattlesnakes (*Crotalus horridus*), took me to dens close to New York City on the understanding I kept the locations secret.
Photo by Edwin McGowan.

A timber rattlesnake (*Crotalus horridus*) prepares for hibernation. Already threatened in Raymond Ditmars's lifetime, this beautiful species has now disappeared from much of its former range. Photo by Dan Eatherley.

A banded water snake (*Nerodia fasciata*) captured more than a century ago by Raymond Ditmars in the swamps of the Deep South. This nonvenomous but notoriously irritable customer wouldn't have come quietly. Photo by Dan Eatherley.

I was keen to inspect the preserved bushmasters at the Smithsonian Museum's Support Center in Maryland. After all, this might be the closest I would ever get to one. Photo by Ken Tighe.

Dean Ripa—herpetologist, writer, artist, jazz singer, and bushmaster obsessive—with one of his friends, a black-headed bushmaster (*Lachesis melanocephala*), at the Cape Fear Serpentarium, North Carolina. Photo by Dean Ripa.

In Trinidad the bushmaster is known as *mapepire z'anana*, the pineapple viper, a reference to the roughness of its scales. Photo by Dean Ripa.

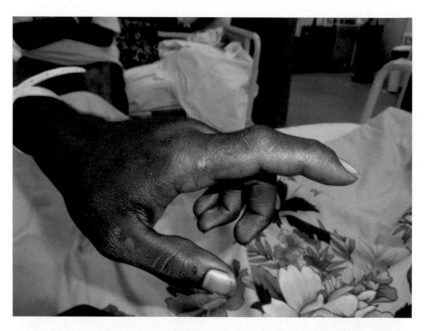

"I felt a sting like a scorpion." Bitten on the finger by a fer-de-lance pitviper (*Bothrops sp.*), the farm laborer's first response was to swallow some earth. Four vials of antivenin administered at Trinidad's Sangre Grande Hospital may also have played a part in his recovery. Photo by Dan Eatherley.

Dr. John Murphy and Mukesh Ramdass examine the frozen corpse of a bushmaster (*Lachesis muta*). It was bludgeoned to death by a farmer soon after my arrival in Trinidad. Photo by Dan Eatherley.

The Simla research station, Trinidad. In the 1950s, Ditmars's colleague William Beebe converted this former British Governor's house into a base for the study of forest life. Walt Disney was among friends who'd drop by for a rum or two on the terrace. Photo by Dan Eatherley.

Driving Trinidad's back roads at dusk was a great way to find tropical snakes, which loved sprawling on the still-warm blacktop.
That was the theory anyway.
Photo by Dan Eatherley.

We approached a former cocoa plantation in Trinidad, said to be crawling with bushmasters. Would I find one here at last?
Photo by Dan Eatherley.

*"Pseustes poecilonotus!"* announces the energetic Tom Anton. It wasn't a bushmaster,
but knowing that Trinidad had at least one living snake came as a relief.
Photo by Dan Eatherley.

Looking for a bushmaster in the jungles of Trinidad. The proficient snake hunter would
have brought a machete to clear vegetation. I wasn't a proficient snake hunter.
Photo by Dan Eatherley.

The bushmaster is a patient killer. One individual in Costa Rica is known to have
waited in ambush in the same spot for twenty-four consecutive nights.
Photo by Maik Dobiey.

Bushmasters are under threat across much of their range. The most exquisite of venom, the most perfect of camouflage is no match for bulldozers, logging, and dynamite. Photo by Dean Ripa.

The beauty of the bushmaster captured by Peru-based photographer Maik Dobiey.

During the 1930s, Gloria accompanied her much-loved grandfather
Raymond Ditmars on snake-hunting jaunts in the tropics. "He was just delicious!"
Photo by Dan Eatherley.

Charles Urban, the British movie mogul with whom Raymond
Ditmars cut a lucrative distribution deal for his educational
films. c. 1914 (Courtesy of Luke McKernan)

Raymond Ditmars dons the appropriate protective equipment to
film a skunk, c. 1916. (Courtesy of Luke McKernan)

A postcard depicting the Strand Theatre on Broadway, New York, where Ditmars's film *The Book of Nature* ran for a record-breaking thirty-seven weeks, early twentieth century. (Courtesy of Michael Perlman)

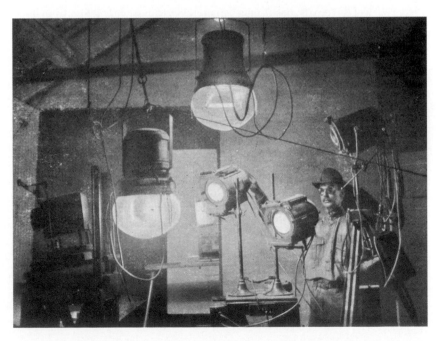

Raymond Ditmars tests an array of lights in his self-built "film laboratory" in Scarsdale, New York, early twentieth century. (Courtesy of Luke McKernan)

Raymond Ditmars with a green mamba (*Dendroaspis sp.*) in 1932. A nine-foot-long specimen of this deadly species once temporarily got loose during filming in his Scarsdale studio. (Courtesy of Mike Dee)

William Mann, director of the National Zoo in Washington, DC, and Raymond Ditmars with a Sumatran blood python (*Python curtus*), 1932. (Courtesy of Mike Dee)

Raymond Ditmars in 1934 flanked by William H. Harkness (left) and Lawrence T. K. Griswold (right), amateur zoologists famed for bringing Komodo dragons to the United States. (Courtesy of Mike Dee)

Raymond Ditmars with a Komodo dragon (*Varanus komodoensis*) brought to the Bronx Zoo in 1934. (Courtesy of Mike Dee)

Raymond Ditmars with spectral, or "carnivorous," bats (*Vampyrum spectrum*) collected in Trinidad, 1935. (Courtesy of Mike Dee)

Raymond Ditmars with a consignment of Galápagos land iguanas (*Conolophus subcristatus*), 1936. (Courtesy of Mike Dee)

thirteen-year-old son Denis with an "exceedingly lively and colorful king snake" as a parting gift. The boy, who had seen and coveted the non-venomous serpent during a recent visit to the zoo, dangled it over his head and wound two coils around his neck to the horror of onlookers.

Despite outward appearances, Ditmars and his colleagues weren't reckless with snakes and took every measure to minimize risk. For protection they sported thick canvas or leather puttees which reached to the knee and high shoes. "If low cut shoes are worn," the zoo man once cautioned, "there are usually several inches of ankle left exposed and this is usually the part of the limb most frequently bitten by venomous reptiles of moderate size." If the worst should happen Ditmars always brought a snake treatment kit. A suction bulb, rubber ligature, several sharp scalpels or safety razor-blades, a jar of antiseptic gauze, and rolls of bandages made from boiled cheesecloth were crammed into an old leather cartridge box carried on his belt or into the capacious pockets of his khaki shooting jacket. A flask of whiskey, potassium permanganate crystals, and even strychnine tablets, were included in the early years but would prove entirely useless, Ditmars later substituting them with tubes of antiserum.

On discovering a venomous snake, the quarry was lured to a favorable position and pinned close to the head with a forked stick. Often Ditmars would carry a pole, fitted at its far end with a specially designed noose that he would drop over the serpent's head and tighten. This device allowed him to maneuver the ensnared quarry with relative safety tail-first into a thick hessian sack. Scissors were used to snip the noose cord, releasing the captive in the bag, which was swiftly and securely knotted. A fellow serpent-hunter once disparaged noosing as "poor sport, the odds being strong against the snake" and, as Ditmars would realize, the method would prove wholly unsuitable for capturing a bushmaster.

ED and I found several more rattlesnakes that day and a possible den site. Descending the talus slopes was slow and unnerving; many rocks wobbled under foot, threatening a twisted ankle and you couldn't be sure a rattler wasn't skulking in the crevices below. Fortunately, as evidenced by the earlier snake, the species tended to avoid striking even when a heavy boot landed close by. A small swarm of hornets patrolling a nearby cliff face added to the perils. Ed meanwhile discussed some of the characters he knew in snake research. Among the most colorful was the late Richard "Dick" Bothner, a biology professor and ardent naturalist.

"He'd go out all day collecting small harmless snakes. Then cram them under his hat, go into a local store and take off his hat so all they all tumbled out." The story echoed those told about Ditmars's contemporary George O'Reilly.

Then there was William H. Martin, someone Ed regarded as "the grandfather" of timber rattlesnake research. "Marty" had spent a lifetime studying the species in the central Appalachians and, when Ed was doing his PhD, had shared with him thirty years' worth of snake reproduction data from Virginia's Shenandoah National Park. Using Marty's figures Ed demonstrated that rattler pregnancy rates rose and fell in relation to the acorn crop two years before. "It's to do with rodents," explained Ed. "Although the snakes can switch diets, the prey of choice is white-footed mice; and the mice themselves like acorns. A surfeit of acorns on the ground means rodents multiply which ultimately benefits the snakes. Acorn failure has the opposite effect, leading to lower reproduction among the rattlers."

Marty was a guru for Ed, and during snake hunts the pair loved swapping tales. Each insisted they had been chased by a male rattlesnake defending a female, a phenomenon perhaps serving as the basis for the timeworn myth that if you kill a snake, its mate will seek revenge. Venomous snake bite in the northeastern states of the US was in fact unusual, perhaps one or two accidents annually. But you didn't work with venomous snakes for as long as Marty had without risking bites.

In August 2008 the inevitable happened. While surveying an oil pipeline in Pennsylvania, Marty trod on a timber rattlesnake that then bit his ankle. Fortunately, the local Lewistown hospital kept antivenin known as CroFab and Marty received four vials' worth within the hour before being taken by chopper to a larger medical center at Harrisburg for further treatment.

"Marty's platelet counts normalized after getting the antivenin and he discharged himself the next day," said Ed. "But that night he started bleeding again through the nose and gums and had to be rushed back to hospital."

Marty Martin's attitude to the incident was relaxed, his sole regret that he hadn't been allowed to enjoy the view during the airlift. He had suffered several further so-called reemergence episodes before fully recovering. I would soon discover that the current strain of CroFab was not very effective against timber rattlesnake bite, something the manufacturer was working on. I was glad to have found that out once my rattler hunt was done. I thanked Ed and headed back to the city.

ALTHOUGH timber rattlesnakes, copperheads, and other species were to be found within an easy auto ride from the Bronx, Raymond Ditmars knew that a different and just as thrilling assortment of reptiles, strange, beautiful, and deadly, was available in the sub-tropical lowlands of the southern states of the United States. Along with alligators were three kinds of rattlesnake including the eastern diamondback, the group's largest representative. There were also the water moccasin, a semi-aquatic cousin of the copperhead viper; the hognose snake, famed for shamming death; and the irascible but handsome red-bellied watersnake.

Ditmars had already learned something of the fauna during his seminal field trip to the Florida Everglades with Professor Smith, and it was in pursuit of such reptiles that in 1899 he instigated what would become regular collecting sprees in the tick- and mosquito-ridden swamps, bayous, and lagoons of the Deep South. Conducted during the spring or summer vacations, these jaunts kindled an appetite for warmer climes, and served as training for the overseas expeditions that came later. In the

1930s, when the hunt for bushmaster was at its height, Ditmars thought back to this hot, sticky, primeval landscape as "exotic in its utter loneliness and strange beauty," considering it "a good area for 'seasoning' experience for the tropics . . . there was a lot to be learned before I felt confident about striking into remote places." The eerie beauty of the landscape was also a draw. "The light is dull in these swamps, not strong enough for the photographic plate," wrote Ditmars in 1932. "Combined with reddish water, and the painting of tree trunks with this hue from freshets, there appears to be a dull red glow, as from an effect light in a theatre—barely discernible, but manifest upon the mind."

At first he explored the wetlands accompanied only by head keeper Charles Snyder, but in time brought along other friends and family, including, from an early age, his daughters. Packing a luggage of canvas bags, fine soft copper wire for noosing and an abundance of quinine, the snake-hunters would head south to Savannah, Georgia, aboard one of many steamers then plying the eastern coast before complet-ing the trip by wagon. Their final destination was the Pineland Club near the tiny settlement of Robertsville in Hampton County, South Carolina. Owned by friends of the New York Zoological Society, this shooting preserve with rented cabins on the northern flood plain of the Savannah River was perfect for sorties into nearby cypress swamps, hummocks, grasslands, pine woods, and cotton fields infested with cold-blooded life.

Ditmars spoke of "a snake's paradise" where "every creeping thing is as the sands of the sea for numbers." Patrolling the swamps, causeways, or narrow deer paths on horses, mules, or a simple buckboard wagon, the curator and his associates would be equipped with wire nooses and, despite the stifling heat, wore "an armor of heavy brown duck, high top boots, and stout flexible gloves." As an added precaution Ditmars always carried a revolver. Having noosed a venomous snake such as a water moc-casin or rattlesnake, he would maneuver "the puffing, thrashing, spitting reptile twixt thumb and forefinger around the neck," dropping it into a fabric sack. The latter would be given "a quick swirl so that the fang that darts forth instantly is embedded in a thick fold of cloth." Not everything was personally collected. As Ditmars had long ago discovered in Central Park, a few pennies were enough to persuade locals to bring him all manner of live specimens. The pick of the crop one year: a six-foot-long chicken snake costing just a dime.

For Ditmars, the alligators of this steamy landscape represented a huge prize, and he trapped many live specimens. In the early years these prehistoric beasts could be found in the big open lakes that connected with the Savannah River during the wet season. This made them easy targets for river steamboats, which "carried veritable arsenals in immediate readiness on the tops of their pilot houses," the appearance of an alligator triggering "a general fusillade." Fishermen also took potshots at them. By 1915 the alligators had retreated into the densest zones of the cypress swamp where, Ditmars contended, they had "multiplied in greater numbers than formerly were seen on the river." He described his team hauling one adult male from a water hole using a steel hook, binding its jaws and feet with a rope before dragging the thrashing, hissing captive a quarter of a mile through thick swamp to the wagon. A week or so later the "troublesome specimen," eight feet in length, two hundred pounds in weight, was on exhibition in a pool at the reptile house.

Alligator eggs were equally sought after. During the summer, a gravid female would scrape together a stack several feet high of mud, twigs, moss, and other plant matter in which she would lay up to fifty eggs. Heat from the rotting vegetation incubated the clutch. In August 1900 Ditmars and Snyder were drawn by the bellows of a mother gator to one such mound close to an ancient rice ditch. Delving into the pile's center they uncovered thirty-seven eggs in a single irregular mass. Ditmars reports that the "entire nest and its contents were packed on our horses, brought to the nearest railway station, and shipped to the Zoological Park." Back in the Bronx, just seven little alligators hatched, of which five survived, the *New York Times* describing the offspring as "tiny, bark-skinned, yellow-eyed fellows, with a baby curiosity for all that is strange and with no clear conception as to where they are."

Nighttime forays, typically for rattlesnakes, were just as productive. They were atmospheric too, taking place amongst moonlit live-oaks dripping with Spanish moss against a backdrop of silhouetted palmettos, the air moist and balmy. Sometimes a silvery haze floated over the swamp. Such outings dismayed the locals. "Well does the writer remember the consternation among the colored folk created by his companion and himself during their nocturnal hunts," wrote Ditmars in 1902 with the casual prejudice of the period. "Nor can these simple people be blamed for evincing astonishment at the apparition of two canvas-clad figures entering the swamps at night, armed with a powerful acetylene lamp, and emerging later with canvas bags which writhed and pulsated with struggling serpents."

The southern excursions always yielded rich pickings, which Ditmars duly recorded in the bulletins and annual reports of the New York Zoological Society. The haul from a 1900 trip comprised "ninety-two reptiles, representing fourteen species, of which nine species were new to the Park collection." Included were various handsome watersnakes, a brilliant blue-tailed lizard, a fine-looking rat snake and water moccasin, the latter giving birth to twenty-three young. This tally was exceeded during subsequent visits to South Carolina. In the spring of 1916 Ditmars and keeper George Palmer snared "over 560 specimens, representing over 40 species, as follows: Crocodilia, 1 species; turtles and tortoises, 7 species; lizards, 7 species; serpents, 19 species; amphibians, 9 species." The snakes alone, ranging "from diamond rattlers to ring snakes no larger than a worm," weighed "over a quarter of a ton," replenishing a reptile house depleted by the existing "war conditions and the consequent lack of Old World specimens."

Halfway into the First World War, the supply of new animal exhibits from European dealers, notably Germany's Carl Hagenbeck, had dried up so Ditmars's contribution was vital. The one downside of the

1916 trip, he revealed, was that "I brought a fine case of malaria, all my own."

When the United States finally entered the war the following spring, Ditmars was forty and too old for the draft. He nevertheless accepted the rank of captain and zealously drilled the forty-eight men of Bronx Zoo's home guard, known as "Company A of the Zoological Park Guards," his father's wartime experiences doubtless an inspiration.

Ditmars's fellow curator William Beebe also played his part in maintaining the flow of new exhibits for the zoo. In early 1916, after squeezing a further $6,000 from the New York Zoological Society's benefactors, he established a scientific station in British Guiana. Located on a rubber plantation, Kalacoon House as it was known marked the first of several field laboratories Beebe would found over his long, peripatetic career. Beebe and his assistants set about harvesting birds, mammals, reptiles, amphibians, and insects from the surrounding forest and, to Ditmars's delight and perhaps envy, soon captured a live bushmaster measuring more than eight feet in length. A hunter had spotted the reptile coiled in the leaf litter near a fallen tree. Its camouflage was faultless: "though I was thinking bushmaster and looking bushmaster," wrote Beebe later, "my eyes insisted on registering dead leaves . . . it was a full three minutes before I could honestly say, 'This is leaf; that is snake.'" He and his assistants lassoed the viper. "Even with the scant inch of neck ahead of the noose," continued Beebe, "the head had such play that I had to pin it down with the gun barrel before we dare seize it. When our fingers gained their safe hold and pressed, the great mouth opened wide, a gaping expanse of snowy white tissue, and the inch-long fangs appeared erect, each draped under the folds of its sheath, like a rapier outlined beneath a courtier's cloak."

The bushmaster's delivery by express wagon to the Bronx Zoo reptile house was celebrated in the newspapers, the *New York Times* noting the tender care with which head keeper George Palmer received and handled the carefully-crated parcel containing "the king of the venomous snakes of northern South America."

Incidentally, Theodore Roosevelt and his wife had visited Kalacoon soon after its opening. The couple moved on to nearby Trinidad, meeting both R. R. Mole and F. W. Urich. Among the serpents, fearsome centipedes, and "bird-killing" spiders, the former president was interested to see Mole's latest *mapepire z'anana*. "The bushmaster is a snake of rather sluggish temper, which dislikes to run, and it is formidable because of the immense quantities of poison which it spirts [sic] into its victim through hollow fangs, which may be an inch and a half long" Roosevelt later observed.

As the years went by and his funds grew, Ditmars pushed into other wild places notably, in the summer of 1922, the Mojave Desert of the southwestern United States. He wasn't just gathering reptiles in the canyons and sands of California and Arizona, the great river swamps of South Carolina, the familiar hills of New York, and Connecticut, Pennsylvania, and Massachusetts. An instinctive journalist, Ditmars was collecting stories too, fertile material for countless newspaper columns, books, lectures, and films, the more memorable exploits resurrected time and again, sometimes decades after the event.

Of course, Ditmars was never going to be satisfied with native reptiles, no matter how colorful or venomous. Since boyhood he'd fantasized about hunting for serpents overseas, especially in the equatorial regions, home to so many remarkable types, snakes such as the anaconda, the fer-de-lance, and above all the bushmaster, the greatest of the world's vipers. Beebe's activities in British Guiana surely both inspired and needled. Ditmars yearned to catch a boat himself to the tropics. But lacking funds, as well as the lobbying skills and obvious scientific credentials of his colleague, such an excursion seemed out of the question. For now anyway.

# 9

# A Messy Business

*"Search as one may among the higher or backboned creatures, on land or in the sea, and no greater perfection in weapons designed to kill can be found than in the fangs of poisonous snakes."*

—Raymond L. Ditmars, *The Fight to Live* (1938)

———◆———

*April 26, 1908. The New York Zoological Park, New York City.*

"Gentlemen, it's past eleven and still no sign of Dr. Danforth. I suggest we start."

The middle-aged man in a bow tie turns to the curator.

"Mr. Ditmars, please proceed."

"Of course, Professor Runyon," says the curator with a grin, seemingly unperturbed that dozens of chemists, physicians, and newspaper reporters are swarming his study. He removes his pipe and hollers down the passageway.

"Charley, bring in the fer-de-lance!"

Ray orders the onlookers to stand back, a request with which everyone is only too happy to comply.

In the hall beyond, zoo visitors gawk as Snyder, in head keeper's uniform, unfastens the rear hatch of a glass-fronted enclosure. He slides his snake hook under the belly of a triangular-headed serpent. Four and half feet in length and as wide as a man's wrist, the reptile is patterned in dark-green diamonds edged in yellow against a background of paler green.

Despite the care with which it is drawn from its quarters and conveyed to the curator's office, the fer-de-lance is alert and angry, flailing, hissing, and squirming. The zoo men are accustomed to such performances but their guests are unnerved, most having assumed the repulsive beast would be brought to the office securely caged.

"Don't get excited!" says Ray, declaring that the serpent cannot strike while balancing over the hook and in any case, the latest snakebite treatment equipment is on hand: cloth strips for a tourniquet, a razor-sharp knife for slashing wounds and Calmette's serum, ready-loaded into a hypodermic syringe (although) the curator privately doubts the efficacy of the Frenchman's antidote against this particular species).

Snyder lowers the fer-de-lance onto a table, the viper coiling in readiness to strike, a shiny forked tongue lapping at the air.

"Now, now, Mr. Snake, lie down and be good for a minute, will you," murmurs Ray as Snyder presses the reptile's head to the table with a piece of wood. Rolling up sleeves, the curator grabs the serpent by its neck between the thumb and forefinger of his right hand, causing the jaws to splay open and scimitar-like fangs to swing out obscenely.

"All right, Charley. Got him, thanks."

Snyder releases the fer-de-lance which again goes berserk, thrashing its body and tail in great arcs and provoking further exclamations of horror from the bystanders.

If the curator is concerned he doesn't show it.

"Professor Runyon, the collection vessel please," he says, pulling the viper's lithe body to his own, careful to keep the treacherous head pointing outwards.

Runyon approaches clutching a small glass beaker, medicated gauze affixed to its mouth. At that moment the fer-de-lance twists powerfully in the curator's hands causing the professor to retreat.

"Come along, Professor, no nonsense now, let him bite the cloth."

Runyon again advances until the receptacle, quivering in his hand, comes within half an inch of the reptile's pointed snout. The snake bites down on the gauze, the audience gasping as cruel fangs puncture the membrane with a pop, spurting twin jets of yellowish liquid. Twice more Ray coaxes the reptile to strike the cloth, each time Snyder squeezing the sides of its head, to ensure the venom sacs are exhausted. Ray holds up the container for all to see, the puddle of viscous fluid within it gleaming.

"There we are, Gentlemen. One measure of *Lachesis* venom — enough to kill us all!"

The spectators clap.

"If the snake lives I expect to repeat this operation in a few weeks' time," continues Ray having returned the fer-de-lance to Snyder. "But I fear the outlook is poor. The specimen has refused food since arriving. It is likely the extraction process will merely further strain what is already a vulnerable animal."

Newspaper photographers now move in on the zoo men asking them to pose with the fer-de-lance. Runyon has meanwhile recovered his composure, and thanking Ray turns to his colleagues.

"At long last," he says, "after eighty long years we now have a fresh batch of lachesis. And not a moment too soon, Dr. Hering's supply is all but exhausted."

The professor places the jar on a miniature set of scales.

"I fancy we have just shy of eighteen grains here, let's say seventeen and three-quarters," he announces after a few minutes. "Truly remarkable! A superb yield!"

More applause.

"Now, no time to waste. The lachesis will rapidly lose its potency in contact with the air so we must act quickly to lock in the active ingredients."

Runyon removes the gauze from the beaker, pouring the precious contents into a small mortar, adding a drop of milk and several teaspoonfuls of sugar.

"I have combined ninety-nine parts sugar to one part poison," he announces. Taking up a small wooden pestle he beats the mixture for several minutes, reducing it to a fine white powder. This he transfers to small glass vials.

The delicate operation complete, Runyon brightens.

"Before you, Gentlemen, sufficient lachesis to satisfy the world's needs *for the next fifty years!*"

—◆—

"WE call these accidents the 'Ts.' They always seem to involve tequila, testosterone, and tattoos." The doctor paused. "Oh, and trucks too. In a typical scenario, the snake owner's having a party, it's gone midnight and he's drunk. He wants to show off so gets out and starts free handling his pets. Then he gets bitten. At least he knows which species it was."

Michael Touger wore a Hawaiian print shirt and a graying beard and sat opposite me in his office. He was talking about the snakebite treatment program he ran here at the Jacobi Medical Center, a hospital close to the Bronx Zoo. Established to deal with accidents in the reptile house, the program now responded to snakebites across the northeast region of the United States, when necessary bringing in plastic surgeons and trauma experts available elsewhere at Jacobi.

"It's a real collaborative effort with the different departments," said Michael, reporting that about half the patients he saw were "innocent bystanders," farmers, hikers, campers, and climbers. In the past summer there had been eight such cases, all copperhead bites, but few needed antivenin.

More problematic were collectors who kept venomous species, often unlawfully, from around the world, and whose symptoms could be difficult to treat. One example was a twenty-five-year-old New Jersey man bitten in January 2011 by an albino monocled cobra. He'd bought it at a reptile show in Pennsylvania where, as Chris Hutson at the Bronx Zoo had mentioned, regulations governing ownership of potentially dangerous reptiles were lax. The victim reportedly believed the venom glands had been disabled through surgery.

"Within an hour of the bite the man has stopped breathing," said Michael. "Luckily his sister knew CPR so he survived long enough to get here. It was a rocky course but he pulled through eventually."

While the Bronx Zoo keeps fourteen different antivenins, hospitals like Jacobi can stock only those antivenins sanctioned by the US Food & Drug Administration. For decades this meant an antidote based on horse serum manufactured by Wyeth. But, to the disappointment of many, production ended in 1996. Five years later approval transferred to CroFab, an alternative made using Australian sheep blood.

"CroFab covers rattlesnakes, copperheads, and water moccasins," said Michael, "but doesn't work for the more exotic venom types we encounter, which is why we maintain our links to the zoo. They can usually get the right antivenin to us within thirty minutes. Elsewhere in the United States it isn't so efficient."

So far the system had worked well without a snakebite fatality at Jacobi since the program's establishment in the 1980s. Admittedly, incidents in the region are few and far between; just five to ten people are treated annually at Jacobi, compared with two hundred or more at a similar facility in Tucson, Arizona.

Discussion of CroFab prompted me to mention Marty Martins's problems following his rattlesnake bite. It turned out that the serious recurrent hemorrhaging Marty experienced happens in just 1 percent of cases, but milder reemergence with CroFab was more common. Medical staff couldn't predict who would be vulnerable so repeated doses were administered until tests confirmed the patient was in the clear. This led to another problem with the current antivenin: the cost.

"Wyeth serum was about ninety dollars a vial. A vial of CroFab is sixteen-hundred," said Michael referencing another recent case in which an elderly man from the Hudson River valley was bitten while picking tomatoes in his back yard. "He ended up needing thirty-five vials."

I now realized that along with the obvious health hazards of my recent excursions with Ed, I'd also taken a huge financial risk and was by no means certain my travel insurance would have covered me.

"Don't worry, I'm proud that Jacobi is a public city hospital," smiled Michael. "The mayor would have paid for it."

But I *was* worrying now. What would happen when I headed down to the tropics to look for bushmasters? Who would cover me then?

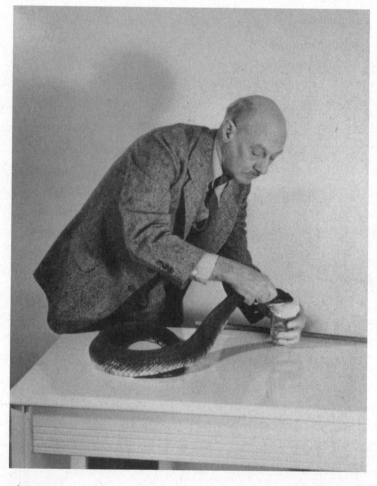

Raymond Ditmars extracts venom from a cottonmouth pitviper (*Agkistrodon piscivorus*), c. 1935. "It's part of my job," he once said. (© Wildlife Conservation Society)

ONE Sunday afternoon in July 1893 a twenty-two-year-old woman was bitten by a diamondback rattlesnake. Newspaper reports told of an "immense" serpent advancing on the girl, "writhing, curving, and bending," rattles sounding, "little beady eyes . . . aglow with anger." Before the victim could react, the creature had "whipped itself into coils" about the "thoroughly alarmed young woman," then sank "venom-tipped fangs" deep into her delicate neck just below the left ear. The reptilian assailant was a native of Florida but the shocking incident occurred in the heart of New York City. And in front of a paying audience.

The victim was a snake charmer known as Dot Sonwell and the serpent, five feet in length and almost three inches thick, one of her props. Dot, who was portrayed as "dark-eyed, frail," and "comely" with "yellow fluffy hair," had been free handling venomous snakes for several years in a number of East Coast cities. At the time of the accident she was drawing crowds at George H. Huber's vast dime museum on East Fourteenth Street in lower Manhattan alongside bear wrestlers, a pig circus, and an armless and legless man. Appearing on a small platform in a short yellow dress, the entertainer was preparing for the latest of six routines she performed daily. Dot gently drew snakes one by one from a perforated wooden chest. Fondling each in turn, she fixed them with a hypnotic stare before draping them over a rail. But the large diamondback, one of three recently shipped north, was in no mood to be charmed. It wriggled free from her grasp and struck.

Dot is said to have given "one terrible scream, and with the slimy coils about her fell to the floor unconscious," her neck and face swelling "to enormous size." As one hundred and fifty panicked spectators along with several "freaks" dashed for the exits, George M. Jansen, the museum's superintendent, carried Dot to the dressing room. There, Eagle Bill, a fellow performer, tried sucking venom from the wound while a pint of whiskey was forced down the patient's throat and ligature applied to her upper arm. Dot was rushed "dying" to St. Vincent's Hospital, although later recovered, which surprised everyone; several newspapers had reported her death.

This wasn't a first for Dot, who had suffered bites four times previously, including one at Huber's not three weeks before, leaving her "weak, and in no condition to handle the deadly diamond-back rattlesnakes." Asked why he allowed Dot to perform again just two days after she'd been discharged from hospital, Jansen, himself a former snake charmer, replied, "We felt bound to re-engage Mrs. Sonwell to give her a chance to recoup the heavy expenses of her recent illness. I particularly asked her if she were ready to go through her performance and although her arm was still black and blue from her last bite she assured me she was perfectly recovered."

Her husband, John Sonwell, was in the same business. Hailing from Cleveland, Ohio, but of German ancestry, "Rattlesnake Jack" had learned his trade in the West and tutored his young wife, a former ballet dancer whose real name was Marguerita Smith, in the secrets of snake charming. At the time of Dot's latest accident, Sonwell was taking a sabbatical, washing dishes in a Sixth Avenue restaurant while living off his wife's earnings. He had temporarily lost his nerve after sustaining multiple bites himself—his standard treatment to slash the wound down to the bone with a dull knife and drink himself silly. Sonwell was an unsavory character who reportedly abused his wife and the pair later separated, although both continued working with snakes.

Dot's employer was also pilloried in the press. "Huber is unquestionably morally responsible for the young woman's injury," railed the *New York Tribune*, among many calling for snake charming to be banned, and Huber's license revoked. "Such a performance is so offensive, so horrible and so revolting to public decency that it should be sharply punished." At the very least, argued the paper, the snake should be first disarmed: "People who enjoy seeing a 'charmer' handle the slimy, dreadful looking monsters would be none the wiser if the fangs were removed." However, those in the trade avoided such procedures which they knew could kill the animal, and in any case, new fangs could naturally replace the extracted ones.

The lady snake charmers from traveling circuses whom Ditmars had known as a teenager worked with harmless pythons and boa constrictors, so he was intrigued to learn of performers free handling venomous snakes. Watching Rattlesnake Jack in action he was astounded by the careless way he fooled about with the deadly reptiles. He nevertheless befriended John Sonwell and asked to inspect his rattlers, discovering them "in full possession of their fangs." When milked the snakes yielded more than a fluid ounce of venom. Ditmars was hardly surprised therefore to hear of Sonwell's demise in July 1902. Days earlier the curator had again witnessed his friend "recklessly exhibiting a writhing and rattling mass of Texas rattlesnakes" and, during a similar performance in Boston, one had struck the charmer's right hand. Within hours Rattlesnake Jack, aged forty-one, was no more.

The accident, if it could be called such a thing, crystallized in Ditmars's mind something that had long troubled him: the lack of an effective treatment for snake bite. The "cures" of the time did more harm than good. Plying the patient with liberal doses of alcohol was standard practice, despite scientists even then regarding it as entirely ineffective. Indeed, soon after sustaining a rattler bite to the finger a few years earlier, Rattlesnake Jack was given "a pint of whiskey" by doctors at New York City's Bellevue Hospital. Following this a "large dose of aromatic spirits of ammonia" was administered and "more whiskey." A "cord was then tightened about his wrist, and hypodermic injections of permanganate of potash and digitalis were given. Then more whiskey." Other remedies were equally hopeless if not downright dangerous, including arsenic, mercury, opium, ammonia, strychnine, gunpowder, saliva, urine, and feces. Bloodletting and suction was also recommended. "I believe in the knife, but not in cauterization," wrote G. R. O'Reilly, Ditmars's hero, in 1891. "If a person is bitten in a fleshy part, and the venom not directly injected into vein or artery, cutting with a knife to the same depth as the snake's fang has penetrated, and afterward sucking the place strongly, will remove nearly every vestige of the poison." Further back in human history the cures were as absurd as they were useless. In ancient Rome, Pliny the Elder cites chicken brains and wine-braised sheep dung as cures, as well as the cutting in half of rats at auspicious times.

That such treatments persisted may be explained by the phenomenon of the dry bite. Venomous serpents did not always discharge a full dose of venom when striking, and sometimes withheld it altogether. Remedies thus gained credibility for "curing" patients who would have anyway survived. Despite study dating back to the Renaissance, no one truly understood what snake venom was, how it acted, and so how to fight it.

Occurring in a quarter of snake species, venom's primary function is to enable a limbless predator to immobilize prey before the latter escapes or retaliates. Derived from saliva, it consists of many toxic agents each attacking in different ways. These active ingredients can be crudely classed into two groups: hemotoxins, which assault the circulatory system and kill by clotting blood cells, dissolving the lining of blood vessels and destroying tissues; and neurotoxins, which act on the nerves and suffocate the victim by paralyzing the respiratory system. The ratio of agents varies widely in different species, hemotoxins predominating in the venom of pitvipers, such as rattlesnakes and bushmasters, neurotoxins more significant in cobras, mambas, coralsnakes, and their allies.

The "vipers are hemotoxic, cobras are neurotoxic rule" is by no means universal. Tropical rattlesnakes, for instance, are known as "neck-breakers" because their venom also contains nerve-targeting ingredients that paralyze the victim's neck muscles, leaving the head left to flop. At the same time, bites from certain African cobras are very destructive of tissues. Thus, to be effective, any antidote would need to neutralize every type of toxic substance within the venom. And to do it fast.

Nature offers an elegant solution to this most formidable of problems. Doctors had long observed that people contracting a weak form of a disease could be protected against a more virulent attack of the same condition. In 1796 the English physician Edward Jenner demonstrated this, conferring resistance to smallpox upon a boy by injecting him with cowpox, a harmless relative of the killer virus. In so doing, Jenner created the first vaccine, the word itself deriving from *vaccinae*, Latin for "from cows." By the late nineteenth century Frenchman Louis Pasteur was producing vaccines against anthrax and rabies from artificially enfeebled versions of the pathogens. Pasteur espoused the new germ theory that identified bacteria and other microscopic agents—not the traditionally blamed"miasmas" or "bad air"—as causing disease. Scientists deduced that when assaulted by these harmful agents, biological cells manufactured antibodies to neutralize the threat. This explained the success of vaccines. Might not this natural immune response now be harnessed to combat the microscopic and deadly elements of snake venom?

Henry Sewall, a young professor of physiology at the University of Michigan, claimed a decisive step toward answering this question. In 1887 he made captive pigeons partially resistant to serpent venom by inoculating the birds with gradually increasing doses of venom from a type of small rattlesnake known as a massasauga.

A decade later, Albert Calmette, a French microbiologist and director of the Pasteur Institute in Lille, developed the world's first effective antidote. He too had administered test animals, in his case rabbits, with tiny quantities of cobra venom. Like Sewall's pigeons, they became resistant. Calmette switched to injecting donkeys and horses, the larger animals generating sufficient antibodies to be "borrowed" by humans. He increased the venom concentration and volume administered until the equines could survive 80 times the lethal dose. Calmette then bled the surrogate animals, allowed the blood to clot and recovered a clear fluid or "serum" that contained the antibodies. When he injected snakebite patients with the serum they recovered. Tubes of "Calmette's Antivenomous Serum" were soon being shipped to snake-infested countries across Asia.

Over in New York, Ditmars followed these developments and was among the first to order tubes from Calmette. But while effective against the neurotoxic bites of African and Eurasian snakes, the serum was inadequate in treating envenomations in the New World, and decades after the Frenchman's breakthrough, a bite from a rattlesnake, fer-de-lance, or bushmaster could still mean death. Although lacking medical training, Ditmars was determined to do what he could to change this and the year 1902, for example, saw him holed up with several researchers in the basement of the city's College of Physicians and Surgeons milking fifty snakes of various kinds to study and compare their venoms. Collecting the fluid was a messy business. "An afternoon was generally consumed in extracting the poison, and during this time the venom was often smeared upon the fingers of the operators," Ditmars reported, "but they were careful that no scratch or cut existed upon their hands when an afternoon's study began."

His collaboration with the brilliant Japanese scientist Hideyo Noguchi was more intensive still. In 1905 Noguchi established a laboratory on Lexington Avenue and Fiftieth Street where he and Ditmars extracted prodigious quantities of venom, some days milking up to a hundred snakes. The effects of the extracts were tested on "frogs, eels, fish, dogs, pigs, guinea pigs, sheep, oxen, and horses." Many years later Ditmars ruminated on these pioneering days "when there wasn't any serum and one took a long chance every minute of the task." He undertook such work for the rest of his life, and it testifies to extraordinary skill that he was never so much as nicked by a fang. Noguchi couldn't say the same, Ditmars reporting that his "invariably cheerful" friend had "lost most of his fingers of one hand from previous accidents." As a baby Noguchi had tumbled into a fireplace, burning and deforming his left hand, so would insist on manipulating snakes with the mutilated hand, remarking that if anything happened he wanted to save the good one.

Ditmars was, however, left with one physical legacy: a right hand that bulged so much that people asked whether he had hurt it.

"Nothing the matter with my hand," the curator would reply, pointing at a cage of serpents. "I've developed that muscle from gripping snakes like these. It's part of my job."

*"Among the important additions to the Reptile collection during the past year were two large specimens of the South American bushmaster (Lachesis mutus), representing the largest known species of poisonous serpent."*
(April 1904)

*"The collection in the Reptile House has been enriched by the addition of an exceptionally fine example of the bushmaster (Lachesis mutus), from the Island of Trinidad. . . . The present specimen has been given a big cage, with a generous bed of damp sphagnum moss, and a rustic shelf on which to climb."*
(May 1910)

*"From Mr. R. R. Mole, who sends us many interesting South American reptiles and insects, we have just received a fine example of the fer-de-lance and a large specimen of the South American bushmaster . . . the bushmaster is about eight feet in length . . . of a beautiful salmon hue, the body crossed by sooty-black bands. The scales are so rough as to suggest the surface of a pineapple."*
(July 1912)

I was back in the Bronx Zoo archives. The arrival of a bushmaster in the reptile house was important enough to warrant a write-up in the New York Zoological Society's reports and bulletins, and in the early years at least, this seemed a frequent occurrence. From 1903 onwards R. R. Mole regularly supplied specimens, and over one six-year stretch bushmasters were arriving annually. Other tropical treasures came from Trinidad too: colorful tree boas, huge anacondas, and venomous centipedes a foot long that Ditmars fed freshly-killed mice.

Each bushmaster was heralded with ballyhoo, often in the New York press, only to refuse food and perish within months. Ditmars did what he could, providing spacious quarters with generous hiding places, tropical vegetation, and plenty of food, but the story with each specimen was the same: "a stubborn, suicidal fast." Force-feeding was counterproductive, as "it seems to benumb the reptile and hinders the subsequent assimilation of the forced meal."

The supply of bushmasters from Trinidad was not inexhaustible; natural populations of all snakes on the island were dwindling thanks to the misguided introduction of the mongoose to control rodents. In the note accompanying a 1910 shipment, Mole's oldest son Howel apologized for upping the charges for a bushmaster. "It is owing to the mongoose, whose destructive work is going on at great pace. Our hunters say that they cannot catch poisonous snakes at the old price, as they are extremely rare, and the risk is too great." The summer of 1915 saw the last bushmaster Mole would send and, save for the spectacular example William Beebe secured in British Guiana the following year, the last to grace the reptile house for decades.

I interrupted my research for a meeting elsewhere on the Bronx Zoo campus. By coincidence the present-day curator of reptiles was among the first to crack the problem of maintaining bushmasters in captivity. Even better, he'd gotten them to breed.

Don Boyer occupied a modest office upstairs in the zoo's administration building some distance from the World of Reptiles. Photographs, paintings, and carved wooden masks dotted the walls and bookshelves. In one small framed photo a younger Don held a clutch of leathery white eggs. Bushmaster eggs.

"The first ones we got," said Don, whose team at the Dallas Zoo's reptile department in the late 1980s was the first to establish routine reproduction of bushmasters in captivity. I was keen to know the secret. What had Ditmars been doing wrong?

Not much it turned out, for the specimens Mole sent were as good as dead before they left Port of Spain. The bushmaster is a remarkably sensitive and fragile snake, and unless caught and handled gently is liable, quite literally, to break. The preferred method for capturing venomous serpents in Ditmars's day—noosing them at a safe distance—snapped the bushmaster's delicate backbone like glass. Pinning them behind the head with a forked stick wasn't much better. Like other wild-caught snakes, bushmasters were also susceptible to parasitic infestation. In their case, the parasites were likely to be the decidedly unpleasant pentastomid worm. More animated screw than worm, these ungrateful hitchhikers specialized in eating their way through their hosts' vital organs. Even modern zoos, with a far better understanding of herpetological veterinary medicine, have trouble removing these.

"The key to maintaining and breeding bushmasters was starting off with healthy ones," said Don. "Snakes without serious parasite infections, hurt necks, fractured ribs, or dehydration."

Once they had fit animals the Dallas team installed females in an artificial "hibernaculum," an old walk-in freezer whose temperature and humidity could be precisely controlled. Males were then introduced.

"They combated a bit and courted the females."

A cool front in the fall really got things going, and the bushmasters started to breed. And carried on. Year after year. With later generations parasite-free, they did even better.

The work at Dallas inspired other zoos to reproduce bushmasters. After a decade in Texas, Don moved to San Diego Zoo, then in 2011 landed the job at the Bronx.

"So how does it feel being the 'new Ditmars'?" I asked.

Don smiled, explaining that he didn't quite fill the same role. In Ditmars's day reptiles were poorly known by the public and the pioneering curator did much to popularize them. The role of zoos had been to exhibit the more spectacular ones. Today, conservation was the goal, and the Bronx Zoo was playing its part with a breeding program for threatened herps, principally turtles and amphibians.

"How about exhibiting some bushmasters here at the Bronx?" I asked.

"I would *love* too," said Don. "But right now it's the Mangs we're concentrating on."

A distant cousin of the bushmaster, the Mangshan pitviper occurs in south-central China. Like the bushmaster, this is a large, beautiful, rare snake that lays eggs. However, Mangs are adapted to cooler forests so are better suited to New York's temperate climate.

I asked Don for his thoughts on Ditmars. Although Gerald Durrell and other recent zoo men had greater direct influence, Don was fascinated by his famous predecessor. "It is humbling to work at the same institution. I think about him walking in these same hallways. I don't believe in ghosts, but sometimes I get a weird feeling."

I left Don's office and returned to the zoo archives. A piece in the January 1909 *Bulletin of the New York Zoological Society* soon caught my attention. "Like all of our other specimens of this rare and deadly snake, the present example came from the island of Trinidad," wrote Ditmars upon the arrival of yet another ill-fated bushmaster. "It is the gift of Mr. Edward Wheelock Runyon, who procured the reptile for the purpose of obtaining some of its venom for scientific purposes." This brief passage was a postscript to one of the most notorious episodes in Ditmars's extraordinary career.

In 1828 a German doctor named Constantine Hering fell ill while working in South America. For a day or so Hering slipped in and out of consciousness, ranting and raving as his wife recorded the symptoms of his delirium. What could have prompted the sickness? Malaria? Yellow fever? In fact, the patient maintained that he had swallowed snake venom in the interests of homeopathic science.

Homeopathy is a system of alternative medicine centering on the maxim *similia similibus curantur*, "like is cured by like." It was founded in the late eighteenth century by another German, Samuel Hahnemann, who surmised that natural poisons could alleviate human ailments by generating symptoms similar to, but which canceled out, those of the disease. He and his disciples set about testing on themselves and others a wide range of nasties including belladonna, mercury, and sulphur. Troubled that his "cures" would aggravate matters, Hahnemann advised diluting them many times over, asserting that the body's "vital force" responded to the tiniest hint of the substance.

Constantine Hering was a follower of Hahnemann. Working as physician-in-attendance to the governor of Paramaribo in Dutch Guiana (present-day Surinam), he learned of a terrible serpent in the area known as the *suru kuku* and supposing its venom to be useful in homeopathy persuaded the local Arawaks to procure an example. A snake was brought, which Hering identified as *Lachesis trigonocephalus*, a now-defunct scientific name for the fer-de-lance viper. The specimen, mangled horribly during a rough capture, was induced to bite a lump of sugar, infusing it with venom. Hering reportedly contracted his fever after eating the sugar.

There is something fishy about Hering's story: unless the person consuming it has an internal injury, a stomach ulcer for example, snake venom is as harmless as raw egg white to swallow. Nevertheless, the German ascribed his reaction to the venom, which he christened "lachesis," later maintaining that in dilute form it might treat infirmities with symptoms like those he had allegedly experienced.

Hering moved to Philadelphia in 1833 taking with him the remains of the snake and the venom extract that was soon embraced by homeopaths the world over. Asthma, bilious fevers, sciatica, diphtheria, sore throats, and bad breath; ulcers around the toenails, deafness, constipation, hepatitis, typhoid, scarlet fevers, smallpox, rabies, nervous breakdowns, and other mental illnesses. The list of conditions which lachesis was purported to remedy was endless. Other snake venoms attracted interest, a "Prof. Barnett of New York" in 1901 reportedly curing tetanus with tropical rattlesnake venom after learning of the remedy from "a native doctor" in Brazil.

Most facets of the lachesis story are fanciful, and like the wider homeopathic principle, were as strongly contested in Hering's time as they are today. Perhaps least probable, however, was the assertion in the early twentieth century that all the lachesis then in use came from Hering's original sample. Whatever the truth, eighty years after the original extraction Edward Wheelock Runyon, the New York–based president of homeopathic pharmacists Boericke and Runyon, set about replenishing the dwindling supply.

Financed by an unnamed millionaire suffering from a nervous malady bordering on "delusional insanity," the project was far from straightforward, requiring the capture and safe delivery of the right kind of snake. Someone would then have to recover the prized extract. This was where Raymond Ditmars came in; the curator's high profile collaboration with venom scientists proved he was the ideal candidate. After enquiries across South America, Runyon secured his snake although, as the *New York Times* reported, his "agent, as a matter of personal safety, was compelled to kill the first specimen taken. The next died in confinement. The third met with mishap." At last, on April 18, 1908, a single fer-de-lance viper caught near the mouth of the Amazon was installed at the Bronx Zoo reptile house. Ten days on, amid much fanfare and before an audience of homeopathic chemists, doctors, and newspapermen, as well as Hering's grandson Ardo, Ditmars carried out what was for him a routine extraction. Runyon contended that the "17 ¾ grains" of venom yielded, equivalent to about a gram, would, when diluted to one trillionth part with milk and sugar, meet global demand for another fifty years.

Within days the medical establishment weighed in, denouncing the operation as "nature faking." Homeopaths bristled at the criticism and passionate exchanges filled the letters pages of national newspapers. The record is silent though on whether the replenished lachesis cured the millionaire benefactor. The fer-de-lance died of a heart attack the following winter "it is thought from overstimulation or excitement" but not before three further extractions were conducted yielding a total of "forty-six and one-tenths grains."

The tale would have one last twist. On December 12, 1908, a brief article appeared in *Scientific American* magazine suggesting that Hering had misidentified the "suru kuku" from which his famous remedy had been drawn: "there is in the Museum of the Philadelphia Academy of Natural Sciences a mounted specimen of *Lachesis Mutus* labeled with Dr. Hering's name." In other words, a bushmaster, not a fer-de-lance, may have been the source of Hering's 1828 extract all along, something corroborated by the fact that *surucucú* is a common indigenous term for bushmasters. Runyon therefore went on to secure a bushmaster (from R. R. Mole) for milking, later donating it to the Bronx Zoo. This was the animal recorded in the society's January 1909 *Bulletin*.

Ditmars's reputation was untarnished by the affair and, although talk of homeopathy is absent in his writings, he continued supporting research into the curative effects of snake venom. During the late 1920s he milked water moccasins for Dr. Samuel M. Peck of New York's Mount Sinai Hospital who had found that sterilized and diluted venom could arrest hemorrhaging in certain bleeding diseases. Another notable collaboration around this time, one that nearly killed him, was with Adolph Monaelesser, a surgeon hoping to cure epilepsy and cancer with venom.

Monaelesser's interest in animal venoms was kindled back in 1898 when he noticed that a leper he was treating in Cuba improved following a tarantula bite. As Ditmars explained, Monaelesser hypothesized that "certain malignant growths were associated with abnormal conditions of the nerve centers" and that an injection of diluted neurotoxic venom might "shock" and thus correct these nerve centers. Working at the Pasteur Institute in the early 1930s with Albert Calmette, the antivenin pioneer, Monaelesser formulated a trial in which modified venom would be administered to 115 cancer patients at Paris's Salpêtrière Hospital. Substantial volumes of neurotoxic venom, of the type found in Indian cobras, were needed and Ditmars was happy to oblige. However, a cobra was far more slippery a customer than a rattlesnake or a water moccasin and, with shorter and stouter fangs, was awkward to milk in the conventional way. The curator instead encouraged cobras to chew on glass plates from which the venom could be scraped when dry. All went well until the day he felt such a pain in his chest that he was forced to walk around "caved in like a pugilist who has stopped a punch he didn't like." The symptoms passed and Ditmars later realized that scraping the dried venom released a fine cloud of toxic dust that he had inadvertently breathed in. From then on he proceeded with far more caution.

Monaelesser wasn't so fortunate. The pioneering scientist died in 1935, reportedly of leukemia, although he too had inhaled venom dust. Hopes of curing cancer also foundered, with none of the Paris patients surviving although the symptoms in some were alleviated. Despite this, Monaelesser, Peck, and Ditmars were ahead of their time, for modern biochemists seeking treatments for tumors, high blood pressure, and other human ailments still study components of snake venom, including that of bushmasters, with promising results.

What drove Ditmars to involve himself in these efforts? Curiosity, undeniably. But also an eagerness to identify the positives in an abhorred group of animals. "I have watched many people look with awe upon the snakes, and I have heard plenty of hostile remarks about them," he once wrote. "But there may come a time when a cobra or moccasin will be thought of as a benefactor."

# 10

# A Sympathetic Knowledge

*"[It] is the writer's hope, ere this book is finally closed, a persistently reigning and unjust prejudice may be completely shattered by the explosion of a long train of erroneous theories; when snakes have been described as they truly are, and the clean, graceful and wonderful phases of their varied structure have been faithfully portrayed by the camera."*

—Raymond L. Ditmars, *Reptiles of the World* (1910)

---

*January 8, 1910. Fifteenth Floor, Waldorf-Astoria Hotel, New York City.*

RAIN-SODDEN TOP HATS and fur coats are removed, old friends and colleagues greeted, spouses introduced. Dining tables have been arranged in neat rows, several positioned against a temporary stage at one end of the handsomely furnished suite. The hubbub of talking and laughter grows as more than one hundred engineers, financiers, lawyers, senators, and soldiers take their seats. A choice of Cape Cod oysters and chicken gumbo, marking the air with their respective aromas, is passed around by liveried waiters.

All the while a male figure is hunkered on the stage, motionless and silent. Knees are drawn to his chest, a turbaned head hangs low as if hiding the face in shame. About his sinewy limbs a great white robe is drawn. Spicy tendrils of incense rise from a small pot beside the squatter. Close by stands a three-foot high basket of green wicker. It quivers from time to time but few notice the movement. Behind the figure is a temporary rail, hanging from which are thick red curtains resembling the Chinese flag and emblazoned with an iridescent dragon. The skin of a large snake adorns the rail, completing the bizarre tableau.

Without warning the house lights dim, prompting the hurried termination of conversations. The dying chatter surrenders to a piped melody, oriental in flavor. Several spectators giggle in surprised delight. The tune comes from the direction of the crouching figure now picked out by a powerful spotlight. He carries no instrument, although one foot taps out the rhythm. Gracefully unfurling, the costumed figure draws the basket close, then in one dramatic movement throws off its lid, plunging both hands deep within.

"Snakes!"

This is the sole word uttered as the performer draws out a writhing ball of serpents, much to the alarm of the onlookers. At first the reptiles, at least a dozen of them, are angry and energized, threatening to liberate themselves and leap squirming, wriggling, and fidgeting into the audience where they would surely wreak havoc. A middle-aged gentleman seated next to the stage—and now wishing he wasn't—slides back his chair in alarm. But with the eerie music rising to a crescendo, the stage performer whispers to his charges, almost brushing their scaly, shiny bodies with his mustachioed lips. He sets about massaging them until at last the snakes lie quiescent in his hands. The charmer now places them one by one into black silken bags.

The main lights abruptly snap on, the music extinguished.

"Thank you, Ladies and Gentlemen of the Rocky Mountain Club!" proclaims the performer, discarding his turban and robe with a flourish. Beneath he wears a pressed shirt, tie, and smart trousers.

"I am Raymond Ditmars, curator of reptiles at the New York Zoological Park. Welcome to this evening's performance of the Bronx Park Reptile Circus!"

This educes warm applause from the relieved onlookers.

"Perhaps, like our serpents, you enjoyed the music?" he continues. "It's an exact record taken in Singapore of the music of the Hindu snake charmer. Of course, at no point was I in any danger, for the type of snakes I handled so freely are a harmless variety."

A pause.

"And now may I introduce my assistant Charley Snyder, head keeper at the reptile house!"

The curtains behind Ray sweep back to reveal a second man standing stiffly in military dress by the outsized trumpet of an Edison phonograph. Snyder bows to the audience before delving into one of several large cases stacked nearby.

"Ours is a circus rather different from the sort with which you may be familiar," says Ray striding about the platform. "As remarkable as the tricks are which creatures learn under the guidance of a skilled circus trainer, they are eclipsed by those that are natural to wild dwellers of desert, jungle, and plain."

By now, Snyder has strung a thin cable at shoulder height between two poles some twenty feet apart.

"Take this black lizard from Madagascar, for example," says Ray as his assistant draws a small twisting reptile from a bag by the tail and places it onto the cord. "Walking this slack wire is hardly an accomplishment, for in the wild state his kind live among trees and jungle growth, becoming expert in running along the creepers and climbing plants."

The animal wobbles, refusing to cooperate, but a prod to the tail causes it to sally forth along the wire, Snyder following to prevent a bid for freedom. The audience applauds in polite appreciation as the lizard attains the far end whence it finds itself briskly seized and handed over to Ray.

"As you can see," smiles the curator upending the animal, "these reptiles have grasping feet well qualified for holding on to slender threads of vegetable growth."

More high-wire artists are put through their paces including Taffy, a ring-tailed lemur, which nimbly draws itself along hand over hand.

Once again in the spotlight, Ray nooses a rattlesnake, reprising the technique by which he catches such beasts in the wild. Soon after, a water moccasin is milked of its venom, the club members at this point tucking into a main of filet sole in a sauterne sauce with Parisienne potatoes. The circus also features croakless frogs and six Japanese waltzing mice each spinning on the spot until returned to their box. Between the acts Ray projects magic lantern slides of his recent snake-hunting trips.

Two hours on and the show is drawing to a close. The audience is enjoying coffees and macaroons, some puff on cigars or Fatima cigarettes. More than sixty live specimens have been exhibited, the latest an iguana which adroitly retains its footing atop a rolling basket. Snyder now parades about the stage clutching by its neck a sandy-colored rodent. The animal's hind legs are twice the length of the forelegs. Longer still is the tail, tipped with a tassel of black and white fur.

"Scientists call this fellow the Saharan jerboa but others know him as the kangaroo rat because he is an excellent jumper," says Ray, his tone as clear and authoritative as at the start. His assistant places the jerboa onto a stool positioned in a trough of water. "This rodent can go for weeks without drinking. Indeed, I'm told that in no circumstances can he be induced to touch water. Look at him here: he's fairly marooned on this stool!"

But at that moment, and to the curator's embarrassment, the jerboa earns its colloquial name bounding clear of the trough, indeed clear of the stage altogether. Screams fill the room as Snyder dives off the stage after the fugitive.

"Please everyone, do not be alarmed!" exclaims Ray. "I can assure you the jerboa is quite harmless!"

The man at the front flushes with rage, slamming down onto his table a lead crystal goblet from which he was about to sip. The latter contains four fingers of brandy and also now one desert rodent, its hind legs jutting in an ungainly fashion from the narrow neck of the glass.

Snyder swiftly retrieves the alcohol-soaked animal which beats its tufted tail about like a semaphore flag.

"Ahem," says Ray attempting to recover his composure. "I guess that proves it, Ladies and Gentleman. Jerboas do *indeed* hate water!"

———◆———

On Wednesday May 24, 1911, the New York Public Library at 5th Avenue and 42nd Street opened to the public for the first time. Somewhere between thirty and fifty thousand people passed through the immense portico that day. While a few borrowed books, most were content just to marvel at the library's resplendent design. Like the New York Zoological Park, the edifice was constructed in grand Beaux-Arts style, but with a budget of nine million dollars at their disposal, the architects, Carrère & Hastings, could truly go to town. Ten years in the construction, the new library boasted three hundred rooms, corridors, and vaults all in polished white marble, and seventy-five miles of shelves with space for three and a half million volumes. Ceilings, desks, and screens were of carved walnut and oak. Topping it all was the world's largest reading room. Located above seven floors of stacks and overlooking the foliage of Bryant Park, the vast chamber could accommodate a thousand readers.

The library is now called the Stephen A. Schwarzman Building in honor of the billionaire financier who had recently donated enormous sums toward the institution. This wasn't the only name change. Patience and Fortitude, the lions of pale pink Tennessee marble crouching guard out front, had originally gone by the nicknames Leo Astor and Leo Lenox after an earlier pair of philanthropists.

For me, a century on, the main draw of the library was its newspaper archive holding a wealth of stories inspired by Raymond Ditmars. Some titles had been digitized and were available via computer terminals, today installed in one half of the reading room. Others had to be summoned up on microfilm, a tiresome process, but worth the effort. As late afternoon sunshine streamed through the reading room windows I selected one year at random, 1901, and listed every article mentioning Ditmars:

BIG ALLIGATOR'S TEETH SHORTENED WITH A SAW

ANIMALS HAVE TROUBLES

CATERING TO SNAKES

MOSQUITO BITES A COBRA

THE SNAKE AND HIS MENU

GIANT PYTHON FED WITH A POLE WHILE HELD BY TWENTY-ONE MEN

PARK BEARS IN A FIGHT

QUEER FREAKS OF SNAKES

BIG SHIPMENTS OF WILD ANIMALS ARRIVE

REPTILES NOT VALUELESS

DANGER IN SNAKE-HUNTING

A DARING OPERATION

THE EXPERIENCES OF A SNAKE MAN

FIGHT WITH A WILD GOAT

SNAKE WITH TWO HEADS

I could have kept going, and 1901 was by no means exceptional. From the opening of the zoo in 1899 until his death four decades later, not a month seemed to pass without mention of the curator's exploits. Part of the reason was that in summer 1901, having proved himself astonishingly capable with animal care, he was put in unofficial charge of the mammals too. As his colleague William Bridges later observed, Ditmars was now responsible for the two animal groups of most fascination to the public. Furthermore, noted Bridges, he had the propensity to deliver a good quote. "I had acquired a nose for news myself," the curator once wrote, referring to his stint as a reporter, adding that "a small clan of newspaper men came to depend upon the park for 'special stuff,' and got it."

A classic example was his October 1909 announcement that a "cricket chirruporium" would be installed at the zoo. Ditmars was raising field crickets, tree crickets, "sleighbell" crickets, and locust crickets in a dozen terraria. The buzzing and chirping of the insect "opera" would make the reptile house more popular for visitors and reptiles alike while relieving "the monotonous silence of the snakes" which grated on the thirty-three-year-old curator's inspiration while writing books in his leisure hours.

An animal collection of the size and quality on offer in the Bronx would have attracted a crowd even without press coverage, but its phenomenal and enduring success was assured in large measure by the thrilling yarns and tall tales drip-fed to reporters. So frequently did the curator appear in the press that at one point during the 1920s an exasperated Hornaday quietly asked the city editor of the *New York World* "to soft-pedal on Mr. Ditmars for a little while and give us, up here, a much needed rest." The stories kept the zoo in the public imagination however with the result that visitors overran the place; for the first twenty-five years, an average of two and half million passed through the turnstiles annually. And not content merely to wait for reporters to come knocking, Ditmars would use every communication tool at his disposal to promote the zoo and its animals. The curator would pioneer an educational outreach program, decades before the term was coined.

Scientific precision seemed rarely to get in the way of a good story. I read in the *New York World* that some escaped garter snakes proceeded straight for the gathered skirts of several young women visiting the reptile house, the serpents reportedly excited by "the new spring hosiery." Ditmars was nevertheless proud of the zoo's "reputation for strict authenticity in publicity." Conceding that an "occasional item may become distorted in some of the papers through the injection of snap into the information to make lively reading," he insisted that the vast majority were "correctly stated and contain instructional points worth remembering."

Of course, Ditmars couldn't resist telling a lot of the stories himself in a succession of well-received books. The grounding in science and his spell on the *New York Times* forged a colloquial style at once precise, readable, and entertaining. As *Time* magazine put it, he "seldom foisted on his public an uninteresting word." Unsurprisingly, the New York Public Library holds a more or less complete collection of Ditmars's own books, and, with first editions fetching high sums, my visit was an opportunity to flick through some of his rarer titles.

I started with his first major work, *The Reptile Book: A Comprehensive, Popularised Work on the Structure and Habits of the Turtles, Tortoises, Crocodilians, Lizards and Snakes which Inhabit the United States and Northern Mexico.* Ditmars's narrative talents were nowhere better showcased than here. Eschewing the turgid descriptions typical of contemporary textbooks in favor of his own colorful observations made of wild and captive specimens, Ditmars shines a new light on a poorly known group of creatures. This 464-page labor of love was years in the preparation and included hundreds of photographs exposed at the zoo and developed by the author himself in the bathroom of his tiny apartment. Writing in the evenings on top of a busy day job, Ditmars credited his beloved Chicky for helping him achieve what sometimes seemed a hopeless task.

On publication in 1907, *The Reptile Book* enjoyed wide acclaim and lent its author the scientific credibility denied by his lack of formal qualifications. Raymond Ditmars was now considered alongside the other leading herpetologists of the time, and was far more prominent in the public imagination. President Theodore Roosevelt was an admirer. "In these days of nature fakers it is genuinely refreshing to come upon a book like yours," he told the thirty-one-year-old Ditmars in a letter, praising him for a volume that could be "understood by the multitude, and which yet shall be true." The reptile man was invited to drop by the White House any time. Similar volumes followed, including *Reptiles of the World* (1910), *Snakes of the World* (1931), and *Serpents of the Northeastern States* (1935), all well received, notwithstanding grumbles in some quarters over the curator's reliance on outdated scientific names. In truth, Ditmars was impatient with the requirements of taxonomy and correct nomenclature, and was often wrong-footed by a fast-moving field of scientific study. More damning were accusations that he exaggerated for effect with scientific accuracy a casualty, and a few "serious" scientists dismissed him as a mere showman.

Less vulnerable to such criticism was his sequence of autobiographical books appearing in the 1930s. Crammed into *Strange Animals I Have Known, Confessions of a Scientist, Thrills of a Naturalist's Quest, The Making of a Scientist,* and *Wild Animal World* are countless entertaining vignettes from his colorful career, which continued to delight readers long after Ditmars's death. The curator also produced, late in life, a series of children's books on natural history topics, with exuberant full-color illustrations by the Canadian artist Helene Carter.

But perhaps most intriguing of all was *The Forest of Adventure,* Ditmars's sole foray into fiction. Before leaving the library I skim-read a well-preserved copy. Published in 1933, the story tells of scientists exploring the wilds of British Guiana, in search of a mythical giant armadillo. I couldn't help smiling. Surely this was a thinly disguised portrayal of the author's own quest for the bushmaster? Along the way his protagonists encounter everything from red ants, poison frogs, and vampire bats to howler monkeys, ocelots, and basilisk lizards. Curiously, snakes are absent but the bushmaster—believed to share the armadillo's burrows—represents a constant menace.

*From Ditmars' picture showing the effect of music upon the bears*

*"Susette"—the intelligent chimpanzee which is the subject of a series of scientific moving pictures made by Prof. Ditmars and released in the Pathé Review*

*The lion listening to a serenade—another of the Ditmars motion pictures showing the effect of music on wild beasts*

Raymond Ditmars's study of animals' intelligence and their response to music, reported in *Reel and Slide* magazine, 1919.

THE force of nature that was William Temple Hornaday retired from the zoo in June 1926 after thirty years' service and was succeeded by second-in-command, Dr. W. Reid Blair. A quiet man, conservative but popular, Blair had joined as a veterinarian back in 1902 and unlike his predecessor cheerfully accepted that most people knew the place as the "Bronx Zoo." The reshuffle at last rubber-stamped Ditmars's promotion to curator of mammals as well as reptiles. Running two departments would fill the diaries of most, yet the curator found time to conduct his own brand of scientific research.

Some experiments frolicked at the margins of genetics, a discipline still in its infancy, notably a 1909 collaboration with "Japanese friends" to breed mice with artificial colors, which produced one with yellow feet and a coat of royal purple. But a fascination with the enigma of the animal mind underlay most of the research. Tirelessly seeking to demonstrate consciousness within even the most primitive of brains, Ditmars was defiantly anthropomorphic. An early study investigated the effect of color on a python's mood, concluding that yellow produced contentment while vanity was obtained by purple. "Color influences upon animals are not rare," he told the *New York Times*. "You know it has become a saying that anything disagreeable to a person is what a red rag is to a bull. With the snake you will notice there is just the opposite effect and it is red that gives delight while green excites to anger." Meanwhile, observation of chinchillas, guinea pigs, squirrels, and badgers convinced Ditmars that such "animals not only play real games, but that they have a sense of humor." When a rhinoceros called Victoria charged her galvanized iron fencing it signaled nothing more sinister than a desire to play. In fact, Ditmars was among many then questioning whether morality and altruism were unique to humans. The British evolutionary biologist J. B. S. Haldane, for example, subscribed to a form of animal ethics; others recognized truth-speaking and lying in animal behavior.

Much work concerned "higher" animals, especially the great apes, whose close kinship with *Homo sapiens* the curator was at pains to illustrate, often quite inventively. In 1922 he took a thumbprint from a spirited orangutan named Gabong. When shown the print, police experts confirmed that it "could not be distinguished from that of a human." In the early years, though, Ditmars would merely train the apes in circus tricks using "kindness, perseverance, and infinite patience" rather than the "long crack-whip." Such projects, he wrote, amused children and "furnished interesting psychological demonstrations of the intelligence of these apes and the facility with which they adapt themselves to manners 'aping' mankind." Rajah, another orangutan, was among the most compliant of early simian students, learning "to perform intelligently on the trapese [sic] and the horizontal bar and to obey spoken commands." Dressed in clothing, and often sitting at a table eating with cutlery, a napkin on his knee, Rajah became a star attraction. The ape enjoyed the run of Ditmars's office, even once threatening several children with an old-fashioned Colt revolver, thankfully unloaded. He was taught to ride a small tricycle, and was learning to roller skate when he succumbed to amoebic dysentery. His teacher was with Rajah at the end; moments before his passing, the orangutan allegedly "caught Mr. Ditmars by the sleeve of his coat, gave one groan and dropped back dead."

This early tragedy did little to dampen Ditmars's curiosity in primate intelligence, and principally the conviction that gorillas, orangutans, and chimpanzees had their own language. In this, he found a kindred spirit in the anthropologist Richard Lynch Garner. A former schoolteacher and Confederate soldier, Garner gained notoriety in the 1890s for living among wild primates in the French Congo protected only by portable steel-mesh enclosure of his own design. After "one hundred and twelve days and nights" spent in the cage along with extensive studies of captive animals, he professed to have discovered ten words of chimpanzee speech. It was possibly at the Central Park menagerie that Ditmars first encountered Garner. The scientist once spent a winter regularly visiting the menagerie in order to get to know the monkeys. "I have the vanity to believe that I was always a welcome guest," he wrote. "We found much pleasure in each other's society."

Garner came in for ridicule but Ditmars was unstinting in his support, confident the "studies were of a serious and interesting nature." When not studying primates in Africa, Garner's "favorite laboratory" became the monkey house at the Bronx Zoo. In August 1914 he famously brought to the zoo a female baby gorilla called Dinah. Just two representatives of the species had before reached America, both perishing within days. Dinah, a vigorous specimen hailing from "the Fernan Vaz district, French Congo" seemed a better prospect, but soon weakened, losing the use of her arms. Despite the strict application of a fresh air treatment involving wheeling the ape around the park in a small carriage for two hours daily, Dinah lasted less than twelve months.

Four years earlier Garner declared he had trained a chimpanzee called Susie to laugh. Ostensibly to prove the assertion he brought the ape by taxicab to the zoo where, before Ditmars and assembled journalists, set about tickling her under the arms. "But Susie only grinned," reported the *New York Times*. The scientist is said then to have poked his chimp in the ribs with a borrowed walking stick causing her to chatter "indignantly" and hiss. "Ah, you heard it," Garner supposedly exclaimed to the skeptical onlookers. "Many medical men have said that it is without doubt a laugh just as a human laugh." The true reason for Susie's visit was rather more mundane: a lecture tour with the ape was proving unsuccessful and Garner needed somewhere to dump her.

Ditmars nevertheless recognized Susie's intelligence and, like Garner, saw inchoate language abilities noticing that she "moves her lips for several seconds when spoken to." Using an "old style phonograph with a cylinder" the curator later produced wax recordings of "monkey talk." One was made with a "battle-scarred" Javanese macaque purchased from a sailor. Unsuitable as a zoo exhibit, the one-eyed monkey with a mutilated hand was brought home as a pet for Beatrice and Gladyce.

"I fixed up a paper horn larger than the normal one and then set out to record the macaque's vocabulary. With the exercise of patience and the assistance of my daughters I succeeded," the curator told the *New York Tribune* in 1920 shortly after Garner's death. He and the professor had played the noises back to the monkeys with remarkable results. "One little Javanese macaque dove straight into a horn in answer to his own voice," asserted Ditmars. "We obtained some reactions which seemed quite positive in separating sounds indicating curiosity, warning and fear."

The reaction of animals to sound had in fact been an enduring line of research for Ditmars, probably kicked off by his interest in snake charmers. The antics of Rattlesnake Jack Sonwell aside, the oriental charmers were of greatest fascination. In 1909 Ditmars obtained from Singapore phonographic records of the music made by "Hindoo snake charmers," which allegedly caused serpents in the reptile house to sway, entering "a hypnotic state." Another time Ditmars invited the poet Edgar Lee Masters to observe snakes under the influence of classical music. As the piece concluded, one serpent "lifted its body until its length was stretched upwards toward the top of its cage." Masters went off and penned a lengthy ode entitled "Beethoven's Ninth Symphony and the King Cobra." Given that snakes are more or less deaf, such stories don't ring true, and Ditmars himself wrote elsewhere that snakes exhibited no interest of any kind in music.

How seriously he took these investigations, far removed from his pioneering work with snake venoms, is debatable, but they made wonderful newspaper copy and publicized the zoo. Incidentally, Ditmars was often addressed as "Doctor," a mistake he grew so tired of correcting that in the mid-1920s he asked well-placed academic friends how he might legitimately receive the title without undertaking an university course. To his undoubted satisfaction, the accolade was at last conferred upon him in spring 1930 by Tennessee's Lincoln Memorial University. Perhaps tellingly, the fifty-three-year-old became a Doctor "of Letters," not "Science."

WITH its pitched roof and Victorian Gothic architecture, the Trinity Episcopal Church of Morrisania is an attractive albeit modest redbrick structure in the southern Bronx. Nestled on an elevated patch of ground among trees and shrubs in the shadows of the great castellated tower of the old Morris High School opposite, the casual passerby would be forgiven for scarcely noticing the place. But on the evening of Thursday, September 21, 1905, a minor miracle occurred here warranting a write-up in several city newspapers. 15 SNAKES BECAME 55 was how the *New York Times* put it, while *New York Daily Tribune* expanded with FORTY LITTLE SERPENTS COME FROM BAG WHERE ONE WAS SUPPOSED TO BE.

The event prompting such excitement was less sensational than the headlines suggested. The church's hall was hosting an event somewhat distinct from the usual christenings, marriages, and funerals. It was a talk entitled "Snakes and Their Habits" and the speaker was Raymond Ditmars. In the course of the lecture before a large audience, made up chiefly of women, the curator and Charles Snyder were drawing serpents from a series of canvas bags when one sack began "to wiggle about in a most astonishing manner." A stream of snakelets soon issued from the bag encouraging a general rush of ladies for the exit. "There's forty of 'em!" announced Snyder after counting the tiny reptiles. During the short journey from the zoo a watersnake had given birth. Ditmars's semi-serious proposal to distribute the offspring among his audience as "souvenirs" did little to calm the situation.

Such incidents boosted the curator's reputation as an unmissable public speaker. The initial faltering attempts at lecturing at the American Museum of Natural History were long forgotten; Ditmars had matured into an accomplished and engaging orator. "In my early twenties the prospect of facing an audience made me pretty nervous," he once wrote. "By the time I was thirty I was addressing a thousand or more people with no feeling of stage fright. This sense of confidence as well as a feeling of pleasure in lecturing comes, I think, from care in arranging illustrative material and a sympathetic knowledge of my subjects."

By the 1930s he had signed up to the exclusive Lee Keedick Lecture Bureau, counting H. G. Wells, G. K. Chesterton, Egyptologist Howard Carter, and Arthur Conan Doyle among fellow celebrity speakers. He once estimated that he had lectured to a combined audience of half a million encompassing all ages, genders, social classes, and educational abilities.

Over the years, his lectures developed as well. At first Ditmars would talk through a series of photographic slides projected via a stereopticon. Popularly known as a magic lantern, this was the nineteenth-century version of a PowerPoint presentation and just as uninspiring. Ditmars wanted to entertain as well as to enlighten and soon enriched lectures with live specimens. As a museum assistant and then journalist he had showed snakes from his own collection, but his appointment to the Bronx Zoo furnished him with an Aladdin's cave of animal treasures to exhibit. Transportation became the sole restriction, solved with the acquisition of a seven-passenger touring car that Ditmars and the ever-faithful Snyder crammed with specimen boxes, spotlights, projection equipment, and folding tables. The mobile menagerie then visited schools, church halls, boy's clubs, prisons, museums, hospitals, and hotels across the city and far beyond.

Talks were largely devoted to scotching erroneous beliefs about snakes, of which there were many. These included the idea that serpents didn't die until sunset; that mother snakes swallowed their young to protect them; that serpents drank milk from cows' udders; that they were slimy; that venomous snakes traveled in pairs; that they stung with their tongues or their tails; that they stung at all when in fact they bite. Then there were the imaginary ophidians: the giant sea serpent; the hoop snake that, tail in mouth, formed a wheel and rolled after you; and the glass snake that shattered when struck only to reassemble itself, this latter myth probably based on legless lizards that will drop their tails when threatened.

Ditmars believed that fact was at least as thrilling as fiction, and enjoyed demonstrating the bizarre and wonderful realities of nature as much as puncturing timeworn myths. Thus, those attending his talks during the first decade of the twentieth century could expect to see snakes swallowing duck's eggs wider than their own body, kangaroo rats jumping hurdles taller than a man, Hercules beetles carrying weights fifty times their own, "waltzing" mice chasing themselves in circles. Ditmars would bring along mammals, insects, spiders, even sea creatures in tanks, but snakes were his first love and remained the core of his lectures. He emphasized the positive in serpents, above all their role in eradicating rodent pests and offered tips on recognizing the few venomous varieties, and, if the worst should happen, how best to treat bites.

Bringing live animals had its risks, however. "I tried taking a few real monkeys to lectures, but after several disastrous experiences gave it up," recalled Ditmars years later, perhaps referring to the time a Brazilian monkey had mingled with the dining audience. The primate partook of several "social glasses" of alcohol, impairing the subsequent performance. "His stumbling utterances and grimaces put him straightaway out of the dignity list," as a reporter had put it.

"Snakes, carried in separate cloth bags which were transported in a suitcase, were practical illustrations if nobody in the audience fainted," went on Ditmars. "However, it got so that whenever I carried a suitcase, even for a week-end party, people would shy away from me."

Fortunately, a new communication medium was emerging which would solve this problem. A medium which would bring hitherto unimaginable aspects of animal behavior to mass audiences in dazzling ways. A medium over which Raymond Ditmars would quickly prove his mastery.

# 11

# The Stage of Nature

*"There is much humor, pathos and tragedy in nature that would fill a vast book that has not yet been written. It was upon this field of wild life that I determined to point the moving picture camera and show animals as they actually live, play and die."*

—Raymond L. Ditmars, *Washington Post*, November 29, 1914

⊰•⊱

*Spring 1913. Scarsdale, in the suburbs of New York City*

A CURIOUS GREENISH LIGHT suffuses the silent nocturnal landscape. Angular shadows are cast across gritty soil, piles of rock, bristly foliage. A fer-de-lance crawls into view, creamy diamond markings running the length of its body. Raising its head, the viper flicks out a long forked tongue in the windless air before probing at the substrate with a pointed snout. Content that nothing is amiss, the reptile draws into a loose coil, resting a yellow chin on a velvety flank. Inky black catlike pupils glimmer in the eerie luminescence.

A raucous mechanical whirring intrudes upon the scene. Though deaf to the racket the snake somehow feels the disturbance, perhaps detecting subtle changes in the ambient temperature with the paired heat-sensitive pits in its face. Puffing up, the fer-de-lance pounds its tail tip against the ground, producing an angry buzz, perhaps as a warning to any aggressor lurking in the gloom. The message seeming to go unheeded, the snake now unravels and advances on the source of the annoyance.

"Watch out, this fellow wants to strike," hisses Ray, a disembodied voice in the shadows.

The viper contorts into an S-shaped loop and without further warning launches itself into the blackness with the vehemence and precision of a steel spring. There comes a shrill cry. The scraping of furniture. The clatter of metal.

"Chicky!" Ray cries, lurching into a tripod stand. The mercury-vapor lamp explodes on contact with the floor, plunging the film studio into complete darkness and releasing a cloud of acrid fumes. His wife screams again.

"*Andy!*" roars the curator. "For *God's sake*. House lights! *Now!*"

The electrician throws a switch to illuminate the fer-de-lance thrashing at the base of the motion picture camera that, moments before, Ray's wife had been operating. Clara hopped back in time but is still in peril having fallen uncomfortably into a small tower of film canisters. Ray, perspiration stippling his high forehead, pins the viper to the floor with a forked stick before it can pounce again.

"Don't worry," laughs Clara struggling to her feet. "It missed!"

"This is getting to be something of a habit for you, ain't it, Mrs. Ditmars?" says Andy, standing by a circuit board. He is a slight young man with freckles and spiky hair. Like the others, he wears rubber boots as a precaution against the powerful twenty-thousand-candlepower electric lighting system. Andy is referring to an almost identical episode a few months back when filming a ring-necked cobra, a devilish species famed for spitting venom. The hooded serpent, double the length of the fer-de-lance, had also flown at Clara, although that time she had provoked the attack by shaking her handkerchief at the snake hoping it would rear and pose.

"The glassy stare of that snake is positively uncanny," she had said. "How wonderful it would be if the camera could look him straight in the eye and picture him as I see him now!"

Chaos had reigned that time as well, Clara jumping onto the housing of an electric coil as the cobra darted under her feet, Ray diving after the snake, Andy racing in horror for the studio door. The resulting footage in which the cobra lunges at the screen into the laps of the audience will however make for one of the more astonishing scenes in the *Book of Nature*.

The goal of tonight's activities has been less ambitious, merely a depiction of the moonlit prowling of the fer-de-lance among the sugar cane plantations of tropical America. But once again the star got spooked.

"Hmmm, this is promising." Ray inspects the camera, having returned the snake to a cage. "Looks like we might have caught the strike again. Of course we won't know till we get the film processed."

With a sigh, he turns to Andy.

"I say we call it a night. It's past twelve and I've a long day at the park tomorrow."

"Sure Doc," nods the electrician, a cigarette now between his lips. "I'll turn off the stove." When running cameras, a copper pan of water is kept simmering to prevent electric sparks that risk marking the sensitive film.

Clara follows Andy, leaving her husband alone in the studio. In the uncompromising glare of the house lights Ray now notices just how cluttered the movie laboratory has become. Everywhere are cameras, projectors, lights, tripods, transformers, motors, lenses, and microscopes. All available surfaces including his ten-foot writing table have been commandeered. Even the floor is a sea of electric cables. Shelves meanwhile creak under the weight of jars and tanks. Most are empty, but in one a pair of tree toads can be seen climbing the glass by adhesive finger disks, in another a black-and-red tarantula rests on a wedge of bark.

The fer-de-lance diorama constructed upon a small movable stage is among several motion picture studies under way. In a different corner of the room a camera is trained on a gelatinous orb of frog spawn suspended in a Bohemian glass jar. Every day without fail Ray has cranked on the film a few extra feet, the aim being to compress two months' worth of metamorphosis—from eggs through tadpoles to froglets—into a minute of screen time. He achieved a similar time-lapse effect with a silken ball of wolf spider eggs carried on their mother's back. Thanks to the close-up lenses he uses, the tiniest animals will be revealed as never before. When the pictures are projected during the talks, he's confident the audience will marvel at the scales of a watersnake shimmering like burnished metal, a lumbering garden mole magnified to the size of a grizzly bear, the nocturnal stridulations of a katydid resplendent in the beam of a two-thousand-candlepower searchlight.

Of course, rarely does a scene work the first time and many successes were preceded by expensive failure. He has lost count of how often a strenuous session ended in one disaster or another. At least tonight's close call promises something usable. Ray reaches for a broom to clear the fragments of shattered mercury light bulb, but with a chuckle thinks better of it. Housekeeping can wait, time for bed.

It was ten in the morning and sunny. Having breakfasted courtesy of a roadside deli called the Stars Bagel & Café, we resumed our journey, my friend Sharyn at the wheel of her ageing black Volvo. Within minutes we were pulling up again. Low-rise, modern, and beige-bricked, the Westchester County Archives & Records Center was sited fifteen miles north of the Bronx Zoo. The building housed public records dating back to 1680 in environmentally controlled vaults, documenting the development of Westchester from farming community to suburbia. The county's historical society was located here too and boasted a wealth of printed material. This boded well for my continuing research into Raymond

Ditmars because by his mid-thirties he was prosperous enough to move his family to a good-sized property in the heart of Westchester. While his new address on Post Road was officially in the town of Eastchester, the Ditmarses considered themselves residents of the more genteel Scarsdale, whose village line lay just to the north.

A female archivist led me through to the spacious reading room, empty apart for some card index cabinets and half a dozen desks. The historical records themselves were stored behind the scenes.

"Now tell me again, who exactly are you interested in?"

"Raymond Ditmars, curator at the Bronx Zoo," I replied. "I can give you his address. He lived in Westchester from about 1913 until his death."

To my surprise, the archivist casually mentioned that Ditmars's will and related documents would be available on site.

A few minutes later I was handed a thin manila file marked "1942," the year of Ditmars's death. The documents within valued the deceased curator's estate at "approximately $30,000." I flicked through an inventory of photographic materials, items such as "2 Kodalite stands," a "Home made phonograph and speaker," a "Simplex projector, approximately 30 years old," along with lights, lenses, and five kinds of motion picture camera. These tools of the lecturing and filming trade were valued at a just $200.

More poignant still were the fruits of his labors: "Approximately 270 cans containing negative and positive rolls of film of various lengths, probably 300,000 feet of film in all." The material, equivalent to 150 hours of viewing, was described as "Natural History and animal studies by the deceased, for illustration of lectures and writings." Noting that once edited and cleaned, a small amount "may turn out to be useable and perhaps also saleable," the appraiser Isaac Sobel believed it could fetch $5,000. Given that Ditmars's nature films were among the first of their kind, the estimate seemed low. But this was an academic point for, as I would soon discover, almost none of the curator's footage had survived.

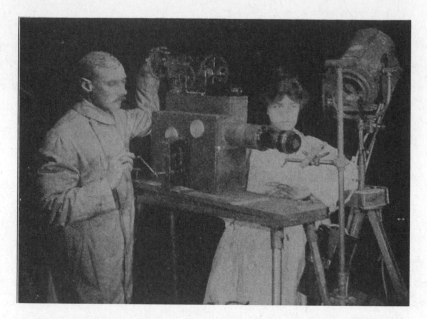

Raymond and Clara Ditmars at work in their film "laboratory," Scarsdale,
New York, reported in *Photoplay* magazine, 1919.

"IF he lived in England he could not escape a decoration or other royal
reward for being the father of kinematographic zoology." Perhaps such
accolades are best reserved for the end of a beneficiary's career but this
pronouncement was made in February 1914, some months prior to the
completion of Raymond Ditmars's first significant motion picture. Its
author was W. Stephen Bush, a fellow filmmaker and writer for the New
York–based trade journal *Moving Picture World*. Bush had just taken a trip
to the curator's studio at Scarsdale in "the wilds of Westchester County"
where Ditmars had wowed him with projected images of a katydid in an
oak tree singing by night, a cobra rearing up and striking at the camera,
a mother wolf spider laboring under her great egg ball that—thanks to a
judicious poke from a blade of straw—spews forth three hundred spid-
erlings. To the modern viewer such sequences would appear mundane,
crude even, but for Bush, Ditmars's achievements were "truly Napole-
onic" and evinced "a vast tenacity of purpose, a comprehensive grasp of

facts, an unswerving devotion to useful work and a fund of vitality which will last for a good deal more than a full score of years."

Ditmars had begun filming the zoo collections in about 1908, perhaps catching the movie bug three years before while assisting the Brooklyn-based Vitagraph Company in shooting a twenty-minute motion picture in the park. The scenes, including *Feeding the Sea Lions*, *Polar Bears at Play*, and *Apes Playing and Walking*, appeared at the society's annual meeting, as well as sixty-seven theaters across America. A skeptical William Hornaday had commissioned the motion pictures after being leaned on by Madison Grant who understood their publicity value. Given that Hornaday paid Vitagraph $340 for the work and apparently saw no interest in retaining the rights to the footage, it wasn't the smartest deal he had ever cut. Ditmars nevertheless relished the experience and with the forbearance of his boss resolved to produce a comprehensive series of motion picture reels for teaching natural history. As a newspaper later reported, Ditmars harbored "a grandiose design of presenting the entire range of life, from the insect up to the man on the screen."

He had already proved himself an accomplished photographer, responsible for most of the pictures in his books. Such skills were transferable to the production of moving images. Handling electricity—"the juice"—was a knowledge gap Ditmars filled by spending a vacation amid "the maze of switchboards and controls backstage in the New York Hippodrome," then the city's newest and grandest theater. Initially he shot subjects on a small makeshift stage in the reptile house, then constructed a studio at his new home in Scarsdale where he could create realistic backdrops and manipulate the lighting. With many of his actors performing best at night this allowed Ditmars to "tumble into bed after strenuous sessions" as he afterward put it.

Although the curator filmed such charismatic species as elephants, polar bears, or musk oxen, it was inevitable that he would also train the camera on reptiles, amphibians, and invertebrates given his instinctive sympathy for the lowly. This preference set apart the zoo man's work from that of his contemporaries. Creepy-crawlies demanded innovative filming techniques, too. Ditmars was not the first to use time-lapse photography to apparently speed up natural processes such as the development of frogs' eggs, or macro lenses to extract close-up detail from intimate subjects — the techniques had been pioneered several years before by the British naturalists F. Martin Duncan and F. Percy Smith. But he was the leading exponent on his side of the Atlantic.

Mastering sophisticated photographic techniques was just part of the challenge in natural history filmmaking. The animals must also perform. Getting a lizard, spider, or ocelot to enter stage left can be extraordinarily difficult. An expensive one too, with celluloid flying through the camera at speeds upwards of sixteen frames per second. An instinct for animal motivations and behavioral eccentricities was fundamental and again, Ditmars had this in spades. Surprisingly, he once pronounced the snake as "probably the least intelligent animal that I have ever trained," but even it could be encouraged "to do what you would like it to do." Tactics included shining strong lights or waving semaphores, although he once admitted that the "promptings of a hungry stomach were found to be the most effective in the stage management of this theatre of nature and many pictures were made at the period of feeding time."

In September 1913 tantalizing excerpts started finding their way onto Pathé newsreels shown at movie theaters: acrobatic tree toads balancing on a twisting string, lizards scurrying about their habitats, close-ups of insects mimicking leaves or sticks. Three months later the curator himself appeared at the American Museum of Natural History to talk through what the *Sun* newspaper called "the most enthusiastically received movie show that New York perhaps has seen." Dazzled by scenes of a king snake swallowing a rat, a hedgehog subduing a venomous spider, and the burrowing activities of a mole, the audience mobbed Ditmars, imploring him "to give the pictures before school and college audiences." But so occupied was the man of the moment with "making the pictures of snakes and mammals and insects and things" that he was yet "to perfect details concerning the showing of the movies." Andrew Carnegie was also offered a sneak preview of the material at his house. So astounded was the tycoon that he contributed $100,000 toward the New York Zoological Society's pension fund.

From the start Ditmars saw his films as an enhancement to lectures, an improvement on the lifeless stereopticon slides, and far better behaved than live specimens. The early movies were not planned as a medium in their own right, and when the "lights went out and the pictures flashed on the screen" the curator was on hand to provide viewers with a running commentary. An obituarist praised Ditmars's performance: "with arduous preparation he so synchronized pictorial matter with the spoken word that his lectures were perfected expressions of information and artistry." Thus, the completion of a picture reel marked only the end of the first phase of a process that saw the curator accompanying the fruits of his labor from venue to venue.

Another drawback of this flirtation with cellulose nitrate was financial; the mounting cost of cameras, lenses, film stock, lighting, editing, and processing exceeded Ditmars's modest salary. Although extra cash trickled in from lectures and writings, he needed more, and later approached prominent figures in the fledgling movie industry hoping to sell them some footage, figures like studio boss Ira Lowry of Philadelphia's Lubin Manufacturing Company and Harold Edel who managed The Strand in New York, among the country's first dedicated movie theaters. Ditmars's lofty scientific ideals now got a bruising. In cinema's formative years short educational films had found a place in theater programs, but scenes of hunting spiders, lumbering tortoises, or chameleons snaring flies with their long sticky tongues were no longer judged commercial. Modern audiences wanted pure entertainment. Where was the love interest? The comedy? The moguls suggested rearrangements and slangy title cards, which, for Ditmars, was unthinkable.

That the zoo man didn't at this point throw in the towel could be credited to his chirpy young assistant, a stage electrician identified only as "Andy," who lacked any scientific scruples. "You've got some swell stuff, but the guys who run the theatres want to hear some laughs from the audience," as Ditmars once paraphrased him. "If you'd hook up some stuff to get a laugh, and shoot in some snappy titles, you'd sell the film — if you gave those guys a chance to make a few changes — just to satisfy them."

The worldly electrician was pushing at an open door. The zoo man's reticence was belied by a sense of fun lurking just below the surface. With Andy's help Ditmars reshuffled a portion of the existing material into an imaginative sequence signposted by title cards and requiring minimal additional shooting. The show starts with seven toads of varying sizes materializing atop white plaster-cast toadstools. (Ditmars took the expedient of first chilling the amphibians in a refrigerator for fifteen minutes, which worked wonders with the cold-blooded animals.) Joining the "audience" are a trapdoor spider, a cock-eyed chameleon, and a rhinoceros beetle which wafts its forelegs in the air. *The beetle beckons to friends — "Come over on this side,"* — the title explains.

Thus begins "The Jungle Circus," scenes of which were borrowed from Ditmars's live stage shows: lemurs springing off trees, jerboas clearing hurdles, whirling Japanese mice, monkeys as trapeze performers. The two most memorable scenes are also the most contrived. In *Graceful Evolutions of the Diving Frog*, the said amphibian teeters on a miniature diving board, folding and unfolding arms and wriggling toes before belly-flopping into a pond. The stilted movements were achieved with rudimentary stop-motion techniques and are as graceful as an animated corpse can be. *The Common Fly as Juggler* was more outlandish still, an inverted housefly manipulating tiny dumbbells with its feet while stuck by the wings to a chair, the latter supported on the carapace of a dung beetle. Here, Ditmars may have been inspired by F. Percy Smith, who in 1911 had produced *The Strength and Agility of Insects* featuring weight-lifting insects; likewise, a Russian professor named Loyshki had been training and filming beetles for decades. Although Ditmars had witnessed in England the juggling fly stunt "for the amusement of a group of children," he denied seeing it "reproduced, close-up, on motion picture film." Whatever the truth, the curator took such concepts to their illogical conclusion. The circus is adjourned by the appearance of a skunk that scatters the audience—although in another version, the party is spoiled by the leering head of a giant salamander. The movie producers loved it, making "but slight projecting room suggestions."

After three long years of painstaking, frustrating, and expensive work, Ditmars at last felt able to exhibit in its entirety the six-reel masterpiece he called *The Book of Nature*. His choice of title followed in the tradition of early philosopher scientists for whom Nature, much like the Bible, was a book to be observed and interrogated. A private showing under the auspices of the Brooklyn Institute of Arts and Sciences took place on October 22, 1914, in the Mecca Building on Broadway. The production was aired publicly the following week with afternoon and evening performances at the Brooklyn Academy of Music. Tickets were priced from 25 to 75 cents, and a percentage of the receipts directed toward the purchase of animals for Brooklyn's own menagerie at Prospect Park. The show moved to Philadelphia whose *Evening Ledger* described the film as the "most remarkable moving pictures of animal life ever shown" and "highly instructive," while the curator's accompanying commentary was deemed "illuminative and quaintly humorous, giving to the exhibition a decidedly popular appeal."

Notwithstanding the surreal frolics of "The Jungle Circus," which came at the end of *The Book of Nature*, Ditmars continued to assert the scientific rigor of his production. Writing in December 1914 he denied that the film, then starting a two-week run at Wallack's Theatre back in New York city, was a "movie show" or "a series of sensational spectacles." Rather, it was "a scientific task" and, as with his lectures, conveyed true animal behavior. "The stage of Nature is vast and replete with humor and tragedy that attend the struggles for life," he went on, "and the story told upon the screen in no way departs from a truthful portrayal of normal existence in the wilds." A contention perhaps hard to reconcile with the juggling flies and chilled toads.

"GET *back!*" growled the husky man in shorts at the German shepherd that, slobbering and wheezing, was contriving a route between the bare legs of its master. Losing patience, the sixty-odd-year-old grabbed the animal by the collar and dragged it into house. The man closed the front door behind him and stepped toward us both. A gleaming black Chevrolet 4x4 dominated the driveway.

"OK, now what was it again you wanted?"

There'd been a lot of things I had wanted to do at the place Ditmars had called home for half his adult life. I would loved to have searched the attic for a long-lost diary or stray reel of motion picture footage, to have scoured the outbuildings for vestiges of the famous movie laboratory, even just to have paused in the hallway in the deluded hope of communing with his ghost. Now, standing here on the doorstep of the large magnolia-colored house in a sunny corner of the Westchester suburbs, such longings were revealed as the absurdities they were. Did I seriously think the present occupant would have cared about a long-forgotten zoo official, let alone permit a total stranger to poke about in his house?

"My British friend here is researching a book about someone who used to live at this house," persisted Sharyn, fearless as ever. It was her idea to show up at the address rather than call in advance. "He was called Raymond Ditmars and worked at the Bronx Zoo. Have you heard of him?"

"Sure," came the guarded reply.

Things were looking up. It was time I said something.

"Did you know that he used to make natural history films in a studio at this property? Probably there." I pointed at an outbuilding adorned with boxwood topiaries.

"No, but I think the guy who lived here before me was a photographer."

A stilted conversation was thus begun. The current owner had acquired the property in the 1980s. By then the precious contents of Ditmars's studio were long gone, the space converted to a residential unit.

"I heard that there used to be cages there where he kept his snakes," he went on, indicating a concrete slab in his front yard, close to the former movie laboratory. "And when I moved in there were a whole bunch of metal sinks lying about. Not sure if they were from Ditmars, or the photographer."

There was no question of being let into the house, but a stroll about the perimeter denoted by mature red oaks was sanctioned, as was the taking of photos from the outside. Neither added much to what was already available on Google Street View and two minutes later I was done.

As we were getting back into Sharyn's Volvo, the man rushed over.

"There was something else," he said. "An old lady in the neighborhood once told me that when she was a girl she was scared to walk past."

"Oh yes?" This was interesting.

"Everyone said that this was the snake-man's house," he said with a half-grin.

THE *Book of Nature* was a phenomenon, showing for a record-breaking thirty-seven weeks at the Strand Theater on Broadway. With the proceeds Ditmars improved his studio and added chapters—Charles Snyder sometimes contributing ideas—so that by the early 1920s the production, renamed *Living Natural History*, ran to forty-two reels embracing mammals, birds, amphibians, insects, spiders, and marine life. The serial was distributed across the country and beyond. In 1925 he sold a complete set to the New York Zoological Society for $3,500. Ditmars also donated to the American Museum of Natural History a "motion picture reel showing the anthropoids and collection of wild equines in the Zoological Park." In return he was elected a Life Member of the institution.

Ditmars worked the material into other productions such as *Modern Truths from Old Fables*, a 1921 series of shorts distributed by Charles

Urban, a British film producer. The fables were based on stories by the seventeenth-century French poet Jean de La Fontaine and included *The Hare and the Tortoise, The Evil of Gossip,* and *The Bird Wounded by an Arrow.* La Fontaine's works had first been recommended to Ditmars by Theodore Rooscvelt during a visit to the ex-president's Long Island home. Additional stop-motion photography was needed, by whose magic a katy-did powdered her nose with pollen and a line of frogs shuffled on hind legs in true Charlie Chaplin style. *Modern Truths from Old Fables* was another minor triumph, the *New York Tribune* reporting that the animals "portray humor and tragedy, they mimic and originate and they apparently have all the resourcefulness of $1,000 a week stars. After seeing them one is minded to say that Mr. Ditmars is a great director."

The curator's agreement with Urban also encompassed *The Four Seasons,* documenting the influence of spring, summer, autumn, and winter on wildlife, a formula since adopted by countless nature programs. Premiering alongside other Paramount releases at the Rialto Theatre on September 25, 1921, the film was a hit and ran for weeks. The forty-five-year-old Ditmars grew hoarse with the lecturing. Critics praised *The Four Seasons* as "one of the worthwhile works of the year," extolling the acting of the frogs as "truly remarkable." The film was shown with titles coast-to-coast, in many theaters forming a double bill with Harold Lloyd's first feature, *A Sailor Made Man.*

More ambitious still was 1922's *Evolution,* based on a lecture Ditmars had given for several years telling the story of life "from the birth of planets to the age of man." For one reviewer, the highlight was a dinosaur which "ambled across a plain, reared his ninety-foot bulk up a cliff and chewed off a few pine trees." Some supposed the prehistoric giant to be an alligator with spikes glued to its back; in fact Ditmars knew that a rhinoceros iguana, when shot against miniature backgrounds and tiny trees, could do the job without a lengthy spell in make-up. Perhaps more mischievous was the curator's choice of venue for the first airing of a film about evolution, All Angels' Episcopal Church on Manhattan's Upper

West Side. The film was re-released in June 1925 to coincide with, and capitalize on, the hullabaloo over the Scopes Trial, in which a Tennessee high school teacher was accused of teaching human evolution in violation of state law. The film composer Hugo Riesenfeld, in whose Rivoli Theatre the re-edited *Evolution* was shown, denied he was taking sides in the controversy: "I am only presenting it as I would any other film at a time when I believe persons reading the newspapers will be especially interested in the subject."

The New York Zoological Society loved Ditmars's films, which helped promote the zoo, and they often formed the star attraction at lavish annual meetings. A 1924 *New York Times* article reported that the motion pictures made by Ditmars and his zoo colleagues were now "shown all over the world and it is impossible to estimate how many millions of people see each year the films prepared from the [Society's] collections."

"YOU'RE getting a tour of all our machines today," Dorinda said, reverently threading the film about various sprockets. The viewing table was reserved for the more delicate material. Dorinda was a technician in the Motion Picture Reading Room at the Library of Congress in Washington, DC, and had seen hundreds of archive films. She nevertheless shared my excitement at the prospect of watching and hearing for the first time Raymond Ditmars introduce one of his talkies. Of the few motion pictures that had survived, most were in poor condition, and this print was no exception, hence the need for apparatus which would be gentler to the film.

I had viewed other short movies over the previous hours. As well as a 1917 version of the *Jungle Circus*—renamed *Jungle Vaudeville*—I had seen studies of the silk worm moth whose wing markings resembled mournful human eyes, underwater tube worms releasing acid to defend themselves, monitor lizards eating eggs. In one film an orangutan sat in a metal bucket before wearing it as a hat: *"Like naughty children the young orangs delight to play in the dirt."* In another, an emu was straddled by a portly zookeeper who pulled out one of the flightless bird's stumpy wings for the camera. Each picture was short, not much longer than two minutes in duration, and most ended abruptly. They felt distant and alien, an impression compounded by their silence, albeit drowned by the clattering spools. The title cards at least captured some of the filmmaker's character, veering between didactic and populist, but I suspected his voice was needed to breathe life into the pictures.

Two days earlier had seen me leaving New York City for good, catching the Northeast Regional Amtrak to DC. As the train emerged from the Hudson Tunnel into a sunlit New Jersey, the pale blue outline of Manhattan could be glimpsed through the smudged window. The Empire State and Chrysler buildings were recognizable, as well as the partially built monolith of One World Trade Center, topped by antennae-like cranes.

A trip to Washington made sense. This was the best place to see what little remained of Ditmars's motion picture output while the city's Smithsonian Institution held specimens donated by the curator a century ago, as well as an assortment of preserved bushmasters, although none associated with Ditmars. Traffic permitting, a comfortable morning's drive would have been enough to cover the two hundred and forty miles separating New York City from the capital. Flying there was easier still. Pricewise, there wasn't much in it.

But neither speed nor cost had influenced my choice of transportation mode; in taking the train I was revisiting Ditmars's most notorious exploit. The story begins in July 1930 when the curator took delivery of two huge king cobras from the Far East. One of these was intended for a new reptile house, then under construction, at the National Zoo in Washington. The importer was none other than the Bartels company, the same Bartels company whose snakes had caused Ditmars and his assistant Charles Snyder so much trouble back in 1900. By now the firm was operating out of Jersey City and the transfer of animals to the Bronx was more dignified than the chaotic episode in Greenwich Village. One cobra, a thirteen-footer, came by express mail. The other, longer and perhaps livelier, Ditmars fetched himself by car, "keeping well within the speed limit," as one newspaper noted.

The difficulties really began the following March. With building now complete at the National Zoo, the time had come to install the star exhibit—the larger of the two cobras lodging in the Bronx. Mailing the snake was risky in the cold winter months so Ditmars decided to escort it to the capital himself aboard an overnight train. This would also give him a chance to exhibit to his Washington colleagues a new five-reel motion picture he had produced. The fourteen-foot cobra was bagged and locked into a sturdy traveling case, from which the curator was certain the snake would not escape; he later insisted that the satchel "had traveled thousands of miles," "withstood the rough treatment of baggage slings, been shot down slides, and banged by luggage smashers of at least six nations."

The train proving colder than expected, Ditmars felt obliged to share his Pullman berth with the warmth-loving snake. The journey was otherwise uneventful, curator and cobra reaching Washington the following morning with fellow passengers none the wiser. All would have been well had Ditmars not divulged his secret during the film-lecture. Newspapers from coast to coast picked up the story and, true to form, embroidered it. "A stout gentleman in an upper berth bound to Washington from Manhattan last week was annoyed by what he thought were sizzling snores from the lower berth," said *Time* magazine, envisioning the "kindhearted snakeman of the Bronx Zoo" asleep below with his feet "resting on the leather traveling bag in which was a 14ft. king cobra." The chilled snake was "sizzling happily like a peanut stand, grateful for the warmth of the Ditmars feet." The incident even inspired verse: "The cobra is a funny snake. / He likes to travel far. / He's happiest when riding in / A Pullman sleeping car," went one well-syndicated poem.

The *New York Times* was less amused: "What if the train had been wrecked, the Pullman telescoped, the bag burst open and the snake turned loose among the passengers, all helpless in their pajamas? We may be prejudiced, but we feel, personally, that a Pullman car is no place for a king cobra." The New York Zoological Society was also dismayed, one member resigning in protest, while the rail company reprimanded Ditmars for violating railroad rules and ethics, exposing passengers and crew to danger, and shocking the traveling public. Ditmars bridled, pointing out that the cobra was an exemplary passenger which "slept silently, rustled no newspapers after hours, didn't explosively cough in a crowded washroom, or splatter the mirrors with a toothbrush."

As we rolled by industrial Trenton, over the Delaware, and on past the gleaming steel and glass of downtown Philadelphia I tried to picture Ditmars taking the same trip seventy years before, a deadly snake secreted in his luggage. But something about the functional carriage fittings, the quiet patter of laptops, and the cell phone conversations thwarted such imaginings.

Now, in the dim viewing room at the Library of Congress, I thought once again of the cobra, for this was the subject of *Killing the Killer,* a talkie produced in 1930. The reels spun and Ditmars appeared on the screen, standing in a richly appointed chamber, all wood paneling and antique furniture. On a table before him is a row of hefty books, a candelabra, and a wicker basket. Dracula's lair. Now in his mid-fifties, the curator's elegance matches his surroundings. He sports a gray three-piece suit with white pocket square.

"It appears that I am to be referee at a combat between two strange jungle dwellers that I have known for a long time: the mongoose and the cobra!" When the voice comes, the tonality is higher than I had expected, the New York inflection obvious, but the delivery imbued with the relaxed authority that comes from years of practice.

Having discussed Rikki-Tikki-Tavi, the mongoose — "a serious menace to poultry" — Ditmars inveigles a cobra from the basket with a walking cane. The curator holds his left arm smartly behind his back, a smile playing about his mustachioed lips. He then discusses the use of snake venom for preparing antivenin, as well as the fashion possibilities of snakeskin—"Eve appears to have conquered her aggression for the serpent of late in adapting its skin for pretty things to wear and to carry"—before we were transported "to the Orient where the action properly occurs."

The cobra and mongoose set to it feinting and darting at one another. The entire film lasts eight minutes, but the duel is short, vicious, and staged. I later read that the footage of the fight itself had been shot by a German named Milton B. Kolb and released in silent form two years earlier to much acclaim. In addition to producing and hosting the talkie version of *Killing the Killer*, Ditmars recorded the cobra's "vocals" at a Long Island studio where, at some risk to himself, he goaded the hooded serpent with a stick "until it drew itself up into a fighting pose and hissed." For me it raised troubling moral questions. Even if modern documentary-makers were guilty of "helping things along a bit," these days only the most unscrupulous would purposely set one creature upon another to capture predatory behavior on film.

Rikki-Tikki-Tavi won, by the way.

DESPITE releasing many of his films with title cards, Ditmars continued to narrate untitled versions in schools, theaters and halls across the country. The work was exhausting and could be futile in the larger auditoriums where those at the back would struggle to hear his voice. It was therefore unsurprising that Ditmars would be in the vanguard of those embracing the new technology of talking pictures. In June 1927—four months before the premiere of *The Jazz Singer*, the first feature-length movie to include audible speech—the curator told the *New York Times* that accompanying the film reels with "the voice of a known authority" would bring "not only the personality of the specialist to the classroom but also the increased conviction that all the details of the lesson are authentic." In a subsequent article he highlighted the possibilities of background sounds: "the beating of native drums, the jumble of sounds from a rabble of natives, the roar of a great cataract, the swish and rustle of wind through palms, surf breaking on a beach, steamer whistles."

He was soon going from cage to cage recording the calls, roars, and chirps of the zoo animals. It wasn't always easy. According to *New Yorker* magazine, the lions were "disappointing—they sound like a cow, no majesty, only vaguely sad," the tree toads "won't perform until you begin sawing up a piece of bronze with a hacksaw—and that spoils the record," and "a man named Phil Dwyer" was hired to reproduce the "mournful and very loud braying noise" of a camel. Back home Ditmars would synchronize the recordings to the pictures. He once hooked up his studio radio to a loudspeaker, blasting the normally tranquil neighborhood. According to the *Scarsdale Inquirer*, "cars stopped and people got out and looked for the entertainment. Even Eastchester expected to see the brass band which was playing come over the hill."

By 1931 a new corporation called Talking Picture Epics was releasing movies by Ditmars with audio tracks. In six of them, with such rousing titles as *Monkey Whoopee*, *Like a Beaver*, and *In the Realm of Goblins*, his older daughter Gladyce poses as a glamorous young reporter in fur coat, asking the curator questions. Her father narrates the ensuing footage, some newly shot, most borrowed from his now-extensive back catalogue.

Talkies offered Ditmars a further advantage: "the lecturer can be in twenty places at once and yet be at home, or plunging through the wilderness gathering material for another lecture." Now, as he entered what would be the final decade of his life, the curator turned his attention to the tropics. Down there somewhere in the South America rainforest lurked bushmasters. It was time to go get one.

# 12

# A Naturalist's Paradise

*"There is one lure that is always pulling me: my love for the tropics. Each trip to the neighbourhood of the equator seems to strengthen my passion for the jungle and its denizens."*

—Raymond L. Ditmars, *Strange Animals I Have Known* (1931)

---

*April 1928. Somewhere east of San Pedro Sula, Honduras.*

TWILIGHT IS ALL TOO brief in the tropics. Just as the forest visitor senses a cooling of the humid air, a lengthening of shadows and the flashing glimpses of a lowering sun through the canopy, so the curtain of darkness falls. The soundtrack changes too as croaking howler monkeys, chirruping insects, and shrieking parrots hand over to songsters of the night. The mating calls of a thousand frogs now form the dominant rhythm overlaid by an eerie counterpoint of cries, hoots, and strangulated rasps.

Ray and his nature-loving companions would normally enjoy the Honduran night—but not this night. All day the two Ford autos and their Honduran drivers have done well to negotiate the tortuous, narrow, and muddy excuse for a road. But returning from the lagoon has proved especially awkward. An hour ago both front tires of the lead car exploded after striking a big pothole and had to be replaced. Soon after, the second automobile also succumbed to a flat, the front suspension springs knocked out of alignment. Then the first car slid up to its radiator in another hole. With two-thirds of the journey back to San Pedro Sula still to complete, such interruptions were disquieting. The failing daylight heightened the concerns, for there was only one functioning searchlight between the two Fords. A further eight miles were completed when disaster struck. The front car again piled into a hole and, swerving to avoid a collision, the second rammed a large root stump, fatally bending the steering rod.

"We're not going to be able to repair it this evening," translates Waller after a lengthy conference with the drivers in Spanish. "We'll have to abandon it." The sky is purple, the forest track cloaked in darkness.

It had all started so well. A couple of weeks earlier, Ray had traveled down to Honduras accompanied by Clara, Gladyce, and their friend Arthur Gillam, founder of the Reptile Study Society of America. The New Yorkers had passed an enjoyable few days at the Tela snake park, entertained and astonished by the fearless antics of Douglas March. The station's young manager regularly descended by ladder into his serpent pit to collect venom from the dreaded *barba amarilla* vipers, a duty he relished.

Then at three-thirty one morning the visitors had made for the interior aboard a customized Ford. The tires had been removed and the wheels shod with flanges allowing it to motor effortlessly for sixty miles along narrow gauge railroad to the end of the spur at Tuloa. The United Fruit Company's banana trains had been sided in advance. March had teased his guests with stories of recent spectacular derailments courtesy of boa constrictors and five hundred pound tapirs on the track. In the event, the only species identified were opossums and tropical whippoorwills, their eyes blinking in the beam of the car's searchlights.

Sunrise had seen the party transfer to a waiting power boat that took them more than twenty miles down the fast-flowing and silty Ulua River. Caimans were sprawled on the bank, and egrets and spoonbills were plentiful. The last leg of the journey was completed by conventional railroad. At San Pedro Sula, contact was made with Dr. William Waller. Hailing from Memphis, the physician has set up a practice in the small town. He too was a keen naturalist and over subsequent days took his guests on excursions into mountains reminiscent of the New England hills where the *barba amarilla* gives way to the *cascabel* rattlesnake, notorious for its paralyzing bite.

Finally, this morning Waller had led the party in two automobiles along eighteen miles of logging trail cut through lowland forest. Parrots and macaws flitted in a canopy of ceiba trees and corozo palms, army ants swarmed the ground. Ray filmed a decent study of leaf-cutter ants and, together with the shots of the Tela serpentarium, exposed some five thousand feet of film, enough for several lectures. Lake Ticamaya was their goal today, a bamboo-fringed lagoon extending over many square miles and home to giant iguanas and colorful bird life. Explorations were made aboard two *cayucas*, round-bottomed canoes hollowed out from tree trunks, which threatened to pitch the party into waters infested with fifteen-foot-long crocodiles. Manatees were also known to be here although no examples of the large aquatic mammal were seen today. In the late afternoon the party started back hoping to reach San Pedro before nightfall. That was when things started going awry.

Mosquitoes present the greatest worry. At Tela the visitors slept in neat little houses, well-screened against the biting insects, but stranded out here in the forest nothing save repeated slaps would stop the infuriating things bleeding them all dry. The decision is made to send Clara and Gladyce ahead on foot accompanied by two Hondurans.

"There's a screened Carib house a few miles down the track," says Dr. Waller. "The women will be better off there than battling these infernal mosquitoes—and walking will be faster than these flivvers."

The curator regards the two guides doubtfully. One is sharpening his machete.

"I know what you're thinking," Waller murmurs. "Rest assured my men are thoroughly trustworthy and their night vision is excellent."

"Don't worry, Pop," says Gladyce brightly, "I'll look after Mom!"

A small fire is lit providing illumination by which the bent suspension leaves can be hammered back into place on the operational Ford.

With *barba amarilla* and *cascabel* on the mind, the men gather kindling from the forest floor with extreme prudence, not least as the flickering flames set the twigs' shadows dancing in a way unnervingly reminiscent of a slithering serpent. The minor repairs complete, the group moves off again, pitching and rolling at a sluggish pace.

Suddenly all is darkness.

"Goodness! What's happened now?" It's Gillam.

"The bulb's probably burnt out," answers Ray. "Must be the low gears we've been using, and the high generator voltage."

"Right, so what now?"

Waller has a plan. "All right, I need some spare clothing."

By the glimmer of match lights Ray and the others hand over socks, outer shirts, and empty snake bags. Waller ties the material to a long pole and pours gasoline over it. A few minutes later and the car is trundling forward again, a man on the running board lighting the way with the makeshift torch, pungent fumes billowing in its wake.

An hour or so passes with no sign of civilization. The men have now smeared axle grease on any exposed skin but the mosquitoes continue harrying them—a situation worsened by the piecemeal removal of clothing.

"Let's hope we don't find any *barba amarilla* now," says Ray whose thoughts also turn to the *diabanadore*, a still larger viper that, Waller reports, leaps at victims. No longer an exciting collecting opportunity, such an encounter could be hazardous with medical facilities so distant. Ray reflects on other nocturnal wildlife. This is jaguar country after all, although the secretive cats would doubtless turn somersaults to avoid humans. Marauding gangs of white-lipped peccaries, a dangerous pig-like creature, are also out there.

At that moment a new pin-prick of light appears ahead and then a clearing in the forest

"It's the house!" cries Waller.

Ray is reunited with his family. Despite the time—perhaps three in the morning—the owners welcome the tourists into their simple home, exchanging bread and tinned sausages for a few dollars. Ray and his friends are famished, wolfing down everything. They instantly regret it. What an irony to be finished off by a can of frankfurters.

———✦———

AN unbroken row of eight-foot-high shelving units lined the vast storage room. The ends of the otherwise anonymous gray cabinets were labeled with the taxonomic designation of their contents: Xenodontinae, Colubrinae, Elapinae. We had arrived in the "snake" section of the archive. Ethanol and something more unpleasant flavored the air.

Arriving at "Natricinae," Ken consulted a printout before spinning a three-pronged handle, rolling the unit smoothly away from its neighbor to offer access to the delights within. A bewildering panorama of glass specimen jars of various dimensions crowded every shelf from floor to ceiling.

"OK, here's one," he said stretching for a sizeable pot that he passed to me. It was heavy. I hung on grimly for fear it would slip through my fingers destroying something irreplaceable.

"Have you ever dropped one?" I asked.

"Oh yes," responded Ken casually before moving to another shelf.

A small, dark-colored serpent was stuffed awkwardly in the jar I was holding. Submerged alongside the specimen was a note: "*Nerodia fasciata*. 030903. UNITED STATES: SOUTH CAROLINA; HAMPTON; Robertsville. Ditmars, Raymond L. MALE. 1902."

So here was a watersnake bagged over a century ago by Ditmars himself during one of his first snake-hunting trips down south. In the cool, clinical atmosphere of the store room it was difficult to conjure up cypress swamps and rice ditches, clouds of mosquitoes, the oppressive heat and humidity. Still, as the mummified snake glared at me from the yellowing embalming fluid I could well imagine the fight this non-venomous but irritable customer would have given the zoo men. Ken had meanwhile located something else, an even larger jar containing the preserved skin of a king cobra. He removed the lid and with tweezers extracted several feet of shriveled epidermis from the malodorous fluid. The skin had been donated by the Bronx Zoo to Washington's National Museum sometime before April 1901. This was more exciting still because, assuming the date was right, I was looking at the remains of one of the very animals that loosed itself in William Bartels's Greenwich Street shop way back in May 1900, an incident which spawned breathless newspaper accounts across America.

My visit to the Smithsonian Museum Support Center in Maryland, a fifteen-minute shuttle ride from downtown Washington, was already yielding remarkable treasures. Built in 1983 as off-site space for cataloguing, conserving, and storing the vast collections of the Smithsonian Institution, the secure, climate-controlled facility housed some fifty-four million items, ranging from fossils and microscopic plants to totem poles and meteorites. Bearded, friendly, and looking to be in his sixties, Ken Tighe was a database coordinator here with responsibility for herps and had agreed to show me the handful of specimens that Ditmars had donated.

"We affectionately call it the Death Star," Ken had grinned as he had guided me through a zigzag series of warehouses, known as pods. I could see what he meant. Although the warren of sterile tunnels, cold metal pipework, and strip lighting also called to mind villains' hideouts from early James Bond films. I half expected a golf cart to career by, at the wheel a pair of machine gun–toting heavies in colorful boiler-suits. A new pod had been erected after the 9/11 terrorist attacks to accommodate thousands more formalin and ethanol-pickled specimens stored at Washington's Museum of Natural History.

"All of a sudden, keeping gallons of flammable liquids on the Mall didn't seem such a smart idea," said Ken. We moved on. It was time to look at some bushmasters.

Scientists extract venom from a bushmaster (*Lachesis muta*), Instituto Butantan,
São Paulo, Brazil, c. 1925. (Courtesy of Instituto Butantan)

IN 1899 John Toomey, a Bronx native of Irish descent, landed a job at the newly opened New York Zoological Park. The jovial twenty-four-year-old started out pruning trees but soon found himself working as a reptile keeper under Ditmars.

"I didn't want the snakes in the beginnin'," Toomey later admitted. "But one o' the boys in the reptile house died an' I had to take the reptiles. After a month or so, I wouldn't change with nobody. I got to know 'em. None of 'em really knows you, but a few of 'em get to realize they have a friend. The minute you open the cage they'll be all around your neck." That friendship was to be sorely tested.

On the morning of January 27, 1916, Toomey was bitten by a six-foot-long western diamondback rattlesnake. One of five shipped from Brownsville, Texas, a month before, the rattler launched itself at the keeper as he was cleaning its cage, nicking the base of his right thumb. Toomey screamed for help, pain flaming in his hand. Fellow keeper Snyder was immediately on the scene, applying rubber ligatures about Toomey's wrist and arm while sucking venom from the wound as per Ditmars's instructions. The affected area was meanwhile washed in a solution of potassium permanganate, thought to "oxidize" the venom.

Alas, just two tubes of Calmette's serum were held at the zoo, the First World War having interrupted supplies from Europe. Worse still the antivenin was in dried form, requiring Toomey to wait forty-five agonizing minutes for the yellowish granules to dissolve in sterilized water before they could be injected into his stomach by Gilbert van der Smissen, the zoo physician. Calmette's preparation was polyvalent, designed to treat the bites of several types of venomous snake, but it was little tested against American species and, although preventing injury to John Toomey's nervous system, the serum failed to neutralize other effects. The patient was soon sweating, shivering, and vomiting, his hand and arm swelling to grotesque proportions. Such was the pain that Toomey begged for the limb to be amputated, repeated measures of brandy and milk failing to alleviate his suffering. During the afternoon a pronounced weakness had set in and the patient was rushed to the German Hospital on Manhattan's Upper East Side where, mercifully, he slipped into a coma. An unsightly purple hue spread over Toomey's upper body. By now his right arm had ballooned to a circumference of twenty-two inches.

Ditmars and his colleagues frantically tried to locate more serum. By an extraordinary coincidence that very week a Brazilian scientist named, appropriately enough, Vital Brazil was in New York City for a lecture tour at the invitation of the Carnegie Foundation. Dr. Brazil had spent fifteen years developing antivenins specific to New World snakes at the Instituto Soroterápico in Butantan on the outskirts of São Paulo. His techniques improved on those pioneered by Calmette but the underlying principle was the same: venom was milked from serpents and administered in steadily increasing doses into surrogate animals, in his case Percheron horses, until antidote could be extracted and purified. The Brazilian, the first to create a polyvalent serum for times when the identity of the serpent was unknown, also established an ingenious system by which serum tubes and snakebite kits were distributed across the country in exchange for live snakes, ensuring that fresh antivenin could always be produced. Between milkings the reptiles were housed in small beehive-like domes studding a moated enclosure. This snake park at Butantan drew large crowds from the outset, and to this day remains popular with locals and tourists alike.

Ditmars knew Dr. Brazil well. His friend Theodore Roosevelt had visited Butantan in October 1913 and then, just a few months ago, the Brazilian had shipped Ditmars an exceptional haul of South American venomous snakes. The curator and Van der Smissen now tracked down Dr. Brazil who happened to be carrying various liquid serums including *anti-crotalico* for tropical rattlesnake bites. By then Toomey was "in the last stages of collapse," but a single injection reversed the symptoms. Within weeks the keeper was back at work complaining merely of a stiff thumb. The snake did not fare as well, starving itself to death nine months later.

"I still kinda like them," said Toomey of rattlesnakes when questioned about his ordeal. He even kept the yellowing skin of the diamondback that almost killed him as a memento.

Ditmars was less sanguine. The accident was the first at the reptile house in its seventeen-year history and showed just how vulnerable to snakebite was his staff, and indeed the country at large. The limited quantities of Calmette's serum then available were evidently of little value against American species. Furthermore, although dry antidotes kept for longer than liquid ones, they were impractical in emergency situations. The United States urgently needed a reliable supply of effective antivenin.

Thus, on February 5, 1916, as Dr. Brazil headed home aboard a Lamport and Holt steam liner, he took with him at Ditmars's behest a cargo of rattlesnakes, water moccasins, and other venomous reptiles of the North American continent. Hitherto, Butantan had produced antivenins against the deadly snakes of Latin America: tropical rattlesnakes, fer-de-lances, coralsnakes, and, of course, the bushmaster. Within months the

Instituto was rolling out antidotes specific to their northern counterparts, the plan being to supply fifty tubes of liquid serum to the Bronx each year. "There is no reason why the men in the Reptile House should be in danger of death every time a poisonous snake 'goes bad,'" Ditmars told the *New York Times*.

The ensuing decade saw a regular exchange with live snakes or venom going south and antivenin north. A charge of $2.50 was made for the use of each tube, the funds raised purchasing more reptiles for Butantan. As the fame of the serum grew Ditmars found himself contacted at all hours of the day and night, often personally distributing the antidote at short notice across the northeastern region, and witnessing "the saving of life under remarkable conditions" as he once put it. For instance, in May 1926, assisted by his daughters Gladyce and Beatrice, the curator dispatched four tubes of Butantan serum by road and rail to Cornell University in upstate New York. A twenty-eight-year-old local man, Leonard M. Spear, had been bitten by a diamondback while visiting a friend in the zoology department. Spear—who had poked the viper with a ruler through the bars of its cage—received the serum in time and survived. The antivenin was stockpiled in other regions, including at army medical posts along the Mexican border, where it swiftly proved its value as early as 1918 by saving a young traveling showman bitten by a Texas rattlesnake.

Despite such cases, snake bite in the United States was, according to official statistics at least, rare with only several hundred incidents reported annually compared with the thousands dying from envenomations in Brazil. Butantan had already inspired similar operations in Thailand and India, but the US government declined to follow suit and private pharmaceutical companies were similarly loath to invest. Ditmars thought this shortsighted, expecting an upsurge in accidents as the public more often came into contact with venomous serpents. In May 1925 he told a *New York Times* reporter of his concerns: "As hiking, camping, and long-distance touring parties are gathering their recruits by the tens of thousands, the hazard from poisonous snakebite is steadily increasing. In some States we have more poisonous snakes than the infested areas of like size in the tropics." Elsewhere he wrote of fields and woods "filled with novices from the cities, the women wearing silk stockings and knickers, the men shod in low shoes and the children generally running wild." With no effective antidote available Ditmars was convinced that the number of deaths would rise needlessly, and even where the victim survived, bites often led to permanent disfigurement. Venomous snakebite also hurt the agricultural economy in certain parts of the country, with an estimated one million dollars-worth of cattle lost in Texas alone over a two- or three-year period.

If things weren't bad enough, that same year the United States Treasury Department prohibited, on a legal technicality, the commercial importation of serum from Brazil. Butantan went on supplying Ditmars with free antivenin, generosity that impressed but embarrassed the curator. He later spoke of his unease at "pestering my Brazilian friends to send me serum as a courtesy."

But, after decades of campaigning by Ditmars and others, a solution was at hand, and it would come from an unlikely source.

THE preserved bushmasters kept at the Museum Support Center weren't associated with Ditmars but I was keen to inspect them. After all, this might be the closest I was ever going to get to one.

With the corpse of the world's biggest viper unable to fit the jars he had hitherto shown me, Ken instead guided me to a separate storage room. Chains hung from the ceiling, possibly for supporting heavy specimens. At the far end was a single stainless steel tank, perhaps four feet in length, lying on a trolley. It looked like an expensive chest-freezer wheeled out in preparation for a barbeque. But there weren't burgers or beers in it, there were bushmasters.

My guide set about prizing off, one by one, the eight metal clips which secured the container's lid. Was it altogether fanciful to believe

I shared at that moment the apprehension of a teenage Ditmars opening that first crate of Trinidad snakes way back in the 1890s? As Ken plunged his bare hands straight into the stinking preserving fluid, did my heart actually start pounding just that little bit faster? Probably not. Like the fifty-four million other things here, I knew the contents would be very dead and unlikely to leap out and chase me about the room. Nevertheless, a frisson of exhilaration now surged through me as Ken fished out one of the bushmasters submerged in the tank.

The reptilian cadaver was in a neat stiff spiral the size of an extra-large pizza. The snake's mouth was agape, the eyes a milky blue, a cataract-like effect resulting from the preserving liquid. I couldn't see the famous inch-long fangs. Were they folded back? I ran my fingers warily over the wet, knobbly, bead-like scales. The bushmaster's nickname "pineapple snake" was spot-on. Even the head scales were small and knobbly. This armor must have given the bushmaster excellent protection in life. A good thing, too. Any animal lying coiled on the rainforest floor for days on end is liable to be trodden on, sometimes heavily.

Ken handed me several more deceased bushmasters with different camouflage markings. In some the coloration was muted with dull brown lozenges against a lighter shade. Others had greater contrast with darker almost black diamonds on a far paler background. The variation is significant as scientists now recognize several species of bushmaster, and patterns are one way of telling them apart.

Before I left Ken pointed at another fluid-filled specimen jar.

"Know what these are?"

Inside was a mass of peculiar white twisted tube-like structures, several inches in length. An outlandish new form of pasta? No, that was silly.

"Tapeworms?" I hazarded.

"Hemipenes," came the answer. In other words, the paired reproductive organs of a male snake.

"They're not called king cobras for nothing," smirked Ken.

In 1885 the Boston Fruit Company was established to distribute bananas from the plantations of Latin America throughout the United States. By 1901 the re-christened United Fruit Company had revolutionized ocean transportation of the perishable crop using refrigerated vessels whose movements were coordinated by wireless communications technology prefiguring today's globalized supply chains. Painted white to reflect the sun and keep their cargos cool, the fast reefer ships plying the tropical waters were famed as the "great white fleet." At the same time road and rail networks were pushed through the forest to deliver fruit efficiently from plantation to port. The organization flourished, absorbing rival fruit suppliers and acquiring territory and political influence across Central America and the Caribbean.

By 1924 the United Fruit Company owned 1.6 million acres of land. Much of it was prime serpent habitat, the crops attracting rats and opossums, which in turn drew venomous reptilian predators from neighboring forests. Encounters with snakes were frequent and often fatal for the bare-legged, machete-wielding laborers known as *campeños*. An estimated two hundred people were dying annually from envenomations across United Fruit Company plantations. The Central American republic of Honduras was unusually snakey. A census conducted between July 1924 and October 1925 at several plantations by the herpetologist Thomas Barbour of the Harvard Museum of Comparative Zoology yielded 3,439 specimens, a fifth of which were venomous. Examples of the latter included the beautiful eyelash palm-vipers, coralsnakes ringed like peppermint candy sticks, and above all the dreaded local version of the fer-de-lance, whose chin coloration earned it the nickname *barba amarilla* or "yellow beard." The species, which attained a length of eight feet or more, was responsible for many fatalities. And the death could be a horrible one. As the hemotoxic venom dissolved capillaries, the skin and flesh of the victim would blacken, the mouth, nose, and eyes stream blood. At least its distant and even bigger cousin, the bushmaster, was absent from Honduras.

Barbour's research prompted the United Fruit Company to launch a comprehensive anti-snakebite campaign across its vast estates. Antivenin was also needed and Vital Brazil would have been the obvious source were his hands not full meeting domestic needs. Thus in conjunction with the Harvard Medical School and the Zoological Societies of New York, Philadelphia, and San Diego, the company sponsored the Antivenin Institute of America. This new body would be "devoted to furthering the knowledge of venomous animals in general, and to developing means of preventing deaths and relieving symptoms caused by their venoms." The Brazilian Afrânio do Amaral, formerly a director at Butantan and then lecturing on ophiology at Harvard, was appointed to oversee the new institute.

An early priority was manufacturing new serums specific to Central American snakes. Venom would be milked at an experimental station in the Lancetilla valley close to Tela, a busy port on the Atlantic coast of Honduras. The place was modeled on Butantan, with large pits filled with snakes from the region. Other enclosures held harmless, rodent-eating species of economic value to the plantations. From the start, Do Amaral stressed the importance of gathering as many venomous serpents as possible because a single animal, "if properly handled, will surely give enough venom to prepare sufficient antivenin for the cure of at least four or five bitten people." But despite a two-dollar bounty for live specimens, *campeños* often played it safe by battering the snake with a machete first. Once extracted the venom would be dried in an incubator and shipped to laboratories at Glenolden, just outside Philadelphia. Operated by the H. K. Mulford Company, and also serving as the Antivenin Institute's headquarters, the two-hundred-acre Glenolden facility was the perfect choice. Mulford maintained a stable of 1,500 horses there from whose blood it was already deriving a diphtheria vaccine with similar inoculation techniques. Now antivenin would be prepared under the guidance of Do Amaral. Back would go the serum to the plantations of Honduras and Costa Rica, to the forest of Panama's Canal Zone (said to be infested with bushmasters), and further south still to save lives among the miners and oil workers of Colombia and Venezuela.

To Ditmars's satisfaction, antivenin against North American snakes would also be produced. The zoo man was involved from the start, acting as a technical consultant for the Antivenin Institute and heading up its "Nearctic division." In October 1926, the *New York Times* reported on a familiar scene at the Bronx Zoo reptile house, Ditmars and do Amaral milking "nine rattlesnakes and a large number of moccasin snakes" whose venom would "produce American-made anti-snake serum." The vipers were kept in "heavy trashcans" during the extraction process and by the end of the day "enough deadly poison had been collected to kill a score of people." The "North American stations" of the Antivenin Institute as a whole obtained venom from over four thousand rattlesnakes, copperheads, and water moccasins in just three months. It wasn't just about serum though. Education was equally important in tackling snakebite and Ditmars fostered a network of branches across the country to publish, for their respective areas, information on "the character, habits, and occurrence of poisonous reptiles." An added benefit for Ditmars was that Tela offered the zoo a presence in Central America and direct access to interesting new mammals, birds, and reptiles at a fraction of the prices on the New York animal markets.

In February 1928 the *New York Times* reported that do Amaral had "convinced" the curator to visit Tela. This could hardly have been a challenge for the Brazilian. Someone with Ditmars's adventurous spirit was never going to be satisfied monitoring developments from his office in the reptile house. The curator, with his family, had in fact already steamed down to Brazil courtesy of the SS *Southern Cross* in the late summer of 1925, delivering "a fluid gallon of rattlesnake venom" and hoping to bring back "an extensive series of South American reptiles." During this three-week stay, subsidized by his employers, the forty-nine-year-old Ditmars was confined to urban centers, visiting Butantan in Sao Paulo as well as a new venom institute Dr. Vital Brazil had founded at Nictheroy (now known as

Niterói) close to Rio de Janeiro. He picked up several ampoules of the latest rattler antiserum, ten times more powerful than that which had cured Toomey a decade before. The bulk of the snakes accompanying Ditmars home came from Dr. Brazil's own collection, save for a few the zoo man had bagged during excursions in nearby countryside, including "a fiery young *jararacuçu*," a type of small pitviper, which was sunning on some abandoned railroad ties.

The Brazil expedition had nevertheless re-kindled in Ditmars his boyhood fascination with exotic foreign climes. The important work going on in Honduras—a "naturalist's paradise"—was the perfect excuse to indulge these appetites. On Tuesday March 6, 1928, Ditmars, accompanied by his wife, daughter Gladyce and his old snake-hunting buddy Arthur Gillam, traveled south again on the *Orizaba* for six fascinating weeks as guests of the United Fruit Company. Thomas Barbour was nominally in charge of the Tela snake facility but his assistant, Douglas D. H. March, ran the show. Ditmars was astonished at March's cavalier approach. Clad in high leggings, the fearless Pennsylvanian would descend into the pits among a hundred or more venomous serpents, brazenly free handling them to extract their venom. A recent accident with a *barba amarilla*, leaving him partially blind until serum could be administered, failed to temper his reckless behavior. March's luck would run out eleven years later when fatally bitten by a snake in Panama; some accounts point the finger at a bushmaster. It was reportedly his eighteenth venomous snake bite.

Ditmars spent the remainder of the Honduras trip collecting for the zoo and taking motion picture footage. Sorties were made into virgin forest by railroad, automobile, and then dugout canoe. Among the herpetological booty shipped home was a pair of large *barba amarilla* trapped on a plantation, along with coralsnakes, tropical rattlesnakes, and some tree toads with calls evocative of a riveting machine. The curator wrote about the trip in the *New York Times* with typical exuberance and other papers took up and as usual embellished the story. Tales of "leaping snakes in banana fields" irked the United Fruit Company, sensitive to the implication that it might be putting workers at risk, and two months afterward Ditmars was forced to publish another article playing down the dangers. If the Honduras expedition provoked a flurry of interest, his quest for a bushmaster would reap a hurricane.

# 13

# The Main Thing Is the Bushmaster

*"A scientist has to cultivate a philosophic mind and accept failure. The engineers had not been looking for bushmasters, and they had killed eighteen. I had searched hard and had no success."*

—Raymond L. Ditmars, *Confessions of a Scientist* (1934)

———◆———

*September 4, 1933. Chilibrillo caves, Panama.*

"WHAT ON EARTH IS he doing in there?"

Arthur has been gone for half an hour. The curator rebukes himself for allowing his plucky young helper to wriggle feetfirst into the impossibly narrow crevice. Apart from the young Panamanian, Ray is now alone in the cavern's main gallery. Alone, that is, if you don't count the gargantuan cockroaches swarming over the damp walls, their oversized antennae wafting and glistening in the beam of his jacklight. Or the mysterious spider-like creatures which rest here and there. Or indeed the "kissing bugs" lurking in the cracks, their bite said to transmit the life-threatening Chagas disease.

But what there *isn't* right now are vampire bats. And that's the problem, because the blood-feasting mammals are what's lured Ray and his assistant Arthur Greenhall to the caves. This year's search for a bushmaster proving futile, the pair have switched focus to another nightmarish species. Vampire bats are sneaky customers. Local Panamanians told of how, in the dead of night, the mouse-sized beasts would attack livestock and even nibble the toes of sleeping humans, piercing the flesh with lance-like teeth. Victims would wake up in a pool of their own blood. How splendid to bring a tiny monster like this back to the Bronx! The zoo men were advised to try their luck at the Chilibrillo caverns. Bats of a dozen species including vampires made their home in this warren of tunnels, galleries, and fissures carved into the limestone by a subterranean tributary of the Chagres River.

Thus, yesterday saw the bat hunters starting out with nets and mesh cages at first light from a makeshift camp near the Madden Dam construction site deep in virgin forest. Leading Ray and Arthur up a muddy cattle track that wound ever more precipitously through the dense malarial forest was dam engineer R. F. Olds and his chief Sydney Randolph. The men wore open-necked shirts and trousers of light khaki. Their laced boots were knee-high as insurance against snakebite, and beneath the boots each wore thin woolen socks dusted with sulfur to ward off ticks and red bugs. Two young Panamanians in more relaxed apparel had completed the party.

The unprepossessing entrance to the first cave had belied its fantastic interior. Donning jacklights fitted to headbands, the men squeezed through the creeper-smothered opening and filed along a widening horizontal passage slick with red mud. The atmosphere was muggy and suffused with a sugary, choking aroma. Overhead, streams of bats fanned warm air into the explorers' faces. The occasional narrow chimney in the ceiling offered glimpses of the outside world. After fording a chilly torrent of water the group emerged into a magnificent central chamber which in places soared to perhaps seventy-five feet in height. The men discerned thousands of tiny black shivering forms clinging to the great domed roof and chattering like monkeys. The sweet stink of their manure was almost unbearable. These animals were well beyond reach, but forays into lesser side galleries had yielded eighteen large specimens, some with wingspans of up to two feet. Ray had identified the captives not as vampires but as a carnivorous type known to prey on birds, frogs, and small mammals, including other bats. The wicked-looking beasts, each sporting an odd leaf-shaped appendage on its muzzle, were wrestled thrashing, squeaking, and snapping into a mesh box. After a breather back out in the forest, the party had explored a second cavern of more modest proportions that proved the exclusive home of a fruit-eating bat. Still no vampires.

Then, in the late afternoon, as Ray and Arthur had lowered themselves into a third cave, they spied several furry forms scampering into a crevice. Bats again—but this time the bulldog faces and the way they scuttled over the vertical surface like rats marked them out as vampires. At last! Extinguishing lights, the men waited in vain for their quarry to rematerialize. Further investigations revealed a side passage leading to an underground stream of unknown depth and a narrow gap through which a slim person might squeeze. Down there somewhere were the prized bats, but the men were exhausted and time had run out.

The following morning Ray, Arthur, and a local teenager chosen for his slender build were back at the vampire cave with their nets. However, once more the bats had defied their pursuers, withdrawing into the furthest recesses of the grotto.

"What now, sir?" Arthur had whispered.

The older man paused before replying, lighting up his pipe.

"The way I see it, we have three options: wade up the water channel although there's no telling how deep it is or how clean. Try to get through that crevice. Or give up."

"There's no way I'm giving up when we're so close! Let me see if I can get through there."

"Sure," Ray had smiled, "Give it a try."

Arthur had started contorting his lean frame into the narrow horizontal shaft.

"It's easier than I thought," he panted.

"Make sure you keep within earshot!" hissed the curator, but clutching a net and mesh box Arthur had already disappeared into the stygian gloom.

Ten minutes later Arthur had whispered excitedly, "There's several of them up ahead. The walls are solid. I'm going after them. Watch out with your net."

And that is the last Ray has heard from his young friend. Dark thoughts have all but crowded out the optimism of earlier.

"Sheer folly!" he mutters to the smiling but uncomprehending Panamanian. "What will I tell his father? If anyone should have gone, it should have been me!"

He stares at the black crevice as if willing Arthur's reemergence. He dare not call after him for fear of startling any remaining bats.

The silence is at last shattered with an excited yell. A bat flutters out, which Ray instinctively nets. With pounding heart, he examines the captive. It's not a vampire.

Splashing noises come from the opening, then a groan.

"What's going on in there?" cries the curator.

"I'm in the water! It's hard to get out!"

At that Ray sends the Panamanian down the crevice with a lamp, the curator himself following in his wake. The shaft is tight on the older man. His belt rips from its loops and his shirt rides up to his shoulders. The hole soon widens though and Ray sees the problem: Arthur has fallen from a limestone shoulder into a shallow crevasse and is now floundering in waist-deep water, the walls too slippery to scale. Ray and the Panamanian soon haul him out.

The bedraggled Arthur holds aloft the dripping box in the dim glow of the lamp and laughs.

"Look! I got two of them!"

※

SHOPPING malls and fast food joints, drug stores and legal firms, churches and gas stations. Tidy front yards bristled with billboards. Real estate.

Furniture. Politicians. Everything was for sale. VOTE No STADIUM TAX insisted one set of signs, YES FOR THE BALLPARK! GET THE FACTS, retorted another.

Although the highway from my motel was as unremarkable as any in the United States, the historic downtown of Wilmington, North Carolina, whispered Deep South. The buildings were imposing, venerable, and southern gothic in style, the sleepy avenues lined with well-cropped palm trees and live oaks dripping with Spanish moss. *Blue Velvet*, director David Lynch's disturbing 1986 representation of small-town America, was filmed here. I could see why.

I parked at a modern two-story redbrick structure a block up from the river. The casual passerby might have dismissed it as an office unit were it not swathed by a huge banner with the words CAPE FEAR SERPENTARIUM. GET EDUCATED . . . BE AMAZED! DEADLY SNAKES and an illustration of a monster-sized bushmaster. I was tired of reading about bushmasters, looking at pictures and holding corpses. It was time to see a living, breathing, biting one. Yes, this was the place.

Erected on the site of a former iron works, the Cape Fear Serpentarium was an exuberant interpretation of the traditional reptile house. Crocodiles, lizards, and snakes were showcased in glass-fronted displays arranged over two levels. Much effort had been expended in designing, building, and lighting the naturalistic exhibits, and judging from the reconstructed Hindu temple—a setting for king cobras—the Indiana Jones movies had provided more than a little inspiration. This treasury of reptile life was the creation of Dean Ripa, herpetologist, writer, artist, jazz singer, and, by any yardstick, bushmaster obsessive. At the last count he had in excess of sixty in captivity. A handful were on display to the public; most he kept behind the scenes in his apartment at the back of the serpentarium. There were even bushmasters in his bedroom.

My arrival coincided with feeding time. Visitors were clustered around an enclosure which recreated the Costa Rican rainforest, all leaf litter, strangler fig vines, and eerie lighting. The label was adorned with a motif of five red skull and crossbones lined up like Space Invaders and explained that one or more bushmasters were hiding in there somewhere. Dean, who looked younger than his fifty-five years, beckoned me over. He carried a plastic bucket and long-handled tongs, and his black goatee lent him something of the swashbuckler.

"We're going to begin with the longest species of viper in the world, the bushmaster!" he announced, adding *sotto voce* to me, "Come this side with us. You'll get a better picture."

I agreed without hesitation and soon regretted it, for Regina, his wife and assistant, approached with a big portable screen that she positioned so that we three were caged in with the snake. No time to change my mind now.

As the crowd, mostly school-age kids, gazed through the mesh with awe, Dean unlocked the glass front and swung it upwards. After a preamble he drew a dead rat from his bucket and with the tongs waggled it at the entrance to a large hollow log. In a blur of movement the black head of a bushmaster shot from its lair, the maw swinging open by 180 degrees, before burying fangs deep in the rodent. Dean continued shaking the rat. The simulated death struggles encouraged the bushmaster to bite down harder and begin swallowing the prey, rather than letting go and biting him. Alternating the left and right sides of the jaw, the snake began the slow task of ingestion. This procedure is called "fang walking." The freakishly elastic ligaments that connect the jaw bones to each other and to the skull ease the process and are among several adaptations for consuming large meals otherwise off limits to a limbless predator. When the *New Yorker*'s E. B. White watched Ditmars feeding a snake back in 1930, he likened it to "a rubber tube being fitted tediously over a much larger pipe." I could see what he meant.

Later that evening I did some ingesting of my own, Dean and Regina treating me to an all-you-can eat buffet dinner at Casey's, a local purveyor of Carolina cuisine. Over chitlins and chicken, okra and stuffed crab, cobbler pie and peaches, Dean talked of his fascination with the cold-blooded. Growing up in the 1970s he had taught himself to observe, catch, and breed reptiles, and was soon drawn to the "hot" herps infesting the wetlands of his home state, the water moccasins and copperheads, coralsnakes and rattlesnakes. Their beauty, danger, and mystery was irresistible.

Around this time Dean also discovered Raymond Ditmars. Decades after the curator's death his publications remained a stalwart of the biology section of provincial libraries across America, often the only herpetological works available. *Snakes of the World* and *Reptiles of the World* were the first books Dean had ever read all the way through, opening up a vista of world snakes: gaboon vipers and king cobras, puff adders and tiger snakes, and, of course, the bushmaster. The photographic plates were a big part of the appeal for Dean. The monochrome left more to the imagination than color images. The famous close-up of the sneering bushmaster was haunting. "I tried to get a shot like that," he admitted, "but couldn't."

Dean's formal education ended as abruptly as his hero's. Dropping out of high school he hitchhiked to Italy to study fine art, later gravitating to less-developed countries where an artist's life was easier. "In Haiti," he recalled, "models would sit all day for me for three dollars." Of course the tropics were also a paradise for reptile hunters and at thirty, feeling "trapped by paint," Dean downed his brush and picked up his snake hook once more. The bushmaster was the target.

"I would explore hill tops, checking out hollow logs and holes," he said. "It was hit or miss." Then he started paying local hunters to take him to paca burrows, a classic bushmaster hideout, and was soon bringing them home from Panama, Surinam, Costa Rica, and elsewhere. In one year alone he collected twenty specimens.

The quest for bushmasters and other venomous species would take Dean to dozens of countries, but import restrictions proved a nuisance and by the early 1990s Dean was back in Wilmington breeding bushmasters rather than collecting them. Although Donal Boyer and colleagues at Dallas Zoo started routinely reproducing bushmasters in the late 1980s, Dean claimed primacy in observing the act of copulation itself and reported a bizarre breeding ritual wherein the male snake would lie belly up on his mate, stimulating her by rubbing his rough scales against hers.

In fact, Dean loved questioning orthodoxy, and nowhere was this more true than with bushmasters. He was the archetypal *enfant terrible*, whose imaginative theories and blunt pronouncements amused and exasperated the scientific community. Many were compiled in a voluminous monograph on an animal he called the "duck-billed platypus of snakes" for its odd trait of laying eggs.

The bushmaster's diet and feeding behavior represented one battleground. Some assumed that bushmasters, like rattlesnakes, targeted relatively large prey, which were bitten and released to avoid injury by the struggling victim. The envenomated prey could scurry off before keeling over. The snake could then relocate the meal in safety using its exceptional sense of smell. Reports that captive bushmasters could consume prey up to 70 percent of their own bodyweight appeared to support this but Dean didn't buy it.

"Bushmasters can't do this. Their body is too rigid and the throat too narrow. If they eat too big a meal they die," he said, insisting that the viper was restricted to eating moderate-sized rodents, such as spiny rats, which they bit and hung on to.

Not all Dean's ideas were so contentious. Scientists had long suspected that the bushmaster wasn't just one species, with the Central American forms distinct to those occurring elsewhere, but in 1994 Dean was the first to go ahead and publish the hypothesis. Genetic analysis by the distinguished Cornell scientists Kelly Zamudio and Harry Greene three years later confirmed the supposition, recognizing two new species: *Lachesis stenophrys*, or the Central American bushmaster, and *Lachesis melanocephala*, a rare black-headed variety confined to southwestern Costa Rica. The South American bushmasters, including those in

Trinidad, retained the original scientific name *Lachesis muta*. A fourth variety, *Lachesis acrochorda*, from the Chocó region of Ecuador and Colombia's Pacific coast, has since been added to the list.

Arthur Greenhall and Raymond Ditmars with a vampire bat (*Desmodus rotundus*) captured in the Chilibrillo caverns of Panama, 1933. (Courtesy of Mike Dee)

DITMARS loved everything about the 1928 Honduras expedition, from the voyage south, during which he observed fascinating new cloud formations, to the wildlife and people he had encountered. The interest that his adventures received in the press added to his excitement. The jaunt had been self-funded, freeing him to do as he pleased. But the line between business and pleasure was always blurry. Thus, the trip was very much a working holiday that saw the curator collecting animal specimens, contributing to the research on venom at the Tela snake park, gathering anecdotes for future books and shooting motion picture film. He was yet to set himself the challenge of finding a bushmaster in the wild but Ditmars was now hooked on the tropics, heading there almost every summer for the rest of his life in search of adventure.

Panama soon found itself on the curator's radar. On August 17, 1929, the United Fruit Company steamship *Ulua* pushed off from a New York pier, its destination Cristobal in the Canal Zone and calling at Cuba and Costa Rica. Among the passengers listed in the papers that day were "Dr. and Mrs. Ray and Gladys Ditmars." Beatrice was seemingly absent, perhaps because she was now married with a baby daughter of her own, Gloria, which hampered such adventures. Panama's main draw for Ditmars that year was Barro Colorado, an island in Lake Gatún formed by the damming of the Chagres River during the construction of the canal. Barro Colorado's six square miles of pristine forest offered zoological treasures in abundance. According to the *New York Times* the curator returned on September 9 with "motion picture films of tapirs, pumas, peccaries, and other wild animals," while the *Scarsdale Inquirer* was taken by the "fourteen healthy tarantulas each the size of a saucer" that he had brought home.

What Ditmars didn't return with was rather more instructive. His experiences in Brazil, Honduras, and now Panama confirmed that finding serpents in equatorial regions wasn't easy. The density of yellow beards and other species infesting fruit plantations was atypical, a response to unnaturally high levels of prey. In undisturbed habitats snakes were far scarcer than in the New England hills or the coastal swamps of South Carolina. "In the actual tropics," noted Ditmars, "poisonous snakes are not so frequently seen as in the temperate zones. One can explore a jungle for a week and not see a single snake."

But, just as this was dawning on Ditmars a determination to catch a wild bushmaster was also crystallizing in his mind. If seeing *any* tropical snakes was a challenge, how much less likely to bag the most elusive of all the pitvipers? Records showed that 1916 was the last time a bushmaster had been displayed in the reptile house. Why get one now? The reason was that road-building activities and ongoing engineering projects associated with the Panama canal were encroaching into bushmaster habitat as never before. Previously able to avoid human contact, by the 1930s the world's largest viper was being encountered with alarming regularity. And, early on, Ditmars came tantalizingly close to laying his hands on one.

In August 1931 parasitologists from New Orleans's Tulane University declared that they had captured live bushmasters while in Panama. The scientists were based at the Gorgas Memorial Institute of Tropical and Preventive Medicine at Ancón, a town close to Panama city in the south of the country. According to one newspaper report, they were "working on an antivenom" and had already extracted "enough poison to kill eight men." That same August, Ditmars himself was back in Panama, partly on the pretext of gathering tarantulas for Adolph Monaelesser. During the stay Ditmars dropped in at Gorgas but saw no live bushmasters. Perhaps the animals caught by the Tulane scientists had simply perished? If so, he could only have missed them by days. The institute's director, Dr. Herbert C. Clark, a founding member of the Antivenin Institute of America and a friend, did however show off "two fair-sized specimens." They had recently been killed by construction workers close to the Canal Zone. Ditmars now resolved to return to Panama once more. This time the capture of a bushmaster would be the primary goal.

Joining him in the summer of 1932 was a twenty-one-year-old student named Arthur M. Greenhall who was paying his own way. One of an army of budding naturalists idolizing Ditmars, Greenhall had bombarded him with fan mail, even saying he learned to read by studying the picture captions of *The Reptile Book*. Ditmars may have seen something of himself in the bespectacled younger man; the son of a wealthy banker, Greenhall was a native New Yorker, was fanatical about snakes, and had also first collected them in Central Park. The pair struck up a close relationship, Greenhall dropping in at the reptile house several times a week to talk snakes with the great man, and it was Ditmars who suggested that his friend enroll in a herpetology course at the University of Michigan. Greenhall would become Ditmars's right-hand man in the quest for a bushmaster.

In the run up to the 1932 expedition the curator had learned that engineers surveying and clearing forest for the new Madden Dam across the upper Chagres River often saw bushmasters, in the last three months killing no fewer than seven of them. And the snakes were monsters, some upwards of nine feet in length. Newspapers were agog with excitement about the mission: DITMARS HUNTS SNAKE IN JUNGLES OF PANAMA, DITMARS TO HUNT LARGEST OF VIPERS went the headlines. Many wanted to know whether he was afraid. "How do you feel when you go tarpon fishing, when a tarpon is pulling on the end of the line?" was his response. "That's the way it feels, except that it's more exciting."

In the unlikely event that a bushmaster eluded him, other fantastic serpents awaited the curator. The rainforest around Madden Dam, fifteen miles from the relative civilization of the Canal Zone, was also said to be infested with fer-de-lances, palm vipers, tropical rattlesnakes, coralsnakes, jumping vipers—locally known as *tommygoffs*—and hog-nosed vipers. Many could be scooped up at night as they warmed themselves on the new concrete highway connecting the area to Panama City.

Thus Ditmars and Greenhall had reason for optimism as they steamed down to Colón armed with hefty canvas bags, snake hooks, nooses, flashlights, machetes, forceps, boxes, antivenin, and other appurtenances, not to mention motion picture apparatus and weather instruments. On arrival, the snake-hunters were assigned as guides a burly young US Army engineer named Abe Halliday and a Panamanian "woodsman" for exploring the forest. John O'Reilly, a New York scientist stationed at Barro Colorado Island, completed the hunting party.

Halliday had himself recently dispatched a huge bushmaster after its tail vibrations disturbed his nap. "I thought it was some kind of a bug," he told the visitors. "It kept on buzzing so loud that I turned around, and there was a seven-foot bushmaster coiled around and ready to let go with his head, about two feet behind me. I must have jumped up from a sitting position and changed directions in the air, because I landed five feet away with my gun in my hand and I swear I was shooting before I felt myself light."

This was one of a further eleven bushmasters Halliday and his companions had killed in the past eighty-five days. Ditmars did the arithmetic: *eighteen bushmasters in less than three months!* Expectations were surely at fever pitch as the snake-hunters motored in torrential rain toward the Madden Dam area. Yet, despite hunting the hot forest day and night, including a promising series of limestone ledges recalling prime rattler habitat back home, not a single snake of any kind was found, let alone a bushmaster. A wry smile must have played over Ditmars's lips as, stepping back on board the *Calamares* two weeks later, he was summoned to the cabin of the ship's doctor. Nestled among medical books was a tiny boa constrictor.

Ditmars had at least "obtained valuable data on the habitat of the bushmaster" as well as "some giant frogs, a 'dragon' lizard which ran on its hind legs, some iguanas fully five feet long, and a particularly large and black tarantula." But these must have been of scant consolation.

The newspaper headlines attending his homecoming cannot have helped: "Curator Returns Without Big Snake," "Ditmars Fails In Snake Hunt," and so on. "Curator Ditmars . . . returned even more empty-handed than if he had been an astronomer in search of a total eclipse," remarked the *New York Times*. "[His] experience was surprisingly like what it would have been if he had landed in Southern California and it had started to rain . . . it must hurt to be the biggest snake man in the United States and fail to secure a specimen of the kind that simply swarms in the detective novels, where their sting is instant and untraceable death." Associate editor of the *Brooklyn Eagle* John Alden meanwhile theorized—in his trademark verse—that the bushmaster simply knew the curator was coming: "I'm forced to believe that some warning went forth / By wireless from copperhead clans at the North; / Or a Palisades rattlesnake's rattle, broadcasted, / Made the Bushmaster tremble as long as long as it lasted."

As if to compound matters, a month later, two American women ran over a bushmaster on the Panama highway, finishing off the seven-footer with the engine crank.

And it was the same story in 1933, when Ditmars and Greenhall once more went to Panama. Again, numerous recent sightings had sent hopes soaring. "Engineers running transits through the jungle in the Madden Dam vicinity have seen the cobra-shaped head and the rough knob-like scales of its body a hundred times in the last weeks," revealed the *New York Times*. The bushmasters were of record-breaking proportions, several measuring "ten, even twelve feet long and a foot in diameter." More electrifying still were reports that a live specimen had been captured near Colón. According to the *Washington Post*, Ditmars's "encounters with the bushmaster in Central America should add a thrilling chapter to his many tales of adventure in capturing venomous reptiles." Meanwhile, under the headline, ZOO OFFICIAL WILL STALK BUSHMASTER, Connecticut's *Hartford Courant* played up the danger: "It's particularly bad for a human being if the bushmaster should approach from behind. The snake weaves slowly and determinedly from side to side, gaining height to strike, and hits like lightning."

Depressingly, the Colón snake proved not to be a bushmaster but a harmless species of snake resembling a fer-de-lance, and the forest hunts were as unproductive as ever. At least when Ditmars and Greenhall stepped aboard the New York–bound fruit liner SS *Metapan* on September 10, 1933, they were able to wire ahead some astonishing news. For, along with the usual miscellany of exotic snakes, spiders, lizards, turtles, and insects, the zoo men had in their possession two small mammals which could rival the bushmaster. Scientists knew them as *Desmodus rotundus*.

To everyone else, they were vampire bats.

THANKS to Dean Ripa I had seen live bushmasters, but could I find a wild one for myself? I would find out soon enough, as I'd be heading down to bushmaster territory presently.

The following morning, before leaving Wilmington, I dropped by the serpentarium again and found Dean in a storeroom stacking translucent plastic crates. Each measured three feet in length and contained a drinking bowl, pages of old newspaper, and a bushmaster.

"They all have different personalities," Dean said going from box to box misting the occupants through the air holes punched in the side. "Some are very docile, some will jump out and bite you!"

I reflected again on that attic in the Bronx, the snake terrorizing a young Raymond Ditmars all those years ago. "Snakes are first cowards, next bluffers, and last of all warriors," observed Clifford H. Pope, among Ditmars's more notable protégés and the curator himself once stated that venomous snakes never chased an enemy, their attitude toward man merely that of self-defense. But Ditmars was probably talking about North American species.

Nevertheless, modern experts question the curator's interpretation of bushmaster behavior. For instance, during the research for this book, Bill Lamar, a respected tropical herpetologist who, despite "worshipping" Ditmars as a youth, suggested to me that "Ditmars's showmanship invariably led to some excessive or inaccurate characterizations." Bill found that in his experience other venomous species, notably fer-de-lances, were far more willing than bushmasters to advance on a human in order to defend themselves.

I asked for Dean's opinion: was Ditmars exaggerating?

"No, I don't think so," he said. "I've had them follow me all the time. They're not trying to kill me. Perhaps Ditmars's bushmaster just thought he was a rat."

"Although it would have struck him in the same way," he added.

Unlike the curator, Dean hadn't escaped injury, suffering a number of bushmaster bites. He likens the experience to "being set on fire, stabbed with a dagger, and then beaten with a sharp, hard stick," adding that "you can't move after a few minutes, and don't want to either." The most recent bite—remarkably, it was his seventh—happened not long ago. He had received enough venom to drop a cow, but fifteen vials of antivenin put him right, although stiffness lingered in his left hand.

"Would you mind getting the other side of this one?" Dean said. "I need to clean it out."

Lowering the box to the floor, he flicked open the red catches at either end and, with extended arms, lifted the green plastic lid away and toward him so that it acted as a temporary shield. The captive bushmaster vibrated its tail against the plastic walls.

I hoped this snake fell into the "docile" category.

"Don't worry. They warn you when they are going to bite you," grinned Dean reading my mind. "Unless they just snap!"

Sensing freedom, the serpent unraveled and eased out onto the floor toward me, tongue stroking at the air. It looked about four feet long. From what I knew of bushmasters I was well within its strike range, but Dean's composure put me at ease.

"I often wonder what Raymond Ditmars would have thought if he was here now and saw all these bushmasters," he said wistfully as he coaxed the viper away from me with a snake hook. "But if it wasn't for him none of this would be here. Without a doubt."

With his free hand, Dean scrunched up the soiled newspaper and placed in some fresh sheets. Thirty seconds later the bushmaster was back in its box. It was probably for the best, I thought.

RAYMOND Ditmars's 1932 expedition to Panama had concluded with another pilgrimage to Gorgas where Herbert Clark again had freshly slaughtered bushmasters to show his friend. This time, though, something else had caught the eye. Clark and his colleague Lawrence H. Dunn believed that vampire bats, common throughout Latin America, could transmit *murrina*, a trypanosome parasite fatally afflicting certain livestock. To the curator's amazement the scientists kept several live specimens of the bat in their laboratory. The mammals were fussy eaters but Clark and Dunn maintained them on blood from local abattoirs. To keep the blood drinkable, the clotting agent fibrin was first removed—a good stir with a cocktail swizzle stick often did the job.

Realizing that an exhibition of these infamous creatures in the Bronx would be sensational, perhaps almost outshining the capture of a bushmaster, Ditmars had added them to his hit list for the following summer's trip. And, thanks to the efforts of his energetic young assistant, Arthur Greenhall in Panama's Chilibrillo caverns, he was successful. During the 1933 expedition the fifty-seven-year-old curator had contracted tropical fever, but rather than sending the bats on to New York by air, he insisted on personally escorting the precious cargo by ship, bringing two quarts of defibrinated blood, packed with ice, fresh from Clark's refrigerator.

Despite these attentions one bat perished on voyage trip home, its death ascribed to the drenching it received during capture. This minor tragedy failed to dampen the fanfare greeting for Volga, as the surviving vampire was sometimes known. Although a mammal, the bat was installed in a glass-fronted case in the reptile house, Ditmars hoping that the building's warmth together with the soundtrack of dripping water and croaking "boop-a-doop" frogs would suit her.

*Time* magazine stated that the star exhibit receiving coast-to-coast coverage was smallish, with a "face like a miniature bulldog's," adding that visitors would see "an unimposing, tightly curled wad of grayish-brown fur" friendly enough with Ditmars "to take tentative nips at his hand." According to another reporter Volga "attracted so much attention that the big snakes were jealous and sulked under their trees. She was so tiny to be so famous!"

Ditmars spent long nights at the reptile house studying and filming the bat's activity, his family later complaining he had missed dinner for a whole week. The mammal's flying and feeding behaviors were of special interest, so too the peculiar way it stalked about hunched on folded wings and down-thrust hind feet. On December 2, Volga unexpectedly gave birth, sending the curator into further raptures. "The mother is the only one of her kind ever exhibited in any zoo," he told the *New York Sun*. "Now we have the good fortune to be able to study the habits of a new-born vampire bat. The thing is worth its weight in gold." To *Time*, "The spitting image of its mother!"

Although both bats died before the year was out—Ditmars blamed "noisy and mischievous visitors"—for a while they had deflected attention from another unsuccessful bushmaster hunt. On his return from Panama Ditmars had rejected suggestions of failure, holding that "the vampires had been the main object" of that summer's expedition. Likewise, in 1934's *Confessions of a Scientist* he writes that the capture of the bats was the "uppermost thought." Such assertions are however contradicted by what he told the *New York Times* on the eve of the outing: "The main thing is the bushmaster. We have had only three in more than thirty years, one little one, and two big ones. The last of the three died nineteen years ago."

A month on, the same paper accused Ditmars of a "cleverly camou-flaged retreat," and taunted its erstwhile employee: "He did not go down to the Canal Zone for vampire bats, even if the attractive creatures do meet a long-felt want in the Bronx. Our biggest reptile man went down to the tropics in quest of the only object that now matters, the lodestar, the *summum bonum* of his future existence. Dr. Ditmars went down in quest of the deadly bushmaster and he returned without a bushmaster. That is the naked truth of the matter. . . . His heart is set on a bushmaster and he won't be happy till he gets one." The words were as painful as they were accurate and Ditmars himself later ranked the failure to catch a bushmaster in Panama among the major disappointments of his life, right up there with "missing the Palm Beach hurricane; missing the eruption of Mt. Lassen—and missing the engines pumping during the fire at Quinn's Livery Stable."

But his luck was about to change. The very next year Raymond Ditmars would bring home to the Bronx Zoo a live bushmaster for the first time in a generation.

# 14

## Six Feet Long and Vicious

*"Like most poisonous snakes, the bushmaster prefers not to fight. As a rule if you leave him strictly alone, he will do the decent thing and leave you alone. But he knows his own weapons and he takes no insults; if you stir him up, he will take the aggressive side instantly. Then all his most dangerous qualities come into play."*

—Raymond L. Ditmars, *Milwaukee Journal*, April 28, 1935

———◆———

*August 26, 1934. Port of Spain, Trinidad.*

ST. THOMAS AND ST. Croix. St. Martin and St. Kitts. The temperatures climbed as the saints went by. Three thousand tons of steel have passed St. Vincent and Montserrat, Antigua and Guadeloupe, Dominica and St. Lucia. Martinique's Mount Pelee volcano snoozed under a lush green blanket, undisturbed by the *Nerissa's* hisses. Rearward too are the Leeward and Windward Islands. No hurricanes this time, alas. And now, more than a week since the curator's ship pushed away from its Manhattan moorings, the coastline of Trinidad is discernible through the venetian blinds of the porthole. The bow anchor rumbles, winches on the loading deck clank. Time Ray and Clara were packed if they're to catch the first shore-bound tender.

Then comes a sharp rap at the door to their stateroom, which is crowded with portable weather instruments from barographs to barometers, hygrometers to thermometers.

"Yes, yes," calls Ray buttoning his pale linen jacket. "We're almost ready."

Another knock.

"All right, all right. I'm coming!" The curator slips into shiny black Balmorals and pulls opens the door. "Now what is it?"

A steward stands in the corridor.

"Professor Urich is aboard."

"Urich? On board already?"

"Yes, Sir. Waiting for you upstairs."

The curator is surprised but pleased: always useful to be met at an unfamiliar port.

"You go ahead, Ray. I'll make sure the girls are ready," says Clara at her dressing table. The curator thanks his wife with a kiss. Looking over her shoulder at the mirror he adjusts his tiepin—a snake's fang—before smoothing the points of his trimmed gray mustache.

Up on deck the air is hot, heavy, and still. Over the side a motley flotilla of launches and harbor tugs is closing on the cruise liner, all raucous whistles and ugly fumes. Two miles eastward across the otherwise somnolent waters, Ray sees the low red roofs of Port of Spain, giving way on both sides to lines of coconut palms. Rearing up behind are the green peaks of the Northern Range.

The curator enters the small but elegant reception room abuzz with passengers, crew, and welcoming parties.

"Dr. Ditmars?"

A portly man in white linen suit who has been leaning on a black wooden cane picks his way through the crowd, his right hand extended. He is older and balder than Ray with a furrowed brow and deep tan suggestive of a lifetime in the tropics.

"Professor Urich?" grins the zoo man.

Handshaking, backslapping, and an exchange of pleasantries ensues between two men who, despite years of correspondence, have until this moment never met.

"Oh, by the way," says Urich, "I have a nice bushmaster for you."

Ray's heart skips a beat.

"I'm sorry Professor, what was that you said?" He knows full well what Urich has just told him, but needs time to process the words.

"I said, I have a bushmaster for you."

"Why, that's thrilling! Where did you catch him?"

"Err. Well, I didn't catch him. He was sort of left on my doorstep. But we'll get the whole story later. Your man Greenhall has also gathered a beautiful collection of other snakes: ten boxes' worth including a fine *balsain*, I mean, fer-de-lance. A crate of land crabs and some tarantulas. Oh and a giant centipede."

Urich pauses then grins. "They're all at my home waiting for you. As is some jolly nice rum punch!"

"Did someone say rum punch?"

Gladyce has appeared at Ray's side, dressed as if emerging from a Fifth Avenue boutique. Like her father, she's beaming from ear to ear.

"That sounds swell!"

Early the next day, a large touring car makes its way out of Port of Spain and along the Eastern Main Road, an asphalt highway skirting the foot of the Northern Range. Neat clay houses and patchwork frame huts give way to palm trees and banana plantations. The vehicle passes the colossal domes of saman trees and hedgerows garlanded with end-of-season hibiscus. A blueish mist lingers on the wide road, empty save the occasional donkey cart or bicyclist.

"They're not so rare here if you know where to look," says Urich who is driving. "Why, on the Carr estate in Caparo they've killed eighteen in the last three months."

Ray, his sole passenger, has of course heard such tales before. This time, though, the old story will have a happy ending. The original plan was for the Ditmarses to spend just one night in Trinidad before completing their cruise to British Guiana. The snake has changed all this.

Their baggage was immediately ordered off the *Nerissa*. They'll reboard the vessel on its return leg.

The curator trails a hand in the cool slipstream, his pipe smoke sucked through the open window. A painful fog hangs in the brain, a legacy of the previous evening's revelries—those cocktails sure creep up on a man. A headache cannot however suppress his excitement.

He has an appointment with a bushmaster!

Ten miles from Port of Spain, the car turns off the road into a tree-lined avenue, sweeping past close-cut lawns and the administration building of the Imperial College of Tropical Agriculture. To avoid disturbing the fragile species, the Professor has left the bushmaster where it was first deposited here at the college. Ray once more presses for the exact circumstances of the bushmaster's capture.

"Unfortunately, that's really all I know at the moment. I just came back to my office to find the animal in a box. A messenger had brought him up from the oil fields close to Point Fortin in the south but seemed too scared to linger. As soon as I can get the whole story, rest assured you'll be the first to know."

They pull up at a wooden outhouse close to some labs in the shade of a silk-cotton tree.

"We've been keeping him here in our mosquito lab," says Urich unfastening one of the largest padlocks the curator has ever seen—and when you work at a zoo you see a lot of padlocks.

Snake hook in hand, the visitor wastes no time in entering. A heavy wooden box, three foot square, rests on a table. A symmetrically coiled form is visible behind a coarse wire screen that has been stapled to the top of the box. Ray exhales with relief. Despite his respect for Urich, the possibility of misidentification has privately nagged at the snake man. Yet, there is no mistaking the famous pineapple scales iridescent in the morning sun, the bright copper-colored skin saddled with thick velvety black rhombs, the blunt head, the tail spine, which even now is beating out its distinctive tattoo.

"Magnificent, Urich! Simply magnificent!"

―◦•◦―

"THEY'RE definitely in my top three. Up there with boa constrictors and Burmese pythons. They're monsters! But at the same time extremely shy, not like a fer-de-lance. You can hold a bushmaster in your hands. It's not advisable but I have done it!"

Smiling, Junior Charleau gripped an imaginary bushmaster as if fighting an invisible tug of war. The strange beauty of Trinidad's legendary giant viper seemed the main appeal for him.

"I'm picturing a freshly shed bushmaster now," he continued, a distant look in his eyes. "It has pearl white scales and gorgeous black diamonds. Beautiful. It's, like, *glowing!*"

I had arrived in Trinidad yesterday. The flight was surprisingly full given that the Caribbean island's spiraling murder rate and recent imposition of a curfew did little to promote it as a tourist destination. However, the plane half-emptied during a stopover in St. Lucia and for the final short hop to Port of Spain I could switch to a window seat. From this altitude the waves below us looked frozen. At a pinch, the steel-blue pattern had the texture of reptilian skin. Was this a good omen?

Trinidad's Northern Range came into view, crowned in pristine green forest, rusty shacks dotting the lower elevations. Was my bushmaster, my *mapepire z'anana*, waiting for me down there somewhere? We overshot the island, tilting back above the Gulf of Paria before swooping down over the Caroni marshland. Far to the south, a sprawling oil refinery could be seen, white storage tanks like giant golf balls shimmering in the haze.

Passing through customs I'd been asked the purpose of my visit.

"I'm researching a book about snakes." It seemed more credible than "I am looking for the world's largest viper." Momentarily bewildered, the female official inscribed *"Book About Snakes"* on a document, her bored expression returning as I moved off into the air-conditioned arrivals hall.

There I was met by Ian, my wife's cousin and a native Trinidadian, who would shepherd me about his island.

The following afternoon we had headed to the outskirts of Port of Spain and the Emperor Valley Zoo, Trinidad's main animal collection. A swift tour of the small and uninspiring series of reptile enclosures had established that no bushmasters were on display. At closing time I'd got to talking with the reptile keeper. His full name was Delbert Charleau Jr. and he had been with the zoo since 1992. Among a handful of youths placed here on a government training program, Charleau was the only one asked to stay: "You're doing a hell of a job, boy," the then curator Hans Boos had said.

We were sitting on a green bench outside the zoo's main entrance. The evening was humid but pleasant. Parrots chattered boisterously in the canopy of a nearby tree. Handsome and now in his early forties, Charleau had graying hair and a precise goatee beard. He continued to effuse over the splendor of the z'anana: "In the sunlight, the scales look like *beads*, like *crystals* on a well-made carpet—"

"But when did you last have one here?" I hated to interrupt the reverie but was anxious to press on with my inquiries.

He now stroked the goatee.

"Let's see. I think we've had three bushmasters over the last six years. One survived for four years! It went *fantastic!* But the conditions have to be right. The bushmaster love dark, humid but not too hot. It loves a *cool* environment. If too hot and dry there is *trouble*. The bushmaster, it will regurgitate food."

I now knew that obtaining a healthy animal was critical to its survival in captivity and sure enough Charleau's record-breaking snake had been parasite-free when captured. It nevertheless failed to shed and died.

"If I wanted to find another one," I asked, "where should I look?"

"Well, farmers in Christophine Valley see them, and a German lady got bitten by one near Asa Wright. She didn't die."

Located high in the Northern Range, the Asa Wright Nature Centre was the country's premier bird-watching reserve, and christophine was not the name of a valley but a gourd-like fruit cultivated on trellises in the same hills. Perhaps the snakes liked ambushing prey in the tangled vines associated with this crop? It sounded like the Northern Range was the place to go.

Grace Olive Wiley with one of her friends, a Mitchell's rattlesnake (*Crotalus mitchellii*). She would die from cobra bite in 1948. (Undated photo, courtesy of James B. Murphy)

It now seems obvious that Trinidad would furnish Raymond Ditmars with his first living bushmaster in almost three decades. Apart from the snake bagged by William Beebe in British Guiana way back in 1916, every specimen had come from the island thanks to R. R. Mole. Why, then, the curator's obsession with Panama? Perhaps it was Mole's demise in 1926. The sixty-six-year-old suffered fatal injuries when his hammock support had collapsed, sending him head-first onto a tiled floor. In any case, the supply of bushmasters from Trinidad had long since dried up, while sightings in Panama during the 1930s were numerous and reliable. Eventually though, vampire bats aside, Panama had proved an expensive distraction. Time for Plan B.

Thus, in early July 1934, when Arthur Greenhall had proposed a trip to the West Indies, he had found Ditmars receptive. Greenhall had been researching travel options downtown and, over luncheon at the zoo's Rocking Stone Restaurant, revealed that the British steamer SS *Nerissa* of the Furness-Withy Line was sailing the following month, taking in various sun-drenched ports and offering five days in Trinidad. "I turned that information over in my mind," Ditmars later wrote. "I had never visited that chain of islands, the time for getting away was right, and Trinidad was rich in reptile life."

A plan fell into place. Greenhall would set off to Port of Spain the very next week aboard the July 19 sailing of the *Nerissa*, with the curator making the same journey in August. Like Ditmars, Greenhall would pay his own way but was tasked with reconnoitering and collecting what specimens he could, leaving orders for others. While the bushmaster was again the main object, other tropical species were on Ditmars's wish list: "the boa constrictor and the big anaconda, or water boa; the yellow tree boa, the beautiful golden tree snake, the vivid green parrot snake, or *chacoya*; the black-and-yellow rat snake, ten feet long but not much thicker than a carriage whip and as shining and smooth as if it had been done up in Japanese lacquer."

In addition, Greenhall was to seek coralsnakes and the irascible fer-de-lance, as well as big tropical spiders, the Hercules beetle, and a horned frog that "looks as if he had been painted with gold radiator paint and barks and bites—painfully." Vampire bats too occurred in Trinidad and a few should be obtained to corroborate Ditmars's earlier groundbreaking observations on the species. A side trip to British Guiana on the South

American mainland was included on Greenhall's busy agenda. The colony's mighty Demerara River was home to a giant freshwater turtle and a toad whose young underwent their entire development—from eggs, through tadpoles to miniatures of their parents—in tiny pockets embedded in their mother's back. Moreover, as Beebe had proved, the bushmaster inhabited British Guiana, where it went by the name *counacouchi*.

William Bridges of the *New York Sun* was among those present at the famous lunch. An Indiana native, Bridges was among many reporters haunting the zoo in the hope of "human-interest stories about animals." Ditmars and Greenhall's enthusiasm for the forthcoming adventure was infectious. Bridges had covered the previous failed bushmaster quests and voiced a desire to come along on this one. The curator suggested that Bridges ask his city editor to assign him to Greenhall's trip. "You've never been in the tropics, you've never been bitten by redbugs or chiggers or dodged malaria mosquitoes, you've never hunted bushmasters or vampire bats," said Ditmars. "Sell him the idea of the fresh viewpoint, stories of your reactions when you're dropped in the lap of the tropics." The gambit worked. A couple of weeks later Bridges was enjoying rum twizzles on the terrace of Port of Spain's Queen's Park Hotel awaiting the arrival of Greenhall's ship, the journalist having leap-frogged the young zoologist courtesy of a Pan-American seaplane. Bridges would file regular dispatches to his paper and went on to document the 1934 trip in *Snake-Hunters' Holiday: Tropical Adventures in Search of Bats and the Bushmaster,* a lively account coauthored with Ditmars.

To smooth Greenhall's way in the tropics the curator gave him cash to buy specimens and letters of introduction to government scientists including F. W. Urich. Ditmars was well aware of Urich's long association with Mole. Then in his early sixties, the professor was a leading figure at Trinidad's Imperial College of Tropical Agriculture, a forerunner of today's University of the West Indies. With his bronzed, sinewy field assistant T. P. Ludolph Wehekind, Urich was investigating whether vampire bats were guilty of transmitting paralytic rabies. Human victims of this condition would lose control of their limbs, their muscles would tremble, their head shake whilst spewing saliva. Death was almost inevitable. Over the previous decade eighty-nine people and thousands of cattle in Trinidad had succumbed, prompting an extensive cull of what Urich termed "the bloody little beasts" thought to be carriers. Ditmars described the scientist as "a man who had penetrated all the jungly areas of that luxuriant island." If anyone knew where to find bushmasters it was surely Urich.

Anticipating Ditmars's own departure for Trinidad the journal *Science* announced that the snake man would "make a preliminary survey of the Lesser Antilles to determine the most desirable place in which to carry on research during the summer of 1935." *New Yorker* magazine took the opportunity to rib the snake man, its Talk of the Town section starting with, "Social Note: A bushmaster is coming to New York to look for Dr. Ditmars." When boarding the *Nerissa* on Thursday, August 16, accompanied by his wife, daughters, and now a granddaughter, Gloria, Ditmars played things cool, however, maintaining that, while he would pick up animals, the trip "was purely a vacation." The papers nevertheless revealed that the zoo man "hopes to return in about twenty-five days with a bushmaster or two and other specimens of snakes, also some frogs, toads, and lizards."

In the event, the 1934 expedition surpassed all expectations. Long before the three generations of Ditmarses began their agreeable voyage south, Bridges and Greenhall had assembled an unparalleled menagerie of tropical beasts. Assisted by Wehekind and fuelled by Urich's famous rum punches—a moreish concoction of sugar syrup, White Star rum, and lime—the student and newspaperman had blazed a trail across Trinidad and British Guiana. They had netted tarantulas and turtles, land crabs and centipedes. They had waded swamps for anacondas, scooped up obscenely fat toads, and snared a slumbering fer-de-lance. They had even eclipsed the previous year's accomplishment, securing four male vampire bats from the Diego Martin caves in the Northern Range, as well as half a dozen of the carnivorous variety. With space at a premium back at the reptile house, Greenhall would keep some of the bats in his own city apartment for the next two years.

But the best was saved for last, for on Sunday August 26, 1934, minutes after the *Nerissa* once more weighed anchor in the tranquil waters of the Gulf of Paria, the fifty eight year old Raymond Ditmars learned that also waiting for him would be a bushmaster.

THE morning after the meeting with Junior Charleau saw Ian and me speeding along the Churchill-Roosevelt highway, the country's main east–west artery. We swept past a beer plant, a cookie factory, and a landfill site with circling vultures, known by locals as *corbeaux*. Hand-painted roadside billboards promised PURE MOLASSES, GUITAR LESSONS, or WOODWORK DONE. NO URINE pleaded another. Several glimmering skyscrapers rose incongruously from an otherwise decrepit waterfront. "The Chinese built them. They're empty," said Ian. China was investing heavily in Trinidad and had also funded the new National Academy for the Performing Arts, Port of Spain's dazzling answer to the Sydney Opera House. The motives weren't wholly altruistic; China wanted access to the vast oil and gas reserves lying just off Trinidad's coast.

I had secured an interview with Charleau's former boss, Hans Boos, who had run the zoo for twenty-five years and was also the country's most prominent snake expert. Encountering legal difficulties of late, he now kept a low profile. We were nevertheless welcomed into his spacious white bungalow in Diego Martin, six miles northwest of the capital. As Ian relaxed with a soft drink on the veranda, the elderly herpetologist and his two terriers, Jack and Lilly, led me into a small office, a confusion of books, pamphlets, compact discs, framed photographs of frogs and snakes, filing cabinets, computer hardware. Lined up on one shelf were Ditmars's titles, moldering copies of *The Reptile Book* and *Snake-Hunters' Holiday*. The tropical conditions hadn't been kind.

Hans was as enthralled with the history of herpetology on the island as with the animals themselves, devoting a portion of his authoritative book *The Snakes of Trinidad and Tobago* to the personalities who, over three and half centuries, had collected and catalogued the slithering forms of this Caribbean nation. Moreover, Hans felt personally connected to key protagonists in Ditmars's quest for a bushmaster. In 1960 he had moved to the capital from his sleepy southern hometown of San Fernando to take up a job at Standard Oil. A keen amateur zoologist, he joined the Field Naturalists' Club and gravitated toward the city's Royal Victoria Institute Museum where he met none other than Arthur Greenhall. Ditmars's former field assistant who had helped bring vampire bats to the United States for the first time was by then settled in Trinidad and an authority on the bats, hugely advancing understanding of their role as disease vectors. Hans also befriended Wehekind, another associate of Ditmars. As Wehekind got older Hans became his eyes and hands in the field. "Ludolph was half-blind, had trouble walking and was going deaf," he smiled. "But quite a character. Still wore his pith helmet!"

If Junior Charleau had raised my hopes of finding a bushmaster, Hans Boos now shot them down in flames.

"I personally have never come across one in the wild."

After a lifetime of snake-hunting he had caught his first *mapepire z'anana* just three years ago in a nearby garden. Even then, someone else had found it first.

Depressing news indeed. What hope would I have in just ten days on the island?

"Dr. Raymond L. Ditmars has a bushmaster! Six feet long and vicious."

On Thursday September 6, 1934, William Bridges broke the news that few could have expected. "And so the Doctor wins," he went on, "after twenty-five years of combing the jungles of Central and South America for the deadliest and most treacherous New World reptile." The story made the front page of the *New York Sun*. Equally excited was the *New York Times*. "Ditmars obtains live bushmaster. Succeeds After 30-Year Hunt and Is Bringing Venomous Snake Here From Trinidad," went the headline. For *Time* magazine the news that flashed from the Caribbean was nothing less than a "metropolitan milestone," adding that the snake "gave every indication of a willingness to bite Dr. Ditmars at the first opportunity." Other papers picked up the story and soon the bush-master was making coast-to-coast headlines.

Given recent history, some, including the curator's own colleagues back in the Bronx, hesitated to accept the reports. Talking to the *Sun*, head keeper John Toomey "wanted it known that he had long given up believing everything he read in the papers," insisting that he "would like to have it right from the snake's mouth before he makes any preparations." Ditmars's secretary Grace Davall was "vaguely skeptical."

This of course hardly troubled Ditmars himself. The man of the moment was cock-a-hoop. "I am sure the folks back home will be delighted to see the bushmaster I am taking back with me," he told the *New York Times*. The paper caused bewilderment by listing "fertile ants" among the spoils. The creatures had been encountered in a canyon forty miles from Port of Spain and "having feasted upon rats, appeared sluggish"—unusual behavior for ants, less so for a fer-de-lance. The homophonic error was fixed in subsequent reports.

Almost a fortnight had passed since Urich first presented the bush-master to the curator. Ditmars had immediately abandoned the final leg of his cruise to British Guiana to fruitlessly scour Trinidad's forests, palm groves, and cocoa plantations for a second snake. A week later, he and his family reboarded the *Nerissa* along with Greenhall and Bridges and steamed home. Twenty-six crates of living specimens were stowed care-fully in the forward hold but, enjoying privileges from the start, the bush-master shared Greenhall's first-class cabin. The snake-hunters were just four days out of New York when they cabled the news during a stopover on St. Thomas in the US Virgin Islands. The prize specimen had yet to feed but this was nothing out of the ordinary for a fresh capture, and in any case it was drinking the "considerable amounts of water" poured through airholes in its green traveling cage. Ditmars was confident his fragile trophy would survive the voyage and, although the snake refused to submit to a dental examination, it was regarded as "in good shape."

His faith proved well-founded and within a week the Trinidad bush-master was placed on public display in the reptile house, the former occupant of its cage, a rattlesnake, unceremoniously moved elsewhere. The newcomer, nicknamed "Lecky" in homage to *Lachesis* the scientific name for bushmasters, was a sensation, an estimated one hundred thousand additional visitors flooding the zoo to see what the fuss was all about. Ditmars meanwhile busied himself filming the viper basking in a specially constructed sunning enclosure. One photograph, much reproduced, shows the curator in the paddock capturing motion pictures of what he interpreted as the bushmaster's "gliding style of attack" as a crowd looks on. Hans Boos later questioned whether the snake was attacking, suggesting instead that the bushmaster was frightened in the open area and had been making for the perceived shelter offered by Ditmars and his tripod.

Over the ensuing weeks the newspapers monitored the serpent's progress. It even featured on radio programs; Dale Carnegie, the author of *How to Win Friends and Influence People*, spoke about the "recent capture of the bushmaster—most dangerous of snakes" on a WEAF show sponsored by the Maltex Cereals Company. For the New York Zoological Society the bushmaster was among the most noteworthy acquisitions of 1934, a bumper year which also included Komodo dragons, two rare Tibetan blue bears, and an orangutan donated by Mr. and Mrs. Vincent Astor. The *Los Angeles Times* called Lecky "the Mahatma Gandhi of reptiles." Such was the interest that Ditmars grew to avoid the reptile house when in a hurry as somebody was sure to stop him and fire a volley of questions about the bushmaster. The American Museum of Natural History also benefited, its reptile hall experiencing a 60 percent upswing in visitor numbers. Other zoos caught the bushmaster bug, launching copy-cat missions for the snake in Panama, Colombia, Surinam, and Trinidad. Within months the reptile houses of St. Louis, Philadelphia, and Washington all boasted specimens of their own, belying the difficulties Ditmars had faced.

ALLAN Rodriguez's head was shaved bald. He wore black-rimmed glasses, checked shorts, and sandals, but no shirt. Serpents were tattooed on each upper arm, the words "Snake Man" inked in green below one of them. Several people in Trinidad claimed the title but, having captured an astonishing fifty-two bushmasters, Allan Rodriguez had more right to it than most. Again, few lasted long in captivity.

"You can't give them what they want in captivity," said Allan. "You can do to the best of your abilities. You can give them the certain temperature, a log, but it's like a man in prison—he still lock up."

Ian and I had met the Snake Man at his home, a self-built three-story structure just outside Sangre Grande, a small town thirty miles east of Port of Spain. Time was limited as he was keen to catch an important soccer match on television.

"Snakemen are not made, you are really *born* to be a snakeman." He was now saying in his heavy Trinidad accent, a distinctive fusion of West Indian and Welsh intonation. "You have that *love* for snakes, you have that love to *care* for snakes, you have that love not to *kill* snakes."

"But why collect bushmasters?" I now asked.

Venomous species had fascinated Allan since he read about them in the public library, snakes like cobras, mambas, and, of course, bushmasters.

"I'd always feel that if I am bitten by a snake with a one in a hundred chance to survive, *I* would be the one person in the hundred to live. So I never had that fear of being bitten."

Learning of Hans Boos's continuing failure to trap the legendary *mapepire z'anana*, Allan was prompted to try his luck and succeeded, catching bushmasters both at night and in full sunshine. One outing yielded ten specimens.

"But how did *you* find them so easily?"

Understanding the animal's habitat preferences seemed to be key. "The bushmaster like deep forest, very cool with fallen logs where they can coil in ambush." A sharp change of weather from dry to wet often lured the species from burrows. Allan believed he could sense when snakes were around and would always grab them with bare hands. To hear that he had been bitten eleven times came as little surprise.

"Four serious. One rattlesnake, one bushmaster, and two fer-de-lance." He indicated several small marks on both hands, the right bequeathed a permanent tremor. "When I sign my name I have to explain that the shaking isn't because I'm uneducated!"

Allan's snake-hunting days were now behind him due to recent heart surgery which had left a thin vertical scar running down his hairless chest. Perhaps it was a good thing the Snake Man had caught his last bushmaster. Bidding him goodbye, we headed to the nearby Sangre Grande Hospital.

As elsewhere, the island boasted a canon of ineffective folk cures for snakebite. In the nineteenth century, the poet and botanist Sylvester Devenish maintained that he had saved a dog, bitten five times about the head by a *mapepire*, with extracts from a specific forest vine. Another response was to eat a mouthful of dirt. Of course the best remedy was antivenin. In Trinidad the only stocks were held at this particular hospital with whose director, Angelie Lochan, I now had an appointment.

While Ian waited in the car, I was waved through the stuffy waiting room to Angelie's office. Small, windowless, and tucked away in the hospital pharmacy, it was modest for a person of her status. Bites, she revealed, were common, about four per month requiring treatment but there had been just one fatality in the last six years.

"And that was due to other complications," she insisted. "The patient didn't come to the hospital in time." *Mapepire balsain*, the fer-de-lance, was responsible for most incidents, but *mapepire z'anana* were implicated in a fifth of cases, many near the Asa Wright Nature Centre, further confirmation of where to focus my search.

By chance, a man in his twenties admitted with a fer-de-lance bite was recovering in a ward having received four vials of serum the previous evening. The young patient, a farm laborer, was sitting up in bed and seemed healthy enough. He brandished an inflamed index finger, explaining that while taming some "bad bush" yesterday he had grabbed a cocoa tree and felt a sting "like a scorpion." The culprit was a *balsain*, not a *z'anana* which he knew had "a black back and the belly orange." The victim's instant reaction was to munch earth. Folk remedies died hard here.

"It kill any kind of poison!"

I wasn't convinced. If a bushmaster found me before I found it I'd be phoning Sangre Grande, not eating mud.

Driving back to Port of Spain, my cell phone buzzed into life.

It was Atkin Isaac, a conservation officer at Asa Wright, with whom I had earlier corresponded by email.

"A six-foot-long *z'anana* has been caught today by a christophine farmer . . ."

"What wonderful news!"

"But the farmer killed it."

Raymond Ditmars films "Lecky," the first bushmaster to be exhibited at the Bronx Zoo in a generation, 1934. (Courtesy of Kraig Adler and Wildlife Conservation Society)

BACK in the fall of 1934, as Raymond Ditmars reveled in the interest surrounding the Bronx Zoo's first bushmaster in decades, a slight disappointment must have nagged at the curator for his failure to snare the viper himself. The full story of Lecky's capture emerged weeks afterward. In the early hours of August 17, the electricity had gone off at a pumping station operated by the Cruze Oil Company in a recently cleared section of forest. A group of oil workers sat in a darkened engine shed adjacent to the derrick, chatting and smoking while the dynamo plant was repaired. When the lights came back on ninety minutes later the huge serpent was revealed slithering across the floor of the shack. As his colleagues reached for clubs, an American engineer, L. A. Thomas, who knew of Ditmars's requirement for a *mapepire z'anana*, had the gumption to noose the viper and box it up. A Louisiana native, the oil man was no stranger to big snakes. "There was a lively tussle, but Thomas won on all points," as the curator put it.

Of course a few curmudgeons sought to dampen the hysteria. "It is the old story of making a mountain of a molehill," wrote Richard K. Sobrian in a letter to the *New York Times*. A Trinidad native, Sobrian insisted that bushmasters were readily found in the land of his birth. "If Dr. Ditmars needs a supply of them, he could very easily get as many as he desires simply by offering to pay five or ten dollars for the best specimens." And things were about to take a turn for the worse.

All too aware of the species's fragility in captivity, Ditmars had done what he could to give Lecky a fighting chance: leafy debris from a rhododendron grove was strewn about the enclosure to recreate Trinidad's forest floor while temperature and humidity were kept at tropical levels. Yet, soon after the serpent's arrival, "it was having difficulty with its old skin," Greenhall later recalled. An inability to shed is life threatening for any snake so Ditmars ordered the bushmaster be saturated several times daily with tepid water from a misting nozzle. The tactic seemed to work and Lecky sloughed off the old skin, the curator helping with a wad of steel wool fixed to a five-foot-long bamboo pole. He described the snake emerging "in a vivid coat of pinkish-brown with cross-bands of black."

More alarming was that Lecky still wasn't hungry. For weeks the bushmaster had been turning its snout up at dead rats trapped for it in the Bronx Zoo's deer barn. "It seems strange he won't eat, because bushmasters are particularly fearless in their wild state," mused Ditmars. "I should say the bushmaster is a snake of mystery." By early October he had enlisted the help of Grace Olive Wiley, curator of reptiles at Chicago's Brookfield Zoo. Wiley was slight, middle-aged and famed for her apparent empathy for venomous snakes, which she freely handled. "Somehow they know very, very soon that I am friendly and like them," said Wiley, who would die in 1948 from cobra bite. "They appear to listen intently when I stand quietly at their open door and talk to them in a low, soothing voice." Praising Wiley's "intuition in dealing with snakes," Ditmars called her a "remarkable woman." Yet, even the feminine touch failed to turn things around.

The last resort was brute force. Anticipating such an eventuality, the *Home News*, a local Bronx newspaper, asked "who in the Bronx Zoo is going to force food down the throat of the bushmaster with his deadly fangs ready to strike at least an instant's notice?" The answer was of course Raymond Ditmars, although his primary concern was the snake's welfare, not his own: "it was a choice of letting him starve or of taking the risk of killing him by a broken vertebra in the process of force-feeding. That chance seemed to be worth taking." On November 10, Toomey pinned Lecky down on a table in a studio at one end of the reptile house and as he grasped the snake securely behind the neck, Ditmars used forceps to shove a freshly killed and skinned rabbit into its mouth. To the relief of all concerned, the snake swallowed. "Out of sheer bewilderment, perhaps!" Ditmars later admitted. The crisis was over.

"We will now feed this bushmaster a rat about every ten days," announced the curator. "When the nervousness passes, I should not be surprised if we could abandon force-feeding."

Lecky would be force-fed six further times before, on the morning of November 22, Toomey found it dead. The cause was mystifying for the serpent had improved of late. An autopsy revealed that the bushmaster had died of pneumonia induced by an infestation of two-inch-long worms. The parasites had accompanied the snake from Trinidad, explaining their host's lack of appetite. Even in death, Lecky attracted zoological attention, the zoo's veterinarian Charles V. Noback, arranging for color photographs of the finding to be made for future research. One worm had attached itself to a wall of the snake's heart. "If I wanted to be sensational about a matter of real scientific interest," wrote Ditmars in 1935, "I could intimate that he died of a broken heart!"

# 15

# We Can Get All We Want Now

*"[B]ehind the scenes in a great zoölogical park there is always an atmosphere of study and quiet observation, of recording habits and aptitudes, of research and questing for information. There are adventures and misadventures, fun and excitement, and a great many puzzles that only long experience can solve."*

—Raymond L. Ditmars & William Bridges, *Wild Animal World* (1937)

⎯⎯●⎯⎯

"I FIRST READ SNAKE-*Hunters' Holiday* when I was in grade school. It was basically, 'Let's go to Trinidad and collect snakes for the summer and have fun!' That was maybe where I got the idea to come here."

We were in the Rituals coffee shop on the campus of the University of the West Indies, ten miles east of Port of Spain. For John C. Murphy, a prominent Chicago-based herpetologist who had been coming to the island for years, Ditmars was clearly an important influence. In 1997 John had published a comprehensive guide to the herps of Trinidad and Tobago and, with Hans Boos retired, was among the few studying the snakes here. He was now updating his guide, as well as gathering evidence for his theory that many of the country's reptiles and amphibians were distinct enough from mainland counterparts to be considered separate species.

John shared my enthusiasm for finding a bushmaster. A veteran of almost a dozen expeditions to the island, he had never seen the viper in the wild. If we caught one he would extract DNA, either from the blood or by snipping the tail, to compare with that of mainland bushmasters. Joining us would be Gabriel Hast, John's wiry young assistant. A zoology student, Gabe's readiness to launch himself up trees or pounce into thick vegetation after a specimen recalled the exuberance of Ditmars's own associate, Arthur Greenhall.

After stocking up at Hi Lo, a small supermarket near the University, we headed for the hills in John's rental vehicle, a tatty Nissan Sunny ill suited to the roads we would face but unlikely to interest carjackers. Our destination was an elegant colonial bungalow high in the Northern Range. Once the summer retreat for the British governor, the building and surrounding estate, known as Verdant Vale, was acquired by the Siegert family who had made a fortune in the nineteenth century inventing Angostura bitters. A prerequisite for the pink gins and rum cocktails enjoyed across the British Empire, the recipe is secret to this day.

During the Second World War, US troops convalesced here and then in 1949 none other than William Beebe, now seventy-two, purchased the property, naming it Simla after the Indian hill town he had visited in his youth. With his longtime partner and fellow scientist Jocelyn Crane, Beebe converted it into a research station for the study of plants, birds, insects, and bats in the surrounding rainforest. According to Beebe's biographer Carol Grant Gould, Walt Disney and his wife were among a succession of old friends and colleagues who would drop by to enjoy a rum or two—"Simla Specials"—on the stone-flagged terrace with Beebe and Crane. After Beebe's death from pneumonia in 1962 Simla fell into disuse and, in 1974, it was donated to the nearby Asa Wright Nature Center, which has encouraged its continuing use for science.

Simla was an hour's drive from Port of Spain, the only difficulty being encountered on the final steep stretch to the research center. The tarmac had disintegrated and the bottom of the vehicle ground ominously against the bumpy track. Our arrival was marked by a brief angry downpour, rattling Simla's copper-roofed building. A sign out front read WILLIAM BEEBE TROPICAL RESEARCH STATION. The place had been rechristened in the great man's honor a year after his passing, although his own choice of name seemed to have stuck. The glory days were long gone but the shuttered windows and stylish French doors lent Simla a faded charm. Best of all, this was *z'anana* territory; Beebe himself had caught one here in 1950.

We didn't hang around long at Simla. The internet was down and John was eager to take samples from the bushmaster killed in the christophine plantation. The snake was on ice up at Asa Wright and within the hour we were on the center's commodious terrace, checking emails and chewing on a late lunch of burgers and fries. Before us fell away a thickly forested valley, in the foreground hummingbirds flitted between suspended plastic feeders loaded with sugary water.

Established in 1967 at the Spring Hill Estate, a former cocoa-coffee-citrus plantation, Asa Wright preserved many acres of undulating tropical woodland in the Arima and Aripo Valleys, including pockets of the mature climax rainforest that once covered the island. The more indolent of ecotourists could while away hours sipping punch and spotting birds from the veranda, although for the complete experience visitors were invited to don hiking boots and take a guided walk in the forest itself.

Mukesh Ramdass, the chief naturalist guide at Asa Wright, now appeared from just such an excursion, binoculars around his neck, a walkie-talkie crackling on his belt. As his bedraggled party congregated at the terrace bar, the fresh-faced Mukesh led us downstairs to a storeroom with bookshelves and a chest freezer from which he retrieved a black refuse bag. Inside the plastic bag was another, and inside that the dead bushmaster.

"Hmmm, I'd say four foot rather than six," said John examining a stiff reptilian coil like those back at the Smithsonian, albeit free of the odor of pickling alcohol. Again I yielded to the insolent but irresistible urge to run my fingers over those rough scales. The rattleless tail-tip protruded from the corpse, perhaps delivering a final silent warning.

The details surrounding the snake's discovery were vague, but according to Atkin Isaac, who later joined us at Asa Wright, the snake had turned up near the Arima Valley road where the christophine farmer had bludgeoned it to death. He had at least refrained from slashing the bushmaster to pieces with his cutlass, a typical response in such encounters, but the battered head and frozen blood stains indicated that he had taken no chances. How maddening to know that just forty-eight hours earlier the target of my quest was on the move not far from here!

Atkin shared my frustration at the bushmaster's fate. "The local community always tells us, especially if it is something rare like a bushmaster. We encourage them not to kill anything."

The find at least proved the snakes were still around.


RAYMOND Ditmars had his bushmaster. Did he ease up a little? Hang up his snake stick? Not a bit of it. Once a collector, always a collector and at fifty-eight he retained the zest of many half his age. On top of curating the Bronx Zoo's mammal and reptile departments, he continued writing books, shooting films, and lecturing, and each summer ventured back to the tropics with family and friends on what the press would call "busman's holidays." Indeed in 1935, the very next year, Ditmars collected a second Trinidad bushmaster, Urich again the provider. The specimen was a "remarkably good-tempered" juvenile christened "Cleopatra Arrima" (the second name a misspelling of the Arima Valley whence it was procured) and proved hardier than its predecessor, gobbling down any food offered. The following June, Ditmars reported that eight months after its introduction to the reptile house, Cleo was thriving and had "devoured its fifty-fourth mouse since entering a life of captivity, which is some kind of record." He spoke too soon; two mice later the snake perished. Parasites again.

The next summer's trip took in Haiti, Colombia, and Panama where the curator was astonished to see a trio of live bushmasters in Dr. Clark's laboratory. "It is doubtful, in the long history of zoological collections," Ditmars observed, "that three living bushmasters have ever before been seen at one time." He departed without the snakes this time, but in April 1938, the reptile house hosted yet another bushmaster, coiled in a bower of dampened leaves and evergreen boughs. Ditmars hadn't even left town for this one; bushmaster number three was caught in Trinidad by workers at the Seismograph Service Corporation and shipped north according to the curator's detailed instructions.

But the importance of bushmasters, and indeed snakes as a whole, seemed to recede. It was as if a lifelong ambition had been realized and Ditmars was ready for new challenges. Indeed, soon after disembarking the *Nerissa* back in 1934 he was already downplaying the achievement. "It's true that I've been looking for a bushmaster off and on for a great many years without being able to bring one back," he told the papers. "Nevertheless, I think we can get all we want now. The bushmaster never has been really rare; he was simply hard to get alive."

ALL around us the vegetation was lit up in strobing red and blue. A large, white SUV rumbled alongside us adorned with the letters TTPS. Trinidad and Tobago Police Service. Two members of the island's finest wanted to know what we were doing. It was the middle of nowhere. It was dark. We were going at ten miles an hour in a scruffy city car. They also suggested — correctly — that we might only have just buckled up.

"We're researchers. Staying at Simla," said John craning his neck from the window. The cops extinguished their flashers and moved away. We had been lucky: driving without a seatbelt attracted a hefty spot fine.

The night closed in once more.

At first we had passed small settlements attended by stray dogs and the sharp odor of burning rubbish, but traces of civilization had vanished as we twisted higher into ever-thicker forest. The mesmerizing yellow beam of the Nissan's headlamps brushed over blown-down leaves, seed pods, twigs, the latter's serpentine form prompting frequent double takes. A heavy vegetal smell now predominated, the squeaks, pips, and chirrups of frogs and crickets were louder.

Exploring the back roads at dusk was a great way to find tropical snakes, which loved sprawling on the still-warm blacktop. That was the theory anyway. We had been running up and down this and other zigzagging routes for three evenings now and had yet to see a thing. That's not quite fair. We had scraped up various squashed serpents including a flat coralsnake, a flat fer-de-lance, and a flat green parrot snake. This last delighted John who suspected Trinidad's parrot snakes to be unique to the island. He needed DNA to test his theory, and road-kill DNA was as good as any.

The apparent paucity of serpent life troubled him. Where were they? Climate change was one explanation. In the tropics the first proper rainfall of the wet season was the meteorological equivalent of a caffeine shot, kick-starting forest dwellers after months of torpor. Herps were particularly active during this period, moving about in search of prey, and we had therefore timed our visit for the first rains. But this year, the supposed dry season had been unusually wet. Perhaps, John reasoned, Trinidad's snakes had already done their feeding, gone to ground. Nevertheless, a nice big storm wouldn't hurt.

Soon after our run-in with the law, the blinking red light of a radio mast could be seen up ahead. This was among the highest points on the island. In less than a mile the road would crest the hill, tumbling down the far side to Blanchisseuse on Trinidad's northern coast. Through gaps in the silhouetted foliage we saw the shimmering lights of the plain a thousand feet below. The air was cooler up here, maybe too cool for snakes.

"OK, I guess we should turn round, we might see something on the way down," said John. We didn't.

The following morning I was roused by a welcome noise. The noise of rain. Proper rain. The air was fresher and redolent of coriander. Locals called the plant responsible *chado benny*, meaning "blessed thistle." Was my bushmaster hunt going to be blessed after all? Today was my last in Trinidad and we planned to investigate two new sites known for *z'anana*.

Joining us was Tom Anton, a friend of John's who'd just flown in from Chicago. Brimming with energy Tom counted scorpions, snakes, crayfish, and the British Lee Enfield rifle among eclectic interests. He also spoke of his "life list"—spectacular animals to see before he died—which included the black mamba, free-swimming great white sharks, and a Mexican scorpion found in the crevices of old lava flows. The bushmaster was up there too.

"Let's get going on this *Lachesis Roundup*! This *Bushmaster Rodeo*!" exclaimed Tom as we drove off from Simla after lunch.

Perhaps our luck truly was in because minutes into the journey Tom yelled again.

"Snake!"

John slammed on the brakes as his friend leapt out to scoop up a beige serpent from the road ahead. Perhaps two feet long, the reptile wound about Tom's arm and chewed on his trouser leg.

"*Pseustes poecilonotus!*" announced John with a grin, a non-venomous species common across Latin America. The captive faced a barrage of camera flashes before being stuffed into a collecting bag. Confirmation that Trinidad had at least one living, three-dimensional snake was a relief.

A few miles down the Arima Valley road we rendezvoused with Abraham Diaz, a photographer for the *Trinidad Guardian*. The country's leading newspaper had learned of my quest, adding pressure to deliver the goods. We also collected Mukesh and Molly Calderon, a fellow guide. Both sported knee-high wellingtons. I now regretted my own choice of footwear, hiking boots that stopped an inch above the ankle and offered meager protection against snake-bites. Ditmars would have tutted at me—or *stupsed*, as they say in Trinidad.

The first potential bushmaster site was a six-hundred-acre former cocoa plantation in a neighboring valley. The property, overlooked by a decaying two-story building, was now managed by Asa Wright. Someone had been busy with a brush cutter and new growth was widespread and dense, obscuring ground-moving creatures. The proficient snake-hunter would have brought a machete to clear vegetation. I wasn't a proficient snake-hunter. Some experts maintained that they were able to sniff out venomous snakes, whose odor they likened to that of cucumbers. All I smelled was mud and rotting vegetation. We traipsed for an hour finding just a tarantula. Abraham looked bored.

We moved on to a nearby village, passing a moldering blue Land Rover abandoned at the roadside. Parking close to a house, we prepared to walk down to another old plantation. Looking for a fillip, I asked a passerby in a Chelsea soccer shirt whether he'd seen any snakes here.

"Yeah, plenty snakes, man."

Abraham wasn't convinced, for at this point he bid us farewell. Perhaps he wanted real news to cover. Sure enough, another two hours of strenuous exploration in the surrounding hills, some thickly wooded, yielded nothing beyond a small frog that excited John and Tom. I was drained, despondent, and drenched with sweat. I would be leaving Trinidad without seeing a bushmaster.

I wasn't surprised. Years making wildlife films taught me that when traveling to a remote location to document a rare species, animal behavior, or other natural phenomenon that had been witnessed for years, including in the days running up to my arrival, the object of the trip would prove elusive. And, yet, within a day of departure, the thing would once more manifest itself. At best my failure at least allowed me to appreciate Ditmars's own disappointments. But this was scant consolation because of course, unlike me, he did finally bring home the goods.

VAMPIRE bats proved an enduring interest for Ditmars, who continued to collect, study, and exhibit what he regarded as an intelligent species, while being troubled by measures to eradicate them from Trinidad — over the years, dynamite, poison, and flamethrowers were used. According to William Bridges, a local slaughterhouse delivered half a gallon of fresh blood to the zoo twice weekly: "each night six small, shallow dishes of blood are placed in the bottom of the vampires' cage. Each morning the floors and walls are splattered with dried blood." Before his death Ditmars devised a dimly lit vampire bat cave in the reptile house swarming with stingless scorpions, giant crickets, and cockroaches, pioneering the habitat-themed exhibits that would become commonplace in modern zoos.

He revisited his earliest passions, too. Ditmars would be forever associated with reptiles, yet amphibians and insects had always been close to his heart, and exploits with them in his autumn years kept him and the zoo in the public eye. In October 1936, for instance, Ditmars brought back from Trinidad's Nariva Swamp a giant tadpole of the paradoxical frog, a bizarre species whose adult form is dwarfed by its young. The *New York Sun* was fascinated: "The tadpole . . . is a freak that sometimes is thirteen inches long, mainly tail, the body being usually the size of a ping-pong ball. As it approaches frog manhood, instead of becoming a monster it hatches into a frog about two inches long, including legs."

And in 1938 the sixty-two-year-old curator returned to Trinidad once more. In his sights this time were parasol ants, named for their habit of conveying aloft leaf and flower fragments like tiny umbrellas. Plantation owners knew of the ants' preference for the more delicate of their crops, and went to war on them with sulfur and arsenic. The insects' nourishment came not from the plant material but from fungus grown on it within the nest. As with so many of Trinidad's zoological curiosities, it was Professor Urich, dead from a stroke the previous year, who had first interested his friend in the ants. Ditmars wanted to establish a colony in the reptile house, the new exhibit timed to coincide with the publication of his latest work for children, *The Book of Insect Oddities*.

That year's trip was as memorable, however, for what didn't make it back. Ditmars had set off home from the West Indies with a dozen frogs of the species *Leptodactylus fallax*, but by the time he reached New York they were gone. The shamefaced curator explained to waiting reporters that on the islands of Dominica and Montserrat, the plump, bronze-hued frogs were a delicacy going by the name "mountain chickens," which could be purchased for a shilling a piece in local markets. Having eaten one, it had been so good that he and fellow passengers polished off the rest. "There will be an empty cage in the reptile house to keep the doctor's conscience pricking," observed the *New York Post*. Populations of *Leptodactylus fallax* were already dwindling thanks to predation from mongoose, and the species is today among the world's most endangered. This wasn't Ditmars's finest hour.

The parasol ants at least were a hit. From a nucleus of two-hundred individuals Ditmars created a colony of ten thousand that became a favorite exhibit at the zoo. The insects thrived on a diet of expensive hothouse rose petals, chiefly the yellow ones, although the ants' numbers had periodically to be replenished. When they descended into cannibalism one winter Ditmars arranged for the airlift of an "under-study colony" from Trinidad; "Ants Flown to Zoo as 'Strike-Breakers'" was the headline in the *New York Times*. The popularity of the parasol ants, as well as the success of the New York Zoological Society's temporary exhibition of spiders, grasshoppers, centipedes, scorpions, and other invertebrates at the 1939–40 World's Fair, spawned a new department of insects with Ditmars in charge. "After you have seen Alice the elephant, Pete the hippo, and the other mountains of flesh at the zoo, the insect house will be an entrancing menagerie of miniatures, with all the fascination that very small things have," promised Ditmars in October 1941. The new exhibit would include insects as "beautiful as perfectly cut jewels," ghost bugs and robber flies, ant lions and electric-light bugs, black widow spiders and tarantulas. Spiders are not insects of course but the curator determined not to "split hairs about these scientific distinctions at the insect house."

Ditmars's career had come full circle. He had started out pinning insects at the American Museum of Natural History and fifty years later was working with them again. He had grand plans: "we shall divide the house into five sections, each devoted to the insects of a different continent,'" but he admitted that "collections of such scope are not easily built up in the middle of a world war."

In the event, he would not live to see the insect department up and running, and it fell to a successor to open the insectarium. Since his early sixties Ditmars had complained of throat infections, aggravated if not caused by the public speaking, not to mention his weakness for pipe tobacco. In January 1942, a bout of streptococcal laryngitis forced him to relinquish his post as curator of reptiles and mammals. For a while new sulfur-based drugs suppressed the illness, but Ditmars relapsed and in February was admitted to St. Luke's Hospital in Manhattan's Upper West Side with pneumonia. He would never see his beloved reptile house again.

Seventy-seven days later, at 7:57 a.m. on Tuesday, May 12, Raymond Lee Ditmars was pronounced dead. He was a month short of his sixty-sixth birthday.

One of the last images of Raymond Ditmars, as he takes delivery of Galápagos tortoises (*Geochelone nigra*), Bronx Zoo, 1941. (© Wildlife Conservation Society)

# EPILOGUE

## My Happiest Hours

*"[T]he intensive scientist—though he might fail to go church—had, in his profound respect for the life he studied, a religion all his own."*

—Raymond L. Ditmars, *Strange Animals I Have Known* (1931)

———◆———

GRINDING GEARS, RUMBLING DIESEL engines, and the warning alarms of reversing trucks formed the soundtrack to my final morning in Trinidad. Exhaust and dust tainted the air. No, I wasn't back in Port of Spain. This was still Simla.

Long a feature of the Northern Range, quarrying activities had intensified in recent years to meet rising demand for limestone, gravel, and sand. Dozens of operations were now blasting, grinding, and digging away the hills from Maracas in the west to Matura in the east. Already, half a mountain of rock had been removed from the immediate vicinity of Simla, obliterating a substantial proportion of the surrounding forest and threatening to undermine the building itself. These days the sterile brown cliffs of a high quarry face were visible through a veneer of vegetation. The Verdant Vale was all but gone.

All terrible news for the bushmaster, of course. That this most sensitive of snakes was scarce in Trinidad was unsurprising given the disturbance. And the story was the same throughout its range, from the coastal forests of Costa Rica and southern Nicaragua to the wilds of Brazil, Ecuador, and Peru. Whether it was the building of vast hydroelectric dams,

271

the extraction of oil and minerals, or the clear felling of trees, the bushmaster's territory was disappearing, taking the snake with it. The most exquisite of venom, the most perfect of camouflage was no match for bulldozers, logging, and dynamite.

A case in point was an isolated population of bushmasters found in Brazil's Atlantic rainforest, a delicate and irreplaceable ecosystem most famous for its golden lion tamarin monkeys. The forest once stretched the length of the eastern seaboard but more than 93 percent of it was now gone, according to the scientist Rodrigo C. G. de Souza, who has started captive breeding the snakes he knows are at imminent risk of extinction. But plans are now afoot to drive a rail line through remaining pockets of this unique forest to take iron ore mined in the Brazilian interior to the Atlantic port of Ilheus. "Chances are there will be a political retaliation against my work because I'm against that railroad," Rodrigo told me in an email a few months later.

Even where good habitat survived, any interaction between human and bushmaster invariably ended badly for the snake. As Hans Boos observed back in Trinidad, "it is the rare *mapepire z'anana* that, once seen, escapes alive from woodsmen or hunters, who view it as their duty to rid the high woods and jungles of this 'menace,' and expensive shotgun shells are spent in killing this snake whenever it is encountered." In the 1983–84 hunting season, a single hunter slew twenty *z'ananas*. Some kind of record. Despite Ditmars's efforts, it still seemed that the only good snake was a dead snake.

Before packing my bags the previous evening I took a last dejected stroll around Simla. I paused to observe ants scampering about a stone wall, when a glossy bronze-colored creature emerged from a crevice. The thing was small enough to be a millipede but lacked legs. I snatched it up and brought it to John.

"*Epictia tenella*, a blind snake," he announced. The animal, which ate ants, termites, and their eggs, would barely have encircled my wrist.

In fact, to get a good look at its scales—reminiscent of fine braid—we needed to use a microscope.

I had come to Trinidad for a giant and caught a pygmy.

A FLURRY of obituaries sought to capture the essence of Raymond Ditmars, but his unusual approach to life defied easy classification. Ditmars was a lecturer and storyteller whose writings inspired a generation of herpetologists; a scientist without formal training; a reptile aficionado who studied insects and bats; a natural history filmmaker before the genre had a name. He brought cold-blooded animals to public attention—if not affection—as never before, providing the template for subsequent popularizers from Clifford Pope and Carl Kauffeld to Archie Carr and Steve Irwin. His venom work advanced medical science and saved lives. He loved hurricanes and steam engines, military history and horses. Ditmars witnessed and embraced unprecedented technological change from the invention of the automobile through the development of long-distance communication and the creation of a multi-million-dollar motion picture industry. From the 1920s onward he guested on numerous radio programs, notoriously broadcasting in 1924 from WOR's station at Newark, New Jersey, the sound of an angry rattlesnake. The terrible buzzing prompted an avalanche of correspondence from across North America. Aged sixty-three, Ditmars even appeared on an early television program; his "Animal Show" was among a number of items broadcast on W2XBS, the Radio Corporation of America's pioneering television station transmitted from the Empire State Building in September 1939.

And his famous expeditions in search of the bushmaster were remembered long after his death. As late as 1950 a radio play was broadcast entitled "A shipment of mute fate" in which an American museum scientist steams home from Venezuela with a prized specimen of bushmaster only for a freak wave to hit the ship and loose the deadly snake. (The viper is eventually killed by a stowaway cat).

Energy and passion were the hallmarks of his life, something recognized by Fairfield Osborn, son of Professor Henry Fairfield Osborn and from 1940 the president of the New York Zoological Society. He remembered that just days before Ditmars's final relapse, his late colleague had discussed new schemes for the parasol ant colony: "As he described the plan, incidental as it was, his voice and manner conveyed an enthusiasm which might only have been expected in a youth who had the making of his career still ahead of him."

But behind the showmanship was a serious man with family values at his core. As early as 1912 Ditmars had written to a newspaper of his horror at hearing two little girls, possibly his own daughters, crooning the chorus of a "very suggestive song." Enquiries at a "cheap music store" revealed the composition to be among several recent popular songs containing "objectionable portrayals of marital infidelity, risqué situations, and crude twistings of coarse phrases." For someone of Ditmars's sensibilities, censorship of such "immoral" ditties was needed.

Above all, therefore, he was a husband, father and grandfather—adored and adoring.

"I don't have to worry about the future, because my happiest hours are spent in the work to which I have devoted my lifetime," Ditmars told his old paper, the *New York Times*. The interview marked his sixtieth birthday, which he planned to spend writing in his Scarsdale study. "Probably the family will come in and give me a slap on the back and I'll say 'thanks.' That's about all that's going to happen."

# AUTHOR'S NOTE

## *Meeting Gloria*

---

RAYMOND DITMARS WAS A gift to newspaper editors. From the earliest days collecting frogs and insects with the Harlem Zoological Society, through the doldrums of the American Museum of Natural History to his blossoming as a public speaker, writer, filmmaker, and curator, countless reports and articles were written by Ditmars and about Ditmars; enough to fill a book far bigger than this one.

He was a man who lived his life in public—his professional life, that is. When I began researching *Bushmaster* I discovered that his private existence had left little trace. For reasons I have yet to fathom, Clara Ditmars, who died in August 1956, passed on few of her husband's personal possessions. Nothing of his extensive library. None of his many motion picture reels. No diaries. No books. No letters. Not a snake skin. Not a fang. According to Raymond Novotny, an Ohio-based naturalist and someone who had also been following the Ditmars trail, the family had simply thrown everything away. And they had been thorough; even the negatives of the curator's innumerable reptile photographs were gone, so too the famous 1907 letter from Theodore Roosevelt congratulating Ditmars on *The Reptile Book*. Perhaps this explains why, over the years, the memory of Raymond Ditmars has all but faded from public consciousness, his celebrity eclipsed by that of his contemporaries, notably William Beebe with his expeditions to the Galápagos Islands, Bermuda, and the bottom of the ocean. One connection to Ditmars's personal life had survived though, someone who had known the man himself: his sole grandchild.

275

Born to Beatrice in 1928, Gloria had accompanied the family on many tropical jaunts, including the famous 1934 expedition to Trinidad. Recollections of the period were now faded, but when I met Gloria in her spacious bungalow in suburban Ohio, I discovered that affection for her grandfather, or "Pop" as she knew him, was as keen as ever. It was the fall of 2012, just days before Hurricane Sandy would sweep in from the Atlantic, swamping lower Manhattan's subway network and flattening homes from New Jersey to Connecticut—a meteorological event that Ditmars would have relished, albeit with sympathy for the people affected.

"He was just *delicious!*" she kept telling me, with luminous blue eyes, striking features that, along with the slim build, fair hair, and angular cheekbones, were inherited from her grandfather. Gloria was also bequeathed the same low boredom threshold, the same penchant for danger and excitement, manifested in a life spent sailing, flying planes, and racing Alfa Romeos. She didn't mind snakes either; as a girl she would bring them to bed with her, dismaying a hapless string of maids and governesses.

"Pop said the snakes were my friends. Leave them alone. I was his only grandchild and he spoiled me rotten. He was a character, a dignified character."

Among pleasurable memories was the time Ditmars gave her a boa constrictor. The family belonged to a yacht club at Larchmont on Long Island Sound, and soon after her grandfather made the gift, Gloria scandalized the club by attending a costume dance with the eight-foot-long serpent draped around her neck.

"It upset the girls because all the boys wanted to dance with me. They wanted to prove they were not afraid," she said. "Then I would take the head of the gorgeous green snake and put it in my mouth."

The yacht club was a favorite haunt of hers, the Bronx Zoo was another. Pop gave Gloria the run of the place, introducing her to reptile house staff including John Toomey and his successor Fred Taggart (her favorite). Some days Ditmars would take her to an Italian restaurant on

Arthur Avenue, or she might dine with the chimpanzees—"They taught me what table manners I have."

When I showed Gloria a photo of the Scarsdale house, new reminiscences flowed. There was the upstairs room shared with her mother. Ditmars helped Gloria tame a robin by mashing worms for it and after a while the bird would hop on her finger. "He must have been an American robin, they wouldn't do that in England. They're too snooty." For someone who loved to bring his work home with him, it was no surprise that the Ditmars household was alive with monkeys, snakes, and other zoo émigrés. More conventional pets included a dachshund called Whoopsie and Hector, an English bulldog. Pop's study had wonderful pictures, stuffed things, and a rolltop desk in which she would hide and scare him. She loved it best when her grandfather gave the rebel yell of the South, an indescribable and frightening sound. "That's good, Pop. I'd say, do it again!"

Gloria was only dimly aware of her grandfather's obsession with the bushmaster, but recalled happy summers in the late thirties cruising the West Indies aboard the SS *Nerissa*. As soon as she could give her latest governess the slip, Gloria would explore the boat, shooting craps with sailors and befriending the captain. "He had one finger missing, and used to say, 'You see this? I use that to pick my nose with.' I think his name was Drysdale. I have no idea why he had a missing finger. Maybe he bit it off."

Gloria's memories of the destinations themselves were fuzzier but Port of Spain's Queens Park Hotel came to mind, so did Professor Urich's legendary rum punches: "I used to drink them. My mother didn't like that much, but my father did. He thought it was *wonderful*, he would finish them up!"

The father to which she referred was a leading New York attorney named John B. Stanchfield Jr., who had adopted her after her mother's first marriage had broken down. Stanchfield was interested in animals but drew the line at serpents.

"Jack thought they were a bloody hell situation. I think he was scared of them like everybody else."

Steaming back north from the tropics Gloria remembered sharing cabin bathrooms with caged vampire bats, containers of blood, assorted snakes and spiders; and when the Ditmars party arrived home she'd derive singular pleasure in hurling things from the ship down at the reporters and photographers invariably thronging the New York dock. "I was a sweet child," she said.

Not every Ditmars heirloom had gone. With the help of her daughter Sherry, Gloria led me around the house. I saw a sizeable oil painting of mother Beatrice and aunt Gladyce as young socialites, resplendent in satin evening dresses; an ornately framed photograph of their own mother, Clara, in the primmer clothing of an earlier era; a soldier's furlough card completed in flowing script by Captain John Ditmars—Raymond's father—in the midst of the Civil War; a yellowing picture from a newspaper showing the Ditmarses of Scarsdale, flush-faced, party-hatted and merry around a restaurant table at the New York Athletic Club; a gold Waltham pocket watch with the initials RLD etched into its rear. And there at the back of a shelf congested with knickknacks accumulated over Gloria's eighty-five years—many of them animals fashioned from clay, glass, wood, textiles—was a portrait of the man himself. Toying solemnly with his pipe, Raymond Ditmars now eyed me through the small menagerie of fish, elephants, doves, monkeys, cats. Snakes there were none but he looked happy enough.

# Acknowledgements

———◆———

DON'T LET ANYONE TELL you that writing is a solitary profession. My quest for Raymond Ditmars and the bushmaster wouldn't have gotten started without the support of countless herpetologists and historians, filmmakers and family members, librarians and literati.

It's hard to know where my greatest debt of gratitude lies. Certainly, a sizeable portion of the thanks must go to the redoubtable Romulus Whitaker for unwittingly sparking my madcap mission. And without the enthusiasm, backing, and guidance of Sophie Rochester, even now I could still be pondering whether to pursue "the Ditmars idea." A more solemn thank you to the late Richard Matthews, a brilliant wildlife cameraman and producer who, not long after giving the book concept his blessing, died while filming in Namibia. Massive thanks also to Sharyn Finnegan and George Prans in Riverdale, New York, and Chloe & Tony Viola in DC for putting up with an amateur snake-hunter in their homes; and to Ian and Sandra Melizan in Trinidad for keeping me safe in the urban jungle of Port of Spain. Special mentions also of three people with unique connections to the Ditmars story who were so generous with their time: Peter Brazaitis, Paul R. Greenhall, and Gloria Fozard (along with her daughter Sherry Hylton).

Others to thank in the USA include: Regina Alvarez; Peter Warny and Erik Zeidler; John C. Murphy and Gabriel Hast of the Field Museum of Natural History; Madeleine Thompson and Donal Boyer at the Wildlife Conservation Society; timber rattler experts Edwin McGowan, Rulon W. Clark, and William H. "Marty" Martin; Michael Touger of the Jacobi

Medical Center; Dean & Regina Ripa of the astonishing Cape Fear Serpentarium; ex-Bronx Zoo reptile supervisor Frank Indiviglio for the best Italian meal of the trip and some lovely stories; Norman Benson for a tale or two of his own; fellow Ditmars aficionado Ray Novotny; Lloyd Ultan of the Bronx County Historical Society; Barbara MacDonald of the Scarsdale Historical Society; Matthew J. Murphy of the New-York Historical Society; Mary Markey, Kirsten van der Veen, Polly Lasker, Addison Wynn, George Zug, David G. Smith, Pam Wintle, Daisy Njoku, and especially James B. Murphy, Kenneth A. Tighe, and Richard Greene of the Smithsonian Institution; Patrick Raftery of the Westchester County Historical Society; Michelle Cadoree Bradley, Matthew Barton, Patrick Kerwin, Josie Walters-Johnston, Janet W. McKee, Robert B. Jones Jr., and Robert Norton of the Library of Congress; Jack Sherefkin and Steve Massa of the New York Public Library; Tom Baione, David A. Kizirian, and especially Gregory A. Raml at the American Museum of Natural History; Andy Lanset of New York Public Radio; Robert Hoch of the White Plains Historical Society; Edward T. Morman of the National Federation of the Blind Jernigan Institute; Sean Kennedy of the University of Maryland; Paul Cerniglia of the US Fish and Wildlife Service.

Those to thank in Trinidad include: Hans E. A. Boos; Delbert Charleau Jr. of the Emperor Valley Zoo; the original snakeman Allan Rodriguez; Atkin Isaac, Mukesh Ramdass, Molly Calderon, Judith Gobin, and Kenneth Fournillier at the Asa Wright Nature Centre; Angelie Lochan of the Sangre Grande Hospital; Eddison Baptiste, Stevland Charles, Elisha Tikasingh, and Selwyn Gomes of the Trinidad and Tobago Field Naturalists' Club; Jemima King of the Trinidad and Tobago National Archives; Roger Downie of the University of Glasgow for an interesting chat about Trinidad's paradox frog; Mike Rutherford of the University of the West Indies; Gerard Ramsawak and Oda van der Heijden at the Pax Guest House; Judy Raymond, editor in chief of the *Trinidad Guardian*, for whom I failed to generate anything newsworthy; and Antony Edwards, Oxford University alumnus extraordinaire.

Thanks also to a bunch of people in Brazil and Panama, and regrets that the budget didn't quite stretch to trips there: huge thanks to Judy and Bob Beer in São Paulo; and *muitíssimo obrigado* to Rodrigo C. G de Souza of the Nucleo Serra Grande, pretty much the only person I know of with a mission to conserve bushmasters.

Other thanks go to Patrick Walsh, Alex Christofi, and Carrie Plitt of the Conville & Walsh Literary Agency; Tony Lyons and Maxim Brown at Skyhorse; Jeremy Seal; Daniel Bardsley for eagle-eyed typo-spotting; Laurence Penney for notes on the type; Andrew Whitworth of the Crees Foundation, Peru; Luke McKernan of the British Library; and Robert W. Henderson of the Milwaukee Public Museum; Mike Dee, formerly of the Los Angeles Zoo; Kraig Adler of Cornell University; and not forgetting the great Bill Lamar whose expertise and enthusiasm for all matters reptilian saw me over the finishing line. Before Bill got his hands on it, this book had more scientific blunders than a bushmaster has pentastomids. Thanks, finally, to the huge support of my wife, Clair, and my dear old Mum and Dad.

# Index

Note: Numbers in italics indicate photographs and illustrations.

inefficient heating, 96
popularity, 105–106
redesign in 1950s, 96
Rocking Stone Restaurant, 104
site selection, 82–84
Bronxdale (New York City), 89
Brookfield Zoo (Chicago), 257
Brooklyn (New York City), 10, 33, 44,
189, 193
Brooklyn Academy of Music (New York
City), 193
*Brooklyn Eagle* (newspaper), 233
Brooklyn Institute of Arts and Sciences
(New York City), 193
Brown, William, 59
brown snake. *see* also De Kay's snake, 9,
32, 49, 61
Brownsville (Texas), 209
Buffalo (New York State), 82
buffalo, African (*Syncerus caffer*), 32
buffalo, American, 78, 82, 87
*Bulletin of the New York Zoological
Society* (journal), 87, 107, 142,
157, 160
Bush, W. Stephen, 188
bushmaster (*Lachesis* spp.)
Bronx Zoo collection, 157, 252
Cleopatra Arrima, 262
Dallas Zoo, 158–159
difficulty of capturing, 230–231
fangs, 95
fragility of individuals, 124–125,
157–158
heat vision, 95
Lecky, 252, 255, 256–258
myths, 5, 50–51
bushmaster, South American (*Lachesis
muta*). *see* also counacouchi, 3,
50–51, 61, 144, 209, 244, 250, 254,
255, 272

Butantan. *see* Instituto Soroterápico de
Butantan

C

*Calamares* (ship), 233
Calderon, Molly, 265
Calmette, Albert, 155–156, 163
Calmette's Snake Serum, 110, 146,
155–156, 210, 211
Canal Zone (Panama), 216–217,
230–232, 238
cancer, 163–164
Caparo (Trinidad), 241
Cape Fear Serpentarium (Wilmington,
North Carolina), 225–226
Cape hyrax (*Procavia capensis*), 124
Carnegie, Andrew, xxii, 191
Carnegie, Dale, 252
Carnegie Foundation, 210
Caroni (Trinidad), 52, 243
Carr, Albert B., 51
Carr, Archie, 273
Carrère & Hastings (architects), 169
Carter, Helene, 173
Carter, Howard, 180
cascabel. *see* also rattlesnake (*Crotalus*
spp.), 205
*cascabel dormillon. see* boa, tree,
Trinidad
*Catalogue of the Lizards in the British
Museum* (1885), 53
cauterization, 153
caves, 221–224, 248
ceiba trees, 205
Center for Global Conservation (at the
Bronx Zoo), 78
centipedes, 144, 157, 248, 268
Central Park Conservancy, 7
Central Park menagerie, 1–4, 7, 14,
80, 176

# About the Type

This book is set in Electra. This typeface was designed for the Linotype machine in 1935 by William A. Dwiggins, an American artist, illustrator, and marionette-maker. Not easily categorized, Electra provides an instantly recognizable texture in book pages and, while narrower than Times and therefore more economical, is just as readable. Electra is widely used in fine works of art, literature, and science.